Sandplay

Sandplay

A Sourcebook for Play Therapists

Susan Perkins McNally

Writers Club Press
San Jose New York Lincoln Shanghai

Sandplay
A Sourcebook for Play Therapists

All Rights Reserved © 2001 by Susan Perkins McNally

No part of this book may be reproduced or transmitted in any form or by any means, graphic, electronic, or mechanical, including photocopying, recording, taping, or by any information storage retrieval system, without the permission in writing from the publisher.

Writers Club Press
an imprint of iUniverse.com, Inc.

For information address:
iUniverse.com, Inc.
5220 S 16th, Ste. 200
Lincoln, NE 68512
www.iuniverse.com

ISBN: 0-595-18650-5

Printed in the United States of America

For the children.

Epigraph

In my experience it is of considerable practical importance that the symbols aiming at wholeness should be correctly understood by the doctor.
Carl G. Jung, 1963

Contents

Illustrations xi
Epigraph vii
Preface xiii
Acknowledgements xvii
One "A Picture Is Worth a Thousand Words" 1
Two An Ideal Playroom 24
Three Working Through 28
Four Cries for Help 31
Five Circumnambulation and the Mandala Form 39
Six T. Rex Meets S. Freud 46
Seven Images of Psychic Attack 57
Eight Roasted In the Fire 63
Nine Working Through Posttraumatic Play 69
Ten Gifts From the Unconscious 78
Eleven Free the Maidens! 96
Twelve When Ends Meet 113
About the Author 117
Appendix A Dictionary of Play Therapy Imagery 119
Appendix B Guide to Resources 197
Glossary 217
Bibliography 223
Index 231

Illustrations

Plate 1 Blocked family rage 35
Plate 2 Don't kill her! 37
Plate 3 Andrew's disorganized world 40
Plate 4 Ken—Under attack 49
Plate 5 The house isn't destroyed! 51
Plate 6 Howard's plight 58
Plate 7 Judith's threatened light child/dark child 60
Plate 8 Kevin—A trial by fire 65
Plate 9 Quest for the green stone 67
Plate 10 Duncan's battle scene 72
Plate 11 Open battle 73
Plate 12 Sharon—Smiling while crying 80
Plate 13 Archetypal parents/fourfold structure 81
Plate 14 Sharon's separated bride and groom 83
Plate 15 Eggs in a volcano 85
Plate 16 Finding Sharon's buried eggs 87
Plate 17 James' couple in danger 91
Plate 18 Play soccer or die! 92
Plate 19 The Rapunzel tower 101
Plate 20 Rapunzel drowned in sand 101
Plate 21 The rainbow girl in the forest 104
Plate 22 A gargantuan meal 105
Plate 23 The day the dragon died 107
Plate 24 The Pink Lady with fawns 110

Preface

Why write one more book on depth psychotherapy in this age of the HMO when many therapists are looking to learn brief therapy skills so they can queue up and receive insurance payments? It is my heartfelt belief that even though brief counseling can be of great value in certain cases, however, in many others it will only provide a superficial Band-Aid. The psyche is complex and multi-layered. Its contents can be restructured. This book demonstrates ways this can happen. The case material that is presented in this book covers play therapy work that done by children over the past twenty-two years.

Over the years many professionals and interns have asked me to help with the interpretation of the sand trays done by their young patients. I have enjoyed assisting my colleagues, and have learned a great deal in the process. During these years I have been shown the actual sand tray that was created by the child, reconstructed sand trays, photos, slides, and have been given verbal descriptions of trays that were destroyed. Many questions have arisen concerning the symbolism contained in the trays.

One of my colleagues asked whether there was a reference available on symbol interpretation for play therapists. At that moment I believed that would not be a good idea since the materials are often so subjective and cannot be rigidly interpreted. I am a great believer in the intuitive process. After thinking about it, I realized that a book on symbolism for play therapists might be a good idea since there has been no single text that provides this information for the clinician.

This volume was written as an introduction to the process of child psychotherapy with special emphasis on the process of transformation. It is the author's conviction that sandplay offers deeper access into the child's dynamics than traditional play therapy alone. In its rich provision of symbols by the therapist, sandplay provides the child's psyche with more appropriate tools for the process of transformation.

It is my hope that this book will be useful to either the novice, or the established child therapist, who would like to understand the process of sandplay symbol interpretation. The Dictionary of Play Therapy Imagery will enable child psychotherapists and other mental health professionals to understand the language of the metaphoric mind in greater depth.

This book is designed as a reference. The subject of this volume is child psychotherapy, however, many of the concepts and information contained within the book are applicable to adult psychotherapy, especially with people who have difficulty with language. As one reads through this text it may become apparent that I believe that a child specialist needs to be trained in play therapy, sandplay, and art therapy. I am not aware of such an educational program that combines all of these methods. A program that includes of these areas would demand that a depth approach be utilized, in addition to a study of psychometrics.

During the years I have followed many cases referred by social workers to various clinics in the Los Angeles area and I have noted to my dismay that the deep therapeutic work that the court and the Department of Children's Services wants done with children is not being done. Because of inadequate funding, some latency-aged children were placed in a group where brief interventions were given and then dismissed as having completed a course of therapy. This perfunctory treatment guaranteed that any deep pathology was left untouched. Others who were referred for severe physical and sexual trauma before coming into foster care were only treated to improve or end their relationship with their foster parents. This is a travesty. One boy, who was referred to neutralize the aggression brought on by years with gun toting, drug dealing parents, was helped to learn his multiplication tables by his therapist. Academic difficulties were not the reason this child was referred for therapy! I have seen more Band-Aids dispensed than I care to mention. It is my fervent hope that sandplay be fully utilized as the potent therapeutic medium that it can be. If this book helps popularize sandplay therapy, and makes Jungian psychology as applied to child psychotherapy less of a mystery to my colleagues, or if it encourages more in-depth work with children, I will feel well rewarded for my effort.

Susan Perkins McNally, Burnet, Texas 2001

Acknowledgements

I want to express my appreciation to Carolyn Abel, Ph.D. for her encouragement, feedback, ideas, and reading of my text in several different stages of its development over many years. Thank you to Kaare Jacobson, and to Mary and Pierce Ommaney for your support. Thank-you to Harriet Freedman for her classes on sandplay. Special thanks to my friend, Cynthia Fichtner, for her careful reading of my text and the long hours she freely spent going over my manuscript with me. Special thanks is due Joe McNair Ph.D. for being such an outstanding teacher, to Sonia Rhia Ph.D. for introducing me to sandplay, and finally, to Mary Dell Smith and Ed McNally for proof reading my text. Thank you to Joe Bongiovanni, Richard Lunetta, Barbara Reinhart, Vicki Badik, Marilyn Avery, Fran Love, Cynthia Trousdale for your feedback and comments.

Much of what I have learned about imagery in sandplay, artwork and dreams has come from extensive reading and my work in the field. Pioneers, such as Dora Kalff, and the children I have worked with have taught me much. I am indebted to each of them.

Many thanks, and never-ending love to Ed and our sons Robert, Michael, and Steven for your love, support, and encouragement.

One

"A Picture Is Worth a Thousand Words"

> Nevertheless, we can learn the language of dreams, for it is not dreams that are obscure, but our understanding of them.
> John A. Sanford 1978

What children do in the sand tray may be easily understood while other sand trays are mysterious. What do they mean? It can be disconcerting to delve into the realm of play therapy only to realize that children are communicating in an unknown language. Right brain thinking is quite foreign to most people. This is particularly true of academics. Intellectuals are typically left brained preferring to deal in words rather than imagery. Parents often dismiss a child's frightening dream with the minimizing statement, "It's just a dream, honey." As clinicians we would be unwise to have such a lack of awareness in our work.

Understanding the non-verbal communication of children is challenging. Unless one is skilled in art therapy, or dream work, is knowledgeable in the language of the unconscious, familiar with the content of children's television programs, movies and slang, much is missed that the child is communicating. A specialist in child psychotherapy must be well grounded and ever growing. While this book cannot provide all the background a therapist requires it should give the clinician a strong foundation in the metaphoric mind.

When adults, or teens, see my sand trays they often experience resistance. I tell them that we have two minds—one communicates in words and the other in images. These two minds do not always agree. Most people seem to accept this notion readily. Unless clinicians understand this second language of imagery our ability to help is limited. We need to understand the way that each "mind" is in conflict.

When we receive our degrees in psychology, social work or medicine, do we immediately rush off to Germany, Italy or Africa and expect to speak in their native tongue? The idea is ridiculous. When we desire to become fluent in another language we study it. Similarly, we need to study symbolism if we desire to interpret dreams or understand sandplay therapy. This book will aid in understanding the language of the second mind. Reading introductory chapters and case studies and using the Dictionary of Imagery (Appendix A) as a reference will help novice or experienced clinicians grow in understanding this symbolic language.

The interpretation of children's art and play is a sensitive art. I hope to give the clinician that works with children, adolescents, or adults, and has access to sandplay, a powerful tool for extending his or her understanding of the language of the second mind. As I discuss case histories later in this book I will be referring to landmarks in the history of child psychotherapy, therefore we need to briefly review the development of play therapy.

A Brief History of Play Therapy

The development of play therapy dates back to the Nineteen-Twenties. Hermine Hug-Hellmuth began using play for diagnosis and treatment of emotionally disturbed children. Anna Freud (1927) maintained that small children could not verbalize their conflicts, but could demonstrate them in the process of play. Eventually, it became traditional for therapists to use toys, small objects, and later games, in the treatment of children. Over the years play therapy has embraced aspects of art therapy, and has expanded to include board games, card games, crafts and other relationship building or ego building activities.

Sandplay is a method of play therapy that is unusually productive. Unfortunately sandplay is a modality used less in the United States than in Europe. This has been changing as more support and training has become available for clinicians, including many sandplay books written during the nineties. The tendency in the United States still favors direct approaches, such as games designed to help overcome a specific problem. The subtly and sophistication of sandplay is often overlooked in our rush to quickly treat our young clients.

Over the years the types of items used in play therapy have increased greatly. Virginia Axline (1947) suggests using nursing bottles, a doll family, a doll house with furniture, toy soldiers and army equipment, playhouse materials, such as dishes and doll clothes, a di-dee doll, a large rag doll, puppets that include all possible family members, crayons, finger paints, clay, water, toy guns, little cars, airplanes, a table for finger painting and clay, a toy telephone, basin, small broom, mop, rags, drawing paper, inexpensive cutting paper, pictures of people, houses, animals and other objects. Other therapists have added such items as, blocks, games, woodworking, and crafts. Violet Oaklander (1978) adds music, pantomime and drama, poetry, movement therapy, the sand tray, projective tests used as therapeutic tools, and the Gestalt empty chair. Eliana Gil (1991) adds sunglasses, Feeling cards, (illustrations of facial expressions), video therapy, and therapeutic stories. Gil (1991) has clearly demonstrated the need for the child to move beyond posttraumatic play, or repetition compulsion caused by trauma. Movement is characteristic of a healthy psyche. Total blockage indicates a severe problem. Gil states the therapist may have to intervene to keep the child from being rewounded should his compulsive play fail to show movement after about eight sessions. Gil (ibid.) has also outlined an excellent approach to children with Multiple Personality Disorder. Art therapy is an excellent modality for children that are comfortable with art materials, and are unconcerned about creating good art. Like sandplay, art therapy can promote depth transformation. For clinicians who want to promote this process vis-a-vis the use of art materials, Art As Therapy With Children by Edith Kramer (1971) is an excellent introduction. Unfortunately, many children believe they are incapable of producing good-looking artwork and shun art materials. Providing sand trays can help bridge this gap of confidence while expanding the arena of non-verbal therapy.

Games: Moving Beyond Win-Lose?

Board games provide interaction between the child and the therapist. Children who are out-going tend to enjoy the involvement with another person. Therapists need to avoid games that take too long to play since children may use them to avoid dealing with their issues. Sand tray therapy and art therapy are inwardly focused compared with interactive games, and may be the natural preference of introverted children. Art and sandplay therapy may not involve the therapist should the child prefer to screen him out. Ideally both extroverted and introverted personality styles should be offered a balance of activities.

The strength of sandplay lies in its power to touch the depths of the personality. Even though one may offer various activities, it seems logical that games are appropriate after deeper metaphoric work has been played-out, and a strong therapeutic alliance has been established. Each child's need is different and that must always be of paramount importance.

During my work in schools with children in the third through fifth grades I use many games primarily because the school wants so many children seen. When I have had small school groups of children from age five to seven I have provided toys from my sand tray collection. School counselors often call for more structured approaches in the belief that more can be accomplished in a short period of time with a curriculum or with therapeutic games than with play or art. The non-verbal approach and power of sandplay has to be seen and experienced to be believed. Amatruda and

Helm Simpson (1997) have found that a short number of sandplay sessions, five to ten, or even just one can be helpful.

Some children play with the full range of play therapy toys, sandplay and games without any difficulty. Many children love competitive games since they desperately want to win in life. Other children prefer to play games because they have an extroverted orientation that places the emphasis upon other individuals. These out-going children enjoy the opportunity to interact with the therapist during the session. Some of these children seem unwilling, or unable, to focus on anything other than the therapist. The inward movement of sandplay can be threatening to those who need to intensely engage the therapist. Certain children have not been safe enough to turn inward and develop the life of the imagination. Other children will focus primarily on sandplay and unstructured art materials. Motivation for these differences will vary greatly with different personalities and different presenting problems.

Play is natural to children and young mammals. Play is the work of the child. A red flag appears when a child's play is blocked. Narcissistic wounds often cause blocks to spontaneous play. Repressed children will not be able to expend energy upon the objects provided for symbolic play until they have found the therapeutic relationship a safe haven. Other children will use sandplay and art materials exclusively while avoiding the interaction of games. This could indicate that a child's fear of failure, or fear of intimacy. It also might indicate a rich inner life.

Many games created by psychotherapists do not place the child in a win-lose situation. The "Ungame" is a classic in the realm of non-competitive therapeutic games. I have found that many children so intensely want to win (feel good about themselves) that they reject this and other non-competitive games."The Talking, Feeling, Doing Game" created by therapist Richard Gardner, is designed to engage resistant and uncooperative children. Gardner's game, and similar games, has grown in popularity among child psychotherapists. It has a familiar format and engages the child's interest with a token reward system that is similar to other games where the emphasis is placed upon winning. The emphasis of these games is upon the creation of therapeutically useful fantasy material A game that includes competition, yet has its emphasis on the expression of feelings, is "My Homes and Places" by Nancy Bohac Flood, Ph.D. This game is a favorite with my young clients. Board games can provoke such a strong desire to win that some children cannot use them in conjoint sessions their rivalry becomes too intense and their egos are much too weak. The Childswork/Childsplay catalog, listed in the Resource section in Appendix B, is filled with an ever-expanding variety of therapeutic board games.

The World Technique Becomes Sandplay

During the thirties sand tray therapy developed in Europe as the Lowenfeld World Technique. Margaret Lowenfeld credits a child with bringing small objects in her room over to the tray of sand. Lowenfeld called sand trays "worlds." A world can be seen as a picture of the psyche. Haim Ginott (1961) and Violet Oaklander (1978) are among the first child psychotherapists in the United States to write about the value of sandplay in child psychotherapy.

As if to underscore one of the theses of this book, Eleanor Irvin (1983, Schaefer and O'Connor, p. 156) writes: "One productive but rarely used activity that can stimulate fantasy play is that devised by the British analyst Margaret Lowenfeld." Irvin's referent is The Lowenfeld World Technique, now known as sandplay.

Margaret Lowenfeld (1979) notes that The World Technique is characteristically a right brain mode. She states that the production of worlds seems to be halfway between that of dreams, that are an unconscious creation, and art, that draws from the conscious, in the creation of structure and form, and the unconscious in the form of imagery.

Sandplay and Child Development

Bowyer (1970) divides behaviors seen in play according to developmental lines, and compared the work of 26 normal children and

24 "clinical" youngsters. She used Kurt Lewin's developmental parameters of (1) increase in life space, (2) increased realism, (3) increased differentiation-integration in (a) use of the tray, (b) the fantasy-reality dimension, (c) use of sand and part-whole relationships. Using the control group as a baseline she observed four chronological stages, two to four years, five to seven years, eight to ten years, and eleven + years. Bowyer (1971) observed burying objects by children over age four was indicative of pathology. Bowyer's control group engaged in intense burying behaviors at age two to three, and this decreased until four plus. "Toys were poked or flung into the sand, so they were buried or half-buried" (p. 26) From two to four children destructively used sand "pouring sand over people or things, or pushing toys into the sand, sometimes with the words 'down, down!'..." (p. 28). Eve Lewis (ibid.) observed that the careful burying of an object seems to indicate acceptance into the unconscious of whatever the object symbolizes.

Charles Stewart (Bradway, et. al., 1981) and Louis Stewart incorporate the work of Erich Neumann, Dora Kalff, Ruth Bowyer, Piaget, and Erik Erikson with their observations of sand trays by children under twelve in an attempt to establish sandplay norms. Stewart's synthesis of Neumann, Erikson, and Piaget's developmental theories resulted in a four-stage construct, which he related to the Sutton-Smith (1974) classification of universal developmental games.

Infancy (Inf. II): 7-10 to 12-24 months
Games of appearance and disappearance (Peek-A-Boo)
Early Childhood I (ECI): 1-2 to 3-4 years.
Games of order and disorder (Ring Around the Rosy)
Early Childhood II (ECII): 3-4 to 6-7 years
Central-person games (Tag, Farmer in the Dell, Mother May I?)
Middle Childhood (MC): 6-7 to 11-12 years
Games of peer sexual differentiation (Jacks, Marbles) Sutton-Smith list games of success and failure. This would now include most board games.

During the ECI phase the typical preschool or kindergarten child alternates between being caught up in the primal relationship with the intermittent budding of ego consciousness. He becomes aware of such dualities as, self and world, yes and no, good and bad, accepting and rejecting, opening and closing, real and pretend. He traverses Erikson's autonomy versus shame and doubt. When both parents replace the security of the maternal matrix this integration is complete. He came to see the behavior of burying and digging up, hiding in the sand than then finding, as analogous to Peek-A-Boo, an Infancy II behavior. This leads one to the notion of damaged object relations.

Stewart states that "The ludic boundaries for ECI are pretend play at 1 to 2 years and imaginative play at 3 to 4 years. With the advent of electronic age babysitters (television and video games), and tight schedules dominating children's lives certain school-aged children now need to be taught how to pretend. Developmental gaps are occurring simply because the normal spectrum of play has become truncated. As a society we have become guilty of over-structuring a child's sacred space within the realm of play. Our children need time to engage in imaginative play.

Relating his synthesis to child development, Stewart differentiates between a child's exploration of the textures of the dry or wet sand and incident patterns that result from a conscious, deliberate manipulation of the sand. He came to see the behavior of burying and digging up, hiding in the sand and then finding as analogous to peek-a-boo, an Infancy II behavior. When these burying, hiding and finding behaviors occur in an older child it leads one to the notion of damaged object relations. This theme will be expanded in the case material.

A Neglected Modality

Sandplay, used in conjunction with other play therapy items, has been widely popular in Europe for many decades. European therapists, of all theoretical persuasions, commonly use sandplay Most research on sandplay has been European or British. This began to shift during the nineties.

During the late part of the 20th Century, sandplay has grown slowly in popularity in the United States. Jungian analyst, Dora Kalff, who popularized the method in this country, named the method sandplay. Since sandplay has been most popular among Jungian therapists in this country, and is classified as a Jungian method, it may be avoided by clinicians with other orientations. This is an unfortunately provincial view. The psyche is not the province of any therapeutic modality; rather it is the heart and core of all depth psychotherapy. Dr. Sonia Rhia, an instructor in my Master's program, introduced her class to sandplay and is a Freudian.

The Jungian view of the transformational power of symbolic material and its emphasis on symbols that reflect archetypal content adds strength to the understanding of sandplay. Unfortunately, many practitioners are both biased against, or intimidated by, the complexities and peculiar language of Jungian Analytical Psychology. This need not be a handicap as the language of the psyche and Analytical Psychology is accessible with a little study. I have defined Jungian terms as they are used. Should you need to review a definition, please consult the Glossary.

A Unique Therapeutic Tool

Fantasy play is the way children obtain as sense of mastery of their world. This type of play needs to be stimulated in our over-scheduled, television and video game oriented children. Sandplay is the single most powerful tool for drawing the metaphoric mind into dialogue. Sandplay stimulates the visual and kinesthetic portions of the mind which is key to learning in the early years.

The medium of sandplay has the advantage of not triggering a child's shame at not being a good artist, a frequent block to art therapy. Energy is freed through this process and individuation is facilitated. Along with freeing the child from a sense of shame at his inability to create art, sandplay provides a specific arena of play or area of containment for the projection of the child's dynamic processes. Jungians refer to the therapeutic alliance and safe space of the consultation room as "a container." When the child has a container for his hurt and rage he may safely discharge these problematic emotions.

The sandplay method generally uses two trays. Later in the text I will explain why I prefer three trays if there is room. Dora Kalff (1966a) recommends a sand tray that is 19 1/2"x28 1/2"x3." The size of the tray corresponds to what the eye can easily encompass. The bottom of each tray is painted blue to represent water. The trays are partially filled with sand. I generally use three to four inches of sand so that mountains may be built, or objects buried. In one tray the sand is moist so it may be molded. Additional water might be added by the client if the therapist is comfortable with this, and the work space permits.

I have used of various sizes not always the size that which Kalff recommended, for example, a large photographic tray. This has worked very well. Molded Plexiglas trays and plastic trays have the advantage of containing watery sand with no damage. A list of resources for trays and other materials will be found in Appendix B.

Miniature houses and buildings, trees, rocks, shells, soldiers, male and female figures, Indians, cowboys, dinosaurs, animals, soldiers, spacemen, dancing girls, fences, bridges, churches, heroes, and villains help an individual create a meaningful world. These objects can be displayed on shelves, kept in baskets, or bins, or contained in drawers.

Another advantage over traditional play therapy is found in the selection of objects not generally considered toys. Useful non-toy items may be obtained from cake decorating shops, aquarium stores, hobby and gift shops, and rock shops, or made, such as the small volcanoes seen in this book. Miniature castles, trees, bridges, rocks, shells, and candles are among the objects that are useful. Most children are delighted with this variety of objects. Suggestions for places to shop will be found in Appendix B.

I have had children walk into my consultation room, spy the sand tray and toys that are so evocative of fantasy, and say, "Oh, we get to do this!" Their joy is a delight to observe. Children that are shut down and intimidated by hostile and controlling adults, or by other children, have responded, "What do you want me to do with this stuff?" Certain children need to be encouraged to play, and some children must be taught to pretend. Television and video games have added enormously to this empty response by encouraging passivity, while absorbing valuable and necessary fantasy play time. A child's development is thwarted when her schedule is filled with too many structured activities and television.

Children and adults who are repulsed by the idea of touching the sand have severe blocks or disturbances. Amatruda and Helm Simpson (1997) have found that alcoholics who are not in recovery have little relationship to the sand. They believe that the addictive disorder keeps the person from going down into the psyche, and this is mirrored in the response to the sand.

During my clinical work with children I have noted that children shift into an altered state of consciousness when involved in creating their personal fantasy tale in the sand tray. This shift is necessary. Reprocessing experiences can be profound as the child plays. Intense play is the most important activity in the world for children. Adults often have forgotten the magical power and total absorption of playtime. Because of this intense absorption I always give the child a five-minute warning before the end of our session. He often has a plan in mind and will move quickly to finish a process when he is aware that the time is drawing short.

The Psychological Needs of the Child in Therapy

Briefly looking at various views of play therapy, child analyst Anna Freud, (1937, 1946) considers childhood neurosis to be the result of an imbalance of intrapsychic forces that has resulted in a rigid and inflexible ego. She also sees failure in ego functioning to be due to prolonged use of defense mechanisms.

Ego Psychologist Donald Winnicott (1941, 1948) is interested in the relation of child's play to trust. Melanie Klein (1948) sees childhood neurosis as being the result of a massive repression of fantasy due the intrapsychic load of guilt and depression that the child developed over the Oedipal problem. In Axline's (1947, 1964) view, the parent, and possibly others, have rejected some part of the child. The therapist facilitates growth by accepting the child.

Bruno Bettelheim (1975), states that when the unconscious comes to the fore in a child it overwhelms, rather than strengthens, the total personality. For this reason a child must externalize his inner processes. The child uses play objects, such as dolls and toy animals, to embody various aspects of his personality that are too complex, contradictory, or unacceptable to handle. This helps the child gain an intuitive sense of mastery. He goes on to state that, "It is always intrusive to interpret a person's unconscious thoughts, to make conscious what he wishes to keep preconscious and this is especially true in the case of a child" (1975, p. 18). I agree completely with Bettelheim. Too much intellectual clarity destroys the power and enchantment of a fairy tale, a work of art, or a sand tray, and can threaten the nascent ego. Understanding what the client is saying and accepting their view of reality is the heart and core of the transpersonal therapeutic alliance.

Bettelheim suggests that the child's experience of entering into a fairy tale is a giving up of the real world for one where fantasy is understood to be foremost. At the end of the tale the hero and the child return to reality, much like our returning to reality after dreaming. Just as the dreamer awakes refreshed, so the child is refreshed "because the stories help the child work through unconscious pressures in fantasy" (ibid. p.63).

A child needs to deal with his inner reality, as well as to develop mastery in the outer world. If the expression of his inner world is denied, he is depleted by the estrangement from his inner life. Bettelheim believes that this estrangement from the realm of fantasy may lead the older child to abandon reality to make up for this lost aspect of his childhood. This void might result in an older child seeking the fantastic in the world of drug induced hallucinations. One young adult shared with me that she turned to psychedelic drugs to keep from losing her childhood fantasy world. As a child's need for fantasy is validated she feels accepted.

As therapists we deal with the practical reality of children who have been neglected, abandoned, physically or sexually abused, and who need depth therapy to neutralize the resulting pain. If our methods are shallow, and the pain of child abuse is not neutralized and safety and trust are not restored, we will continue to see alcohol and other drug abuse used to numb the pain of these wounds.

Looking at the factors listed above as indicative of a need for therapy we have amassed an impressive list. Poor object relations, difficulty with intrapsychic processes, rigidity of the ego, prolonged use of defenses, overwhelming of the immature ego, repression of fantasy, lack of acceptance, and child neglect and abuse are among the many difficulties that might be brought into the play therapist's consultation room.

The child may also bring in a burden that belongs to the parental unconscious. Unconscious angers, fears, or repressed longings that belong to one or both parents may be intuited by the child and appear as the child's symptom. Frances Wickes, in The Inner World of Childhood (1955), gives numerous examples of this psychic burden unconsciously carried by the child.

The medium of sandplay offers the child a wide variety of objects that may be selected repeatedly, used only occasionally, or totally ignored. Each of these responses, including failure to respond, makes a statement about the child's psychological situation. The objects selected by the child reflect her object relations, most favored collective alternatives, objects used to represent the self as suggested by Bettelheim, and universal symbols as suggested by Jung. Ignored or rejected objects represent repressed or rejected parts of the psyche.

The therapist's acceptance and creativity are evident by the wide variety of objects not found in the toy box at home. When shopping for objects psychological balance needs to be maintained. Objects that reflect the masculine realm should be counterbalanced by objects that represent the feminine, dark or evil objects should be counterbalanced by religious or heroic objects, and so forth. Collecting objects in the service of the psyche is an art.

How Do Archetypes Relate to Child Development?

Why study anything so complex as Jungian Analytic Psychology? Jungian Psychology is the only psychological system that extensively explores the metaphoric mind. This second language of ours consists of images and symbols that may be beyond the awareness of the individual's conscious mind. A vivid example of the importance of understanding this unknown, archetypal language of the unconscious occurred to me years ago. I saw my dream mother, my inner mother—not my biologic mother—standing before me with a pig that I raised. She was pleased with me. I awoke puzzled, particularly since my waking ego-mind felt repulsed by the idea of eating pork—my immediate association to the image of a pig. Serendipitously, after this dream I attended a lecture on the Great Mother archetype at the C.G. Jung Institute. During the slide presentation I discovered that the pig is a fertility symbol. With this new understanding I thought about my inner mother as pleased with me for raising a pig. I realized motherhood and the birth of my sons had been deeply transforming growth experiences for me, and had healed a wound in me. Now my dream made sense and had great value to me. I was astonished that this type of information was contained in my psyche. It was totally foreign to my ego-mind, and yet was at least as much value as knowing French would be while touring France. Jung taught that this rich, inner world of archetypal communication is true for all of us. We need to take the time to look within, learn and have regard for this language of the psyche.

An archetype is an original model after which other similar objects are patterned. Jung (1947) differentiates between the unconscious archetype and its representation in consciousness—its imagery. Archetypes create naturally occurring vortexes of energy that cause various images to be thrown up to consciousness. Images that arise from the collective unconscious represent archetypal conditions and tendencies. They are not the actual archetypes themselves. The actual archetypal form belongs to the realm of the collective unconscious, and cannot be totally grasped. James Hillman (1979) speaks of the images thrown up to consciousness as "guiding errors." The image guides the person, but is not exactly right. There is a gulf between the archetypal inner world, and the individuals need to act in the outer world, and move toward individuation.

Jung states, "There are as many archetypes as there are typical situations in life. Endless repetition has engraved these experiences into our psychic constitution, not in the forms of images filled with content, but at first only as forms without content, representing merely the possibility of a certain type of perception and action" (1968, p.48). Archetypes are general, collective a priori categories, and lack the character of individual personalities.

Archetypes are envisioned as vortexes of energy potential, somewhat like the feeling-toned complexes that Jung described. A complex is an integration of impulses, ideas and emotions related to a particular idea or activity, such as the person's mother or sense of self. Complexes contain personal material that an archetype will not contain. In a sense an archetype is hollow. Some of the archetypes that Jung identified and described are the Earth Mother, the Wise Old Man, the trickster, birth, death, rebirth, the Hero, the witch, the child. Many other images, such as circles, mandalas, squared circles, rings, weapons, animals and natural forces are included in his list of archetypes. As Jung explores the consciousness and the unconscious he employs the term, the "objective psyche" to make clear his conviction that the inner world of the psyche is just as much a valid object of study as the outer world of material objects.

Jung sees archetypes as composed of positive and negative potentialities comparable to spheres illuminated on one side by a spotlight. One half of the archetypal form is light/positive, while the other is dark/negative. Jung is so convinced of the universality of this perception that he came to speak of God as dark and light, that is, as an archetype, composed of dark and light portions. Jung used the Biblical story of Job as an example. While accepting his psychology, one might dispute Jung's theology. The notion of God as both dark and light contrasts with the Biblical statement, "Don't be deceived, my beloved brethren. Every good gift and very perfect gift is from above, and comes down from the Father of lights, with whom there is no variation or shadow of turning," (James 1:17). From a Biblical point of view the question of God allowing evil is not to be taken as synonymous with God being evil.

The struggle of good against evil represents an archetypal battle that deeply effects the minds of both children and adults. This battle may be experienced inwardly in one's moral development, or may be enacted outwardly in political struggles against oppressive conditions. This archetypal struggle is ubiquitous to the human condition.

Since Freud's and Jung's early work in psychiatry, fascinating research has been done in the realm of primary process thinking. We now know that there are predictable cycles that influence us day and night. During the fifties, dream researchers, Dement and Kleitman (1957), discovered four or five predictable cycles of dreaming that occurred at approximately ninety minute intervals. These cycles influence the production of dreams during the night, but have a more subtle effect during the day. It is also intriguing that mammal's dream, but reptiles do not. It is undeniable that dreams speak to us in visual symbols, and the visual mind is operating continuously. During these cycles the visual mind tends to be stimulated more intensely. We need to tune in to the communications of the visual, metaphoric mind to understand our clients.

The Archetype of the Self

The total personality consists of the ego consciousness, the personal unconscious, and the collective unconscious. This totality constitutes the Self, the central archetype in the collective unconscious. Jung theorized that a person inherits, in the unconscious mind, memories of certain ancestral experiences, which effect behavior in the present. The archetype of the Self serves as a guide and focal point for the movement of psychic energy from the unconscious to the conscious personality. The Self or self is separate from the ego complex, called the self, in lowercase letters. This larger Self may be likened to the submerged portion of an iceberg. Much vaster than the tip of the iceberg, the ego corresponds to the tip of the iceberg, and is supported and nourished by the totality of psyche, or the Self. If these concepts seem difficult read on. You will find the material on imagery useful, and the case material will help clarify some of these concepts.

Analytical Psychologists believe that children are led in their therapeutic work by the emergence in projected form of the archetype of the Self or potential personality pattern. Dora Kalff (1966b) believes the archetype of the Self is a healing factor in sandplay. "The Archetype as a Healing Factor" (Kalff, 1966a) was the first article to explore this aspect of sandplay.

Jung's typology first postulated introversion and extroversion. Research in child development has confirmed that children are born with dispositions toward introversion, the tendency to react with inhibition, withdrawal, or freezing to unexpected events or new people. An infant who exhibits this type of response is called passive. The extroverted type will approach or do something in response to a new event or person. This type is termed an active coper. Individuals also manifest a greater or lesser tendency toward irritability, and inherited talents and natural aptitudes. Paul Mussen, et. al. (1979, p. 143) says, "The most obvious differences among infants are behavioral, however. Although mothers have always recognized that each of their children is 'different from the first day,' psychologists have only more recently begun to look systematically at these initial differences and their potential significance." Categories of initial differences are motor activity, irritability, and passivity. Some children are placid from birth, while others are physically active even while asleep, thrashing and kicking their arms and legs. Irritability is not solely related to activity. Certain infants are easily stimulated responding more by crying, whining, and fretting. These irritable personality types are more difficult to placate than are the infants who easily tolerate frustrations or unusual situations.

It has also been confirmed that individuals have varied learning styles, as Jung put forth in his typology.

These various hereditary tendencies appear to interact with the archetype of wholeness, and form the archetype of the Self that serves to guide the development of the conscious personality. The spiritual component in the human psyche is of paramount importance in Analytical Psychology. The yearning for something deeper, more profound and transcendent than the mundane life of the ego is basic to human nature. I believe this is true of all of us even if we have no conscious awareness of these impulses. This is as true in child psychotherapy as in adult therapy. You will see from the case material that spiritual issues are of paramount importance to certain children. Direct, quick-fix approaches do not touch upon deep spiritual issues.

The archetype of the Self is represented by an image, or images of wholeness that may emerge spontaneously in artwork, dreams or fantasies. Speaking of the spiritual content inherent in the symbol of wholeness, Kalff (1966b) says, "Symbols speak for the inner, energy-laden pictures, of the innate potentials of the human being which, when they are manifested, always influence the development of man. These symbols of numinous or religious content tell of an inner drive for spiritual order that allow relationship to the deity. This order gives man an inner security and insures for him, among other things, the development of his inherent personality." (p. 29).

The Self carries many archetypal images. These images function in pairs of opposites, for example, the image of the eternal youth, or inner child, relates to the image of the old man. These two images are complimentary. Like most classical scholars, Jung used Latin terms. He named this polarity the Puer/Senex. A Puer is an eternal youth. A Senex is an old man. This was popularized as the Peter Pan complex.

The work of a child is play. Children process visually, tactically and symbolically before they verbalize their understanding. This primary level of understanding is followed by verbalization. The work of the child is also the development of a strong ego. The ego's polar opposite is the archetype of the Self. The ego complex is specific and unique to that individual, while the Self carries a full range of human potentialities. This archetype may serve to feed and enrich the ego-complex, or if all is not developing properly, may present dark and frightening images, such as monsters. These threatening images are demands from the unconscious for change and growth. When libidinal energy has accumulated in the unconscious through repression of feelings, such as anger, an image of a threatening nature will be thrown up to the conscious mind. We are challenged to deal with these forces or suffer the consequences. This is precisely why, "It's just a dream, honey," is an inappropriate response.

Unstructured mediums such as sandplay and art materials send out an invitation to the child's unconscious to continue the process of individuation. The child's natural tendency to project his conflicts is stirred by the wide variety of small, highly symbolic objects, the blank paper, or a formless lump of clay. These materials, contained in a clearly defined space, provide a degree of psychic freedom for the child. This creates an area of focus upon which the child projects his personal and interpersonal conflicts as well as his intrapsychic and collective psychic impulses.

Most therapists know to provide materials that will illicit personal and interpersonal conflicts, such as medical toys, toy telephones or toy guns. Additional benefits are provided when a therapist supplies clearly archetypal objects. Traditional play therapy does not address the archetypal realm and the spiritual realm, and subsequently may fail to support the depth of recovery that is possible.

A wide variety of images representing good and evil, masculine and feminine, joy and rage, constellates, or calls up, the archetype of wholeness that has been blocked in its action due to processes as repression and rigid defenses. Reconnecting to images of wholeness helps to repair psychic wounds and blocked energy.

Play and Healing

Since play is the mode chosen by most child psychologists, then one may assume there is something restorative in play. John Sanford (1978) believes the ancient Greeks were right when they sought the healing power of dreams. Although different, primary process thinking, dreams, and play are closely related.

John Perry (1974) suggests that the psyche has a self-healing tendency that exceeds the expectations of most Humanistic psychologists. He believes an acute psychosis is the psyche's attempt to bring about personality reorganization. When not worked through, the primary process of the schizophrenic becomes a destructive trap, whereas the play of a child in therapy is often restorative.

Regarding the dual nature of the unconscious John Sanford (1978) says, "The unconscious can be either a poison or a medicine, destructive or healing (p. 34)." Deep, therapeutic play in the presence of an adult, who has a strong ego, and who understands the process, serves the process of personality reorganization. Sanford (1977) maintains that healing is psychological wholeness. This view harmonizes with Anna Freud's thesis that the neurotic child is rigidly limited, with Axline's view that some part of the child has been rejected, and does not discard Klein's theory of massive repression of fantasy. The therapist's task is to accept the whole person. The process of personality growth is served when the archetype of the Self is acknowledged in all of its complexity.

Is all children's playing therapeutic? This is certainly not true of play filled with repetition compulsion. If not all play is not intrinsically restorative, why does play in therapy result in significant improvement? Many clinicians believe that it is play in the presence of an understanding, accepting adult that provides the conditions for healing. The literature contains many statements by therapists from different disciplines affirming this belief. Estelle Weinrib (1983, p.29) says, "Experience has shown that without the understanding on the part of the therapist of these stages and their symbolic representations, the process is only minimally effective." This unspoken understanding is key to the bond that develops between the client and the therapist. The therapist's understanding and presence in the reality of the present is the child's anchor in the storm.

Everyday play may contain elements of repetition compulsion, while creative play introduces new elements into the child's conscious or preconscious world. The key difference is in the therapist and child dyad. Edith Sullwold (Stein, Ed., 1982) makes the rationale clearer saying the therapist must bring her understanding of the process of maturation to the therapeutic work. She asserts that the therapist must have an experience of the healing power of the unconscious.

In Memories, Dreams, Reflections, Jung (1961) gives an example of creative play, a solitary ritual he created as a boy that ended the feeling of disquietude and gave him a feeling of safety. A therapist may not always be required, but we can act as facilitators and bring new elements into a child's play experience.

A Therapy for All Ages

The literature amply demonstrates that traditional play therapy can be valuable for the younger child. During the latency period, the value of traditional play therapy drops off sharply as children mature. This unique method, sandplay, has value from age four through adulthood, and has proved beneficial with Multiple Personality Disorder, Post Traumatic Stress Disorder, couples and families. As children mature it is increasingly important to provide a sand tray. A colleague of mine commented that a young teenager that she counseling was extremely difficult to talk to and was contemptuous of the toys that she had provided for play therapy. As soon as I had moved my sand tray and collection of objects into her office he began to respond positively, and worked intensely with the materials. Having the fuller range of sandplay objects is also important for the younger child who is severely disturbed. Speak to a child's psyche with imagery and you will find a richness that goes beyond words.

A few caveats if you use plan on using art therapy or sandplay experience it for yourself first. Become aware of and comfortable with your own metaphoric mind. Examining your dreams will be beneficial. Interpretations of symbolic imagery should generally start with the personal, move toward the interpersonal and be followed last by the transpersonal, if needed. Occasionally, a purely archetypal image will be presented by the unconscious. As we will see in the clinical case material, children will open their work with personal and interpersonal problems, and later on in the process may create strongly archetypal work.

Again, I follow Kalff's and Bettelheim's lead and do not verbalize my interpretation to the child. When you interpret for your own understanding, do not be so rule bound that you throw the baby out with the bath water. Do some investigation if in doubt. I worked with a boy who placed a house (a symbol of the self) in the left side of the tray (symbolic of the unconscious), and put a pool (water indicates feelings/unconscious) in the lower right-hand portion which associated with the ego. His unconscious and feelings might be interpreted as overwhelming his ego development, however, I knew this corresponded to the physical layout of his family house and swimming pool. As Freud said, "Sometimes a cigar is just a cigar."

The whole business of assigning interpretations to the four quadrants of a sand tray is hotly debated among sandplay therapists. I often find just focusing of the content and the client's emotional tone and comments is more important than spatial interpretations. See the entry under Quadrants in Appendix A for various theories.

Bonding Breaks and Unattached Children

While dealing with antisocial tendencies in children is beyond the scope of this book with the frequency of school shootings in this country it is important to mention it. In 1987 Dr. Ken Magid and Carole McKelvey published *High Risk: Children Without a Conscience*. Magid has come to believe that if bonding breaks are severe this results in a child who stops trusting and hardens his or her heart. His book suggests that this can be remediated up to age seven, but that it would take nothing less than a miracle to change this mind-set after age seven.

I do not know if psychopathic tendencies can be changed through this method, but Christ-centered counseling has taken a great leap forward with the development of Theophostic Ministry by Ed M. Smith (1999). Smith has had great success freeing clients from the pain of severe ritualistic abuse and other trauma by identifying the source of a lie the client has come to believe early in life and having God minister directly to that place. I have personally seen great and rapid results with adults using this method. Smith claims equal success with children. Since this method is new in my experience I cannot personally verify this, however I believe this method to be a powerful breakthrough for those not adverse to a Christian approach.

Two

An Ideal Playroom

> In providing a bridge to the world,
> the sand tray may serve as a "transitional object"
> as defined by the English child analyst, D.W. Winnicott.
>
> Weinrib, 1983

If I were to design an ideal consultation room, I would want an area for artwork that includes a washable table, an easel, and a deep sink to wash out brushes or to supply water for various projects. Adult and child-sized chairs are a must. I would also want areas for three sand trays. A tray is dry, one that is damp, and a third very wet tray provide more versatility. A large cabinet and stacking bins to contain the sandplay objects is helpful. A large area for floor play is essential for work with preschoolers. I would provide space for a large toy chest, stacking bins with toys and a large chest filled with wooden blocks. It is helpful to have a table for books and games, and projective tests. A special corner can be devoted to music. Since I do not play an instrument I like to have a cassette and CD player and simple rhythm instruments for the children. Other clinicians might have a piano or a guitar in this spot.

Clinicians need to have anatomically correct adult and child dolls for use with children who have been sexually abused. I keep my dolls concealed in a cabinet and take them out for children who need to deal with this specific type of trauma. For children with profound unmet nurturance needs, it is helpful to have baby bottles they can use as Gil (1991) suggests. A puppet theater, a doll house and a rocking chair would round out my selections. A special bonus would be a small patio, with a faucet, so dirty objects might be washed without having clay or sand damage the plumbing.

The art area should include such items as: clay, paint, markers, watercolors, pencils, and finger paints, glue and collage materials, colored paper, white paper, magazines with photos, scraps of fabric, wallpaper samples, etc. to stimulate creative expression. Material for creating puppets and masks is fun, if the therapist is capable of guiding these activities.

For three-dimensional work, it is useful to have both water base and oil base clays available. Plasticine is oil base clay. Sculpy (brand name) clay may be hardened in an oven. I have suggested to children who are having difficulty in balancing an animal or a figure on a house, cave, or mountain that they use a small amount of plasticine clay to temporarily secure their piece. One child used a little clay to adhere a figure that tumbled up side down as he fell off a motorcycle. Water base clay may be reused or fired so that the child can take home his or her finished creation. I have had a local ceramic shop fire the clay sculptures that some of the children have made while in therapy. After the objects are fired the child can use a mixture of watercolor paint, water, and glue to color their sculptures. This shortens the time it takes to complete the project, and dispenses with the need to stock glazes and make the trip to the kiln for a second glaze firing. Of course, a small kiln in the playroom would be wonderful.

If the therapist is skilled in art, and the child is particularly interested in art, then more emphasis can be given to creating something that is artistic for this too can be therapeutic. Children have a tremendous need for a sense of mastery, and creating artwork can be quite a boost to the ego. Mastery can also be facilitated through the use of crafts and hobby materials, woodcarving, puppet making, etc. I have found helping adults create art in addition to psychological counseling has brought some individuals out of a deep depression.

Sand trays on carts with wheels may be moved around the room as the child or the therapist desires. I prefer the use of three sand trays because the children have really enjoyed pushing the limits of what is possible. When we have had access to a sink and a place where excess water can be disposed of, I have allowed children to fill one tray quite full with water. I use a tray made of molded fiberglass that is ideal for use with very wet sand (see Appendix B). If the child wants to use moist sand, rather than super-saturated sand and water, a pitcher can be used to scoop up the excess water. Sponges may then be used to blot up the remaining excess water. I have several castle molds that have been used by numerous children and teens. Fairly damp sand is required to use molds. A vinyl floor helps at clean-up time.

The arrangement of the sandplay objects is important. I prefer to have toys arranged on open shelves as close to the trays as possible. This has not always met with a positive response. The variety and number of items can overwhelm either developmentally disabled or obsessive personalities. This can be detrimental to their treatment. I recommend a closed cabinet for many of the objects or I place groups of related objects in baskets, while displaying a few special pieces on shelves. A large cabinet can provide an excellent storage space for games, toys, and art materials.

Groupings of similar sandplay objects are placed into baskets or bins that are lined so tiny items will not drop out. Trees, plants, flowers, and related items are all contained in one of the larger baskets. Spacemen with spaceships, cowboys with Indians, fairy tale characters, family figures, shells, rocks, and pebbles are contained in their own separate baskets, or stored together. For example, I have one bin that contains shells, pirates, hula dancers, frogmen and deep sea divers, a treasure chest, fish, etc. This method facilitates play. A child can pick up the basket with cars, trucks, emergency vehicles, policemen and firemen in a single motion and take them over to the tray. Large objects, such as castles, volcanoes, and houses, as well as fragile ceramic items, are best placed on shelves. The most frequently used items may be placed upon the cart shelves on which the tray is housed.

A well-equipped room, like a wide variety of sandplay objects, shows the therapist's interest in and acceptance of the child. Unstructured materials, such as clay and paints, allow for a variety of responses. It is important to have more than just sandplay available so that the child is not forced to use such a potentially powerful method week after week. Some children are overwhelmed by the sandplay materials and need to use them with less frequency. The case material on Bertha illustrates this difficulty.

Three

Working Through

> I know that at least six to eight weeks are
> needed before a situation that is just becoming
> visible as it emerges from the unconscious,
> can push through into the outer life. It is
> as delicate as a newly-sprouting blade of grass
> that needs attentive care. Dora Kalff, 1966

Some children will come into therapy eager to use the materials to work through their conflicts; others may need to test the relationship in order to feel safe before revealing themselves. During the first session, I recommend asking the child to draw a person, then draw a person of the opposite sex, and then draw a tree followed by a house. After the House-Tree-Person drawings, the child can be asked to draw a picture of all the members of his family doing something—a Kinetic Family Drawing. After these two classic projective tests, I would encourage the child to make a picture in the sand tray and then to tell a story about the picture. At times I will ask about a particular toy or object they have used or a situation that has been depicted. Most of the time children quickly respond with information that is helpful in understanding their process. Interviews with the parents, foster parents, teachers and other significant adults, along with a few questions for the child, will provide a baseline for the therapeutic work that will follow.

Dora Kalff (1966) sees interpretation as unnecessary during sandplay therapy. If it is to be utilized it is only after a strong ego is developed and the individual is secure in his or her identity.

Kalff (ibid.) sees a child passing through three stages in sandplay therapy. She calls the first stage, the vegetative. During this period, the child will appear stuck or stagnant. He will often create messy, unformed or watery trays. Once I began to allow children to use copious amounts of water the vegetative stage has intensified for certain children.

The second stage is the fighting or struggle phase. Many boys spend the bulk of their work in this phase. Some children will enter therapy during this stage and then temporarily cycle back to the vegetative. Evelyn Dundas has noted that instead of a fighting phase, many girls pen-up animals with which they identify. Dundas (1978) sees the need for females to move inward and deal with their instinctual nature, rather than outward into conflict. She says, "girls move into the second or struggle phase by containing then freeing themselves from their instinctual identity."

During the third and final phase, adaptation to the collective or, simply, the community stage, the child will tend to create cities, towns, or use construction trucks. My clinical work over years with a wide variety of children confirms Kalff's paradigm. I have found that this stage can be brief. If the child has completed the process of working through, the play will cease to be as compelling. At this time I believe it is ideal to switch over to games designed by therapists to improve therapist/child communication. Intense play followed by brief periods of verbal consolidation is ideal for this process corresponds to the way a child learns. With other children the community stage is often followed by another vegetative stage and a new cast of symbolic characters and themes are introduced.

When the therapeutic process is complete, or has to be terminated early for some reason we review what the child has done. Some therapists that use art as therapy or sandplay make slides of every piece of art or every tray. These can be shown in a projector during a review of the previous sessions. I usually do not go to this expense. I make notes and diagrammatic drawings as the child plays. From these I will either refer to key points in the child's work, and help the child reconstruct an important sand tray. This review is generally very well received.

Four

Cries for Help

> Conflict of opposing urges, feelings, duties, etc., thus suffered, eventually calls forth what Jung calls the reconciling symbol. This appears, not from the imagination or the fantasy of the analyst, nor from the inventiveness of the patient, but spontaneously from the unconscious itself. Whitmont, 1969

The next chapters include case studies illustrating the process of ego formation, artwork in service of defense, portions of depth work that utilize sandplay, and includes the creation of a personal myth. Special emphasis will be placed on the importance of the symbol as a vehicle for transformation. Play in service of the child's need for mastery will not be covered, even though it can be an important part of the child psychotherapist's approach to the total child. Most of the case material consists of short vignettes taken from my work with children. Occasionally I have used a fragment from a colleague's case material. The story of Jennifer, in Chapter Eleven, clearly illustrates the process of working through a difficult mother complex. These children range in age from four years to twelve years old. Their names are fictitious.

Assessment, Diagnosis, or Treatment?

When asked whether the sand tray is to be used for diagnosis or for treatment, my reply is an unequivocal, "Both." When I see a new client my first question is, "Who owns the problem?" Is the child acting-out the family's problem or has she internalized family pathology and needs treatment separate from helping the parents?

In many ways the sand tray is an excellent projective instrument since the child is freed from such structures as the Children's Apperception Test cards, nor is she or he presented with such vague stimulus as the Rorschach cards. Family figures, animals, heroes and villains all can be manipulated, as can the sand. Children may dramatically play out their interpersonal or intrapsychic situation in a way that is natural and appealing. The trays don't have the structured artificiality of certain of the commonly used diagnostic methods. Diagnosis can flow into the process of depth psychotherapy without a sharp demarcation between the two processes. If the child refuses or seems unable to engage in symbolic play it may be helpful to do an assessment of the child's maturation.

I prefer to work with children in pairs if I have a number of children that I am working with at a single location, such as a school or child guidance center. By doing this I can see how the child relates to his sibling or to another child. For these conjoint sessions I do initial assessments so I can match the children as to intelligence, gender, age and style of play. Generally, I match boys with boys and girls with girls. I have paired a boy with a girl when the two children were well matched in style of play, age and intelligence. When I work with a child who is cross-gender identified, I will pair him with a girl or, her with a boy if that seems workable, or I will see the child individually.

Assessing Intelligence

David was five years and four months when first seen. He was adopted as an infant. David's behaviors and initial sand tray work convinced me that he is an extremely bright boy, much more so than indicated by his WPPSI I.Q.

score of 115. During his intake session David created a Human Figure Drawing indicated that was crude and impressionistic, but was not bizarre or inhuman. His play behaviors are sensitive and self-confident.

David frequently intruded on Andrew's play. Treatment goals centered primarily on his learning to respect the work and boundaries of his partner in sessions and continuing the process of separation-individuation.

Much of his initial session was concerned with a mutual establishment of the rules of sandplay therapy. David informed me that "fish and shells belong at the beach, not ducks." He reassured me that he would be careful with my ceramic houses, and asked about the function of the volcanoes, "Why these mountains got fire? Where do they live?"

David showed interest in the pretty and delicate toys, such as the "pretty girls" and the deer, yet he seemed to feel that he has to reject these objects as they did not fit his developing masculine ego. He rejected the girls saying, "Na", and the deer by saying, "I don't want any deers. They are ugly."

His careful shaping of the sand a behavior that is not usually seen in a five-year-old immediately demonstrated David's high intelligence. Intelligence is also seen in his unusual and inventive creative play; his comments as he plays, and his ability to construct an elaborate zoo scene complete with fences.

The beautifully constructed zoo that he created during his eleventh session was an appropriate place in which he could use the deer without threatening his manhood. David's zoo was complete with a cave. He told me, "Lions go in there at night."

The use of fences was another indicator of David's intellectual capacity. Although a few children use fences earlier than others, Buhler did not observe the use of fences much before age eight. Since David was five and a half, this is significant.

Finding an appropriate place in his world for the feminine, pictured by the deer, without having to reject it wholesale is a distinct accomplishment in such a young child.

Cries for Help

When a child is the identified patient, I ask questions about the family's home life, and encourage the parent(s) to look at their own process. Whenever appropriate I encourage the parents to work on their own issues in therapy. If they do not, I will work with the child, and counsel with the parents briefly whenever I need to inform them of their child's progress. I will refer them to books on parenting and communication skills.

Seven-year-old Susan was referred to a colleague of mine, because of behavior problems at home and at school. She came from a broken family. Her mother claimed that she had adjusted to the new situation. Susan was now living with her mother, while her brother lived with their father. Susan's mother was overly solicitous and intrusive into her daughter's child's activities and feelings and she seemed to be smothering Susan.

During an early session Susan chose four volcanoes, four family figures, four corks and a heroic figure for her tray. What is both striking and disturbing is that she stopped each of the volcanoes with a cork. What a powerful visual demonstration of the family's blocked rage this was. Without a word she informed the therapist of her family's need for treatment. It is important that cries for help are heeded. The therapist can see the family as a unit, or make a referral to other professionals. I have seen a number of separated parents attend parenting classes. Hopefully, the family will join the child in recovery rather than sabotage her growth.

Plate 1 Blocked family rage.

Eight-year-old Louise was brought to me by her mother for diagnosis. Her parents divorced earlier that year. She had begun having problems with asthma. I asked if she were getting enough attention from her parents since there is often a correlation between poor family relationships and childhood asthma. Her mother replied that the child's father gave their children enough attention but she, the custodial parent, has not. I agreed to see the child for a diagnostic evaluation while encouraging Louise's mother to spend more time with her daughter.

When she walked into the room Louise was immediately delighted with the sand trays and the art materials. During her session she created two sand trays and two paintings. First, she piled the sand up into a large, circular hill. Louise picked a dramatic couple that I had just purchased in a fantasy role playing shop (Dungeons and Dragons, etc.). The male stood over the woman, while the she knelt with her hands bound before him. He holds a knife menacing the woman. Most children did not select this piece. She placed these figures in the center-right portion of the tray. The rest of the figures were placed around this couple in an irregular circle. Louise said that the man was going to kill the woman. The skeleton was a person that had already been killed. The king, unicorn, and the dwarves tell the man to stop. These inner figures are quite positive in terms of her inner resources.

Asthma often is associated with a threat, or fear of death. The man threatening the woman has many potential meanings. Her parents' divorce was a deep heart wound, and a threat to her identity. Was there a battering situation between her father and mother before they separated? Her mother did not share this with me. Obviously, Louise felt a tremendous sense of loss, with further losses possible. The king, unicorn and dwarves are positive inner animus figures, which soften the threat indicated by the man with a knife. Was the death indicated by the skeleton the death of her parent's marriage?

Plate 2 Don't kill her!

The next tray was much more positive. In the center of the tray upon the hill, Louise created a vegetable garden. This second tray's theme centered on family, instinctual feelings, mothering, and the feminine principle. This tray was much more typical of an eight-year-old girl than her first tray.

Louise's first painting demonstrated conflicting feelings. She painted a man who appeared to be agitated. White drops of paint that represent tears surrounded him. Louise pointed out that he was smiling while crying. Above the figure, and to the right, she painted the word "mad." She appeared gleeful as she repeated that the man is smiling, crying, and mad. This is a high level of awareness for an eight-year-old. A verbal acknowledgment of these conflicting emotions is rare in a child this age. What is not unusual is that these emotions are projected, rather than acknowledged as her own. Was she identified with her father who carries these conflicting emotions? Why would she be gleeful? Was she identified with her mother who happily rejected her spouse? This was puzzling.

Looking at her first tray and this painting I thought, This child seems to be burdened by her parents' unconscious. This hypothesis seemed to be confirmed by her second painting of a man starving to death in a desert. The man's torso is skeleton-like. Drops of blood scattered about the figure represent his dying. She pointed out the sad expression.

Louise wanted to share her work with her mother. It is only after the child asks that I will have her share sand trays or paintings with a parent. I prefer not do this every session, but only occasionally since the session is the child's private time to vent and find her own strengths. When I spoke to her mother, I stressed Louise's work was unusually strong for a first session. Louise clearly internalizes her family's pain. Internalized family pain is one of the chief criteria for child psychotherapy. I encouraged Louise's mother to bring both Louise and her brother in for therapy. We discussed finances. Since her mother was already in therapy with another therapist, I offered to see both siblings in conjoint sessions at a low fee. Unfortunately, as much as the child cried out for help in her sand tray and paintings, her mother decided against therapy for her children. One can lead a horse to water…

Five

Circumnambulation and the Mandala Form

> "The goal of psychic development is the self. There is no linear evolution; there is only a circumnambulation of the self."
>
> C.G. Jung, 1963

The first great task in life is the development of a strong ego that is differentiated from the Self, or undifferentiated wholeness, and freed from the unconscious of the parents. In dysfunctional family systems this is a difficult. The process of separation and individuation is reflected by the child's work in the sand tray, and by his drawings and play. Ego formation usually proceeds quite rapidly, however one may see a child whose energy remains scattered and unformed. Andrew was such a child.

Unformed Trays

Andrew was five years and one month when he entered therapy. He was a charming, sensitive child. His Full Scale I.Q. was 101. Andrew's Human Figure Drawing was extremely primitive. Ghostlike, it was notable for its lack of arms and legs. As clinicians trained in art therapy are aware this indicates a lack of grounding, and difficulties with parents. Andrew's behaviors were disruptive and difficult to manage. He was easily influenced or overwhelmed by other children. Andrew's play behaviors showed indicators of creativity and intelligence, but in a half-formed, amorphous fashion. It is notable that he was adopted as an infant.

Kalff (1980. p. 24) states that in about the third year of life the "Center of the Self is stabilized in the unconscious of the child and begins to manifest itself in symbols of wholeness." These images of wholeness may appear as squares, circles or religious figures.

Edith Sullwold's comments (Jungian Analysis, Murray Stein, Ed., 1982) may have a bearing upon Andrew's unformed trays. She maintains that when the child has failed to experience a sense of unity with the parents, the image of unity with the archetype of the Self may be absent. Andrew's adoptive parents were loving, but over-extended since they had several small children at home, and both parents worked full-time. Their work schedules often include weekends—a less than ideal situation.

Plate 3 Andrew's disorganized world.

Andrew used the sand tray toys provided by the guidance center before I brought my research project and sand tray objects. It took very many weeks of Andrew's asking, "Is this yours?" for this child to sort out which objects were mine. He was more relaxed after he had gotten this clear in his mind.

Andrew's object choices were masculine (female figures made only a fleeting appearance). He played intensely, creating appropriate and interesting sound effects. This in itself could be said to be indicative of some separation from the maternal matrix of the unconscious, and a strong sense of masculine identity.

Andrew's Machine Age Totem

The toy motorcycle was his most cathected object. It represented his sense of manhood, and was the closest to a symbol of the Self that he produced. Whenever I think of Andrew, I recall the toy motorcycle—a constant point in a sea of change. Once I observed the ubiquitous motorcycle secreted in a cave. Here was a place that offers some protection. A cave symbolizes a place of renewal and transformation, or place of fear and dissolution. The positive interpretation of a cave seems appropriate here.

Andrew's motorcycle serviced as a machine-age totem. It appeared to serve a similar purpose for Andrew. Ancient man used animal figures as objects upon which they could project and focus their psychological characteristics.

Andrew's intelligence was evident by his shaping of the sand; his intuition by his unusual fantasy play, by his frequent playing with airplanes in the air above the tray, and by the very scattered quality of his play. That these patterns remain constant through out the process of therapy illustrated that this unformed and disorganized quality was typical of Andrew's intuitive and fluid psyche.

During the months we worked together Andrew's trays remained chaotic and unformed. In Buhler's terms they were "disorganized." Most children create trays that have more form. He was in what Kalff would term a vegetative stage. Andrew struggles to form a strong ego. Greater structure in his school and home life, adult help with clarifying his thinking processes would improve this child's ability to focus and help him feel less scattered. More physical play, including eye contact with his adoptive parents would enhance bonding. Working in the sand tray provided an excellent opportunity to begin to focus and contain his energies and form a more adequate sense of self.

During the brief time I had to work with Andrew, he seemed to be finding the process useful in terms of establishing his developing ego and masculine identity, represented by the motorcycle. The process of sand play served his growth needs admirably. Continuing the sandplay process along with specific guidance in helping him focus his energies would benefit Andrew. Andrew might be encouraged to just make one story during a session.

After only four months of working together, his next Human Figure Drawing was a recognizable little boy. Although it did appear more doll-like than lifelike, the basics were there, and it was a great step forward for a five-year-old.

Images of Centering

Images of centering and mandala-like forms occur in the work of children who enter therapy with a strong disturbance as well as in trays of children who have resolved their major conflict. Spiral, circular movement is natural to the psyche. Ego development is proceeding when this occurs. The next few cases highlight this phenomenon.

Camellia, Overwhelmed and Overburdened

Camellia was a pretty, eight-year-old who gave the impression of greater maturity. She appeared to be an extremely sensitive youngster who was working quite hard to please her mother. When her mother was busy in therapy sessions, Camellia bore the responsibility for her infant brother and younger siblings, usually without complaint. As therapy progressed she seemed to show signs of resenting the burden of the younger children.

Camellia's behavior indicated that she wanted to play more, especially with the other children who visited the counseling center.

Her first sand tray was remarkable since it showed an overlap between conscious and unconscious that is global. Analytic Psychologists believe that a young person has access to unconscious contents in several ways. The first connection with the unconscious occurs during the earliest years. This is the matrix from which the ego emerges. The child is in a fused state with the parents' unconscious, most particularly with the mother's. The second type of connection results from a deep psychological wound. This wound allows an intrusion of unconscious material. The unconscious may flood and contaminate the conscious mind, bringing up images that would not occur to the nascent ego. It is this wounding that brings so many borderline personalities their uncanny psychic abilities. This wounding of the psyche brings in images from the psyche that are usually unconscious. These images are then projected. A third type of contact with the unconscious occurs when images from the parent's psyche invade the child's dreams and fantasies. These images may appear as monsters or as images that speak to the parent's problem. The fourth possible connection to the unconscious relates to a specific personality type. Jung's typology postulates four styles or types of consciousness, or learning styles: thinking, feeling, sensation and intuition. An intuitive personality is quick to perceive things best known through the realm of unconscious—out of the air, if you will. Several methods of receiving unconscious contents may occur within a single individual. It is likely that in Camellia's case that at least two of these factors were operating.

My sense was that Camellia's unusual initial tray indicated a wounded intuitive. Even though her tray contained many objects, it retained an aesthetic quality that is lacking in the work of less talented individuals. The tray's contents formed a spiral mandalic form. Signs of an abandoned or destroyed treasure hunt are evident throughout the tray. Two rock walls form protective grottos. Each grotto served to protect one or more animals. Animals are generally interpreted to be symbolic of the instincts.

Next to the grotto on the left side of the tray stood an owl, a rabbit and a mouse. The grotto on the right shelters a second owl. A seated fawn was nestled next to a clam shell (a symbol of the feminine) in the center of the tray. These objects all speak of the feminine core of her personality. Two horses stood in the upper rear of the tray, while two antelopes stood in the lower center/front. A third antelope was lying almost totally buried in the lower right front corner. Only his horns and a part of his head show. This indicates some damage to the instinctual self. A kettle, a feminine symbol, was half-buried on the far left.

A helmet of a worker was half buried in the lower right corner. Partially buried treasure-hunting equipment (a pick and shovel) were placed in the upper right corner. A lifeboat was half buried in the lower left-hand corner. Right above it, in the upper left-hand corner, we find the treasure. It is notable that the signs of this treasure hunt are on the outer circle. The feminine core was unaffected.

What is the treasure—her childhood? Is it a loss of appropriate relationship to her parents, particularly her mother? This first communication was deep and poignant. After seeing many trays by both adults and children, I found the contents of this tray to be deeply moving. The toys had to be returned to the shelves and baskets at the end of the session since other children would be using the tray right after her session. Camellia and I did this together. I wanted to honor her creation, yet all I could say was, "There was a lot that lived in this tray." She seemed pleased.

After my initial assessment of the group of children I was assigned conjoint therapy sessions were begun. During her second session Camellia observed a tray that impressed her. Subsequently she created a whole series of trays based upon his concept. While she modified the content to suit her own psychology, and carried through a psychologically relevant process, I felt uneasy about the strength of the outside influence.

She created a world in which a little girl could develop and was cared for by many inner figures. A nurturing family, parental figures and an archetypal Wise Old Man cared for her little heroine. This was a positive way of dealing with her nurturance needs. During the creation of one of her last trays she asked me to help her search for the "right" little girl. She described this little girl as being four or five years old. This inner self was quite a contrast from eight-year-old Camellia's real life responsibility of being the second mother in an over-burdened household. Finding and nurturing her inner child was key to the treasure that was lost. My concern about the outside influence disappeared.

If Camellia and I had worked together longer she might have used the trays to express some resentment at her position as one of the family's primary caregivers. I recommended to her parents' therapist that they need to be more aware of this burden, and to allow her more time to play.

During our last session together I reviewed the work she had done in the sand tray. From these past trays she took a little of each and created a composite scene. This was a loving and delicate way of saying good-bye to the process and experience.

Six

T. Rex Meets S. Freud

> Any body can become angry-that is easy; but
> to be angry with the right person, and to the
> right degree, and at the right time, and for
> the right purpose, and in the right way—that
> is not within everybody's power and is not easy.
>
> Aristotle: Nicomachean Ethics

During my Master's program, I had one Freudian and one Jungian instructor. The Jungian by far was the greater influence in my life not only because he taught more courses in the program than she did, but because my dreams and life experience validated Jungian psychology. During the process of working with children so I could learn sandplay therapy certain basic concepts of Freudian psychology reared their primitive heads in the sand.

The human brain core contains a mass of primitive structures that are similar to the reptilian brain. This group of structures has been alternately termed the reptilian brain and the R-complex (MacLean, 1973). The brain stem is remarkably similar in all vertebrate creatures. This reptilian core is the primitive, instinctual portion of the brain. Research indicates that this area contains the neural impulses for violence, ritual, mating, forming social hierarchies, obsessive behaviors, selecting leaders, territorial behaviors, insistence on routine, and lavish imitation of fashion. Emotions are not present in this system, nor is appreciation of the past-future time continuum. These findings are especially important when interpreting primitive, regressive imagery, obsessive or ritualistic play behaviors, and in work with acting-out, antisocial adolescents.

This portion of the brain may be responsible for the will to power. When domestic cats exhibit intense territorial display behaviors as the stiff-legged, arched-back, hair-raised response when a strange cat strays into their territory, the R-complex has been triggered. MacLean found that only lesions to the R-complex would inhibit display behaviors in such advanced animals as the squirrel monkey. The higher areas of the brain are not responsible for these behaviors.

Damage to the R-complex results in an inability to initiate and carry out routines. Animals with massive destruction of this area lost their species specific behaviors. MacLean suggests that it is the R-complex that is largely responsible for our non-verbal behaviors. Some non-verbal behaviors that have been attributed to the right brain belong to the brain stem.

The midbrain, or mammalian brain, is termed the affective brain. This area is composed of those subcortical structures that include the limbic system. The hypothalamus and the pituitary gland that control the endocrine system are included. The limbic system is the seat of our emotional responses. It is involved in the feeling-toned complexes that Jung described. MacLean believes that it is this area that unites internal and external experience, and is vital to our reality testing.

MacLean states that the triune brain suffers from a design weakness since the older centers, the R-complex and the limbic system, have few neural connections linking them to the neo-cortex. He maintains that this results in our being afflicted with a quasi-schizophrenic split between reason and emotion. Charles Hampden-Turner (1981, p. 82) says, "Famous psychoanalysts might rightly insist that deep within us is a quite different, dumb, dark, yet powerful mind, binding us to some ancestral superego, and which, full of resistances, fastens tenaciously on symbols which express its feelings." Dr. J.P. Henry (1977) believes that subcortical structures are involved with the psychological experience of archetypal forms that create much of our experience of the collective unconscious.

Working Through Rage and Self-Hatred

Asian American eleven-year-old Ken had been to a lot of therapists, and didn't like being sent to one at school. He wandered around the playroom brooding, stopped at the playhouse and examined the basketful of playhouse furniture. He selected the miniature mop, broom, and rake, and jammed them into the chimney of the playhouse—pure phallic aggression. Next he stuffed all the furnishings into the dollhouse in a total jumble. As satisfied as psychopathic rapist might be, he moved to the sand tray and selected a house. He placed this in the center of the tray and surrounded it with tanks, airplanes, and other weapons. He proceeded to bury the house, and then buried all the weapons in this configuration. This initial tray appeared to be the embodiment of pathological burial. After these extreme behaviors he announced that he would not work with me, and he left the room.

Fortunately, a child Ken admired enjoyed working with me. He relented after several months and began to come to my consultation room for a weekly session. Because of the extreme pathology and his late start, he was seen alone.

His initial session was most destructive I had seen up to that time. I reviewed his files and found that he had just been recommended to UCLA's Neuropsychiatric Institute, and that he was receiving special education services.

I visited his classroom. Ken had to work at a desk by himself because of his inappropriate and disruptive behaviors. I spoke to my supervisor and told him that I suspected that this child might be a borderline personality who might lapse into psychotic episodes. Since I was doing these sessions as an internship in a public school, I was surprised at the severity of Ken's pathology. I thought the prognosis to be abysmal and wondered if I could be of service.

Plate 4 Ken—Under attack

Burying the house symbolizes Ken's demoralized state and overwhelmed ego. Burying weapons indicates aggression that is piling up and turned inward. Together both are indicative of severe pathology as Buhler (1941) noted. This tremendous rage, self-hatred and aggression is forced back into the unconscious/R-complex. This back up of energy serves to give the destructive powers of the unconscious even greater strength.

Houses are interpreted as being symbolic of the individual. In a child's world the house is also associated with the parents, especially with mother. The attack upon the dollhouse chimney with the mop, rake, and broom followed by the stuffing of the interior of the house with a jumble of furniture suggested a symbolic raping and defiling mother combined with intense self-hatred. He verbally challenged and assaulted me during that initial session saying with contempt, "You must be at least forty years old."

I was not yet that age, and knew that I looked years younger. Obviously, a virulent transference emerged. To clarify the situation I asked, "Is your mother forty or older?"

Ken replied, "Yes." I informed him that I was not forty to help him differentiate therapist from mother.

His artwork was immature and his play often was poorly organized. Ken created many crude glue men on white paper. He usually asked me to show them to the boy he liked.

As he came to feel comfortable and safe with me, he began to value our time together. Months later, after a positive therapeutic alliance had developed, Ken placed the Oriental house in the middle of the tray. Weapons stood on either end of the tray facing the house. He stood there motionless.

I asked quietly, "What happens to the house?"

He replied, "It's alright, it isn't destroyed."

Plate 5 The house isn't destroyed!

As the school year was ending I spoke with the aides on the playground and found that the destructive boy's games in which Ken was the victim stopped during the time we worked together.

Ken came to regret that he had not started working with me earlier in the school year. During our last few weeks together he counted off each session that remained.

Deep-Seated Rage Creating A Resistance to Sandplay

Nine-year-old Bertha had a behavior problem in the classroom. When I began working at this school I asked several teachers to refer children to me who were poorly socialized and withdrawn or poorly socialized and overly aggressive. Bertha was one of those who was overly aggressive. She had just a few friends, other Black girls. Bertha was significantly overweight. She was bossy with most children, as well as difficult to manage in the classroom.

Bertha liked both the sand tray and the dollhouse, but chose to spend most of her first session playing in the sand like a small child might at the beach. She seemed fascinated just shaping the sand, and had me play a simple guessing game with her. I had three different sized plastic scoops. She spent time carefully hiding a scoop in the sand. She asked me to guess where the scoop was hidden, almost as if she still had to deal with the basic experience of object constancy.

After she tired of the hiding game, she placed dollhouse furniture and family figures into the sand tray. I have often observed dollhouse furniture used in the sand tray during many girls' play. These objects are rarely chosen for sandplay by boys, and are never used to the same extent as by the girls, except by males who are cross-gender identified.

Bertha began to play that she was feeding the family figures. As her play progressed she became increasingly aggressive. Eventually the whole family was engulfed in an earthquake. One by one family members were killed and buried by the earthquake. The older son and a young infant are all that remained. He hears the infant crying. In attempting to rescue the baby he was killed. Last of all the infant dies. Bertha was the youngest child in her large family. Clearly these burials seem to indicate severe dysfunction and pathology.

During her third session she played appropriately and peacefully with toys girl's usually choose, i.e. the family figures, flowers, containers, dancing figures, gentle animals. I noticed only one problem; she crowded the tray with too many objects. Crowding the tray may reflect: 1) low intelligence, 2) anxiety and obsessive defenses, 3) a poor aesthetic sense, 4) a combination of these factors.

It is my habit to give a five-minute warning as the session is drawing to a close. When I told Bertha that we only had a few minutes remaining in the session, she picked up a plastic meat cleaver and gesturing, cuts off the head and legs of an adult female figure. Bertha kept glancing sideways to see my reaction. Bertha's rage at her mother might have been the cause of this behavior, and she was wondering if I would be judgmental or offended as an adult woman. I accepted the mayhem without appearing shocked or disturbed. The intensity of Bertha's rage was difficult for her to accept. Fear of reprisal and guilt can often be closely associated with this type of primitive rage. Once more, here is the pathology that was initially seen in the earthquake/burial sand tray.

Bertha's artwork and sand trays were messy, and lacked careful planning. Occasionally her designs were quite good, but she would continue too long and create a mess. This is a problem even skilled artists have to resist. When I added a wet tray to the consultation room she mushed around in the sand, making mud pies, much as would a preschooler. Bertha loved to be praised for her efforts. She was so competitive with other children that I stopped conjoint sessions and worked with her alone. Rather than missing the other child, Bertha seemed to love having all of my attention. Was all that rage a result of feeling neglected in a large household?

Most of her sessions were spent doing trivial artwork, such as sentimental Valentine cards, and simple bands of color filling a page. These activities are indicative of Bertha's resistance to the therapeutic process. Resistance is not always problematic in therapy. It often reflects the psyche's need to slow down the process. I let several sessions past in this manner, and then asked her to work in the sand tray. Bertha used the sand tray each time I asked. Powerfully destructive trays resulted in every incidence.

It was during these times that she talked about liking such horror movies as, Blood Beach. She talked about Lois Lane being buried during an earthquake in the movie Superman I. Here was another reoccurrence of the theme of burial during an earthquake that emerged during her initial session. While she talked she buries a fat, old Oriental sage. This image seemed to relate to her family. Obesity was typical in her family—primitive feelings encased in adipose tissue.

I had not seen a child who would avoid the sand tray so long, and then produce such destruction in the tray. It appeared that the sandplay's evocative potential, and the multiplicity of the toys that I provided were overwhelming to her for several reasons. Bertha's I.Q., that I would estimate was about 85, seemed to be a factor in her reaction to the number of items that sat exposed upon the open shelves. My impression was that the sheer number of objects overwhelmed her. Most crucial was her intuitive fear of the depth of sand tray work. The banality of her artwork was a resistance to, and a buffer against, the power and threat of the sand tray that triggered her unspoken rage at her family. It was notable that her rage was not projected onto fantasy figures or animals. In using family figures she failed to adequately distance herself. Murderous, primitive rage is a threat to the developing ego. Symbolic representation has great psychological value. Bertha might have benefited by guidance to help her project her feelings onto animals or fantasy figures. Family therapy was recommended.

Years later I worked with two boys that reminded me of Bertha. Problems that were seen in her play behaviors will be addressed when the play of Brian and Geoffrey is covered later in the text.

Transforming Suicidal Feelings

Before I was able to set up a sand tray in this next setting I began to see a young client. Jeff was eleven when he began work with me. He asked to speak to a counselor because he was having suicidal thoughts. Jeff believed that he was the bad person in the family. I asked about his family life and found that he was a scapegoat. Both his mother and grandmother took turns blaming and criticizing him. Once his grandmother chased him out of the house with a broom. Jeff was clearly depressed.

I explained that depression is anger turned inward, and suggested that during his session with me he could safely express some anger at his mother and grandmother. This idea frightened him. I convinced him that his anger would be something that just he and I knew about. I asked him to draw his angry feelings at the way he was treated. Initially this idea scared him, but with some reassurance he began to draw.

Jeff began by drawing a house with his grandmother and mother inside. Far above the pair he drew an airplane with himself as the tiny pilot. From the plane a single, silent bomb falls toward the house.

"What happens next?" I ask.

Jeff drew the house exploding. Mother and grandmother were flying out through the explosion.

"What happens next?" I ask.

Jeff drew a long, phallic column and grandmother and mother falling down on each side of the column. They were falling down toward a group of jagged marks that looked like sharp mountains.

"What happens next?" I ask.

Jeff drew a conveyer belt, and explained that they were ground up into hamburger.

"What happens next?" I ask.

Jeff drew himself going to the meat counter where he bought the hamburger.

"What happens next?" I ask.

He drew himself relaxing by a barbecue while the hamburgers cook.

"What happens next?" I ask.

The consequence of his train of thought was too intense. Jeff could not totally identify with the oral sadistic rage he felt. He drew a cannibal with a hamburger in his mouth. This is the kind of displacement that would have helped Bertha.

"What happens next?" I ask.

The last drawing was of a stomach with the hamburger in it. A cartoon style balloon contained the plea, "We are sorry, please forgive us!" We arrived at a point of resolution, and this was a first session.

His initial sand tray was done in the second session. For this he brought in a partially burnt toy submarine in which he said a boy was trapped. The session focused on his rescue. Long cycles of work would be needed to deal with his feelings of rejection and inferiority.

Jeff had not recovered, but the rage directed inward had been redirected, and his imagery was now focused on rescue and help. He never complained about feeling suicidal again during the remainder of the time that we worked together.

Seven

Images of Psychic Attack

> The ego of the child is still too unformed to be able to set up barriers against the invasion of forces that move in the unconscious of the adult to whom he is still bound in an identification....
>
> Wickes, 1927

The idea for this book grew out of a question from a colleague who asked, "What do snakes mean in a sand tray?" What do snakes mean in a sand tray? As I explain in Appendix A, the Dictionary of Play Therapy Imagery, snakes can be a positive or negative image, healing or poison. In the next few stories we will see several snake images. As mentioned earlier, one type of contact with the unconscious may occur when images from the parent's psyche invade the child's dreams and fantasies. These images may appear as monsters or as images that speak to the parent's problem.

A Mother-Complex and a Chaotic Family

Howard was a slender seven-year-old boy who came from a shattered family situation. He had been in therapy with a colleague for several months previous to this particular session. On this particular day Howard came to his session and knew exactly what he wanted to do. He created a sand tray in which a snake was wriggling toward a bird's nest that contained unprotected eggs.

Plate 6 Howard's plight

Eggs carry hidden potential. They represent the concept of rebirth or renewal, and as such are symbolic of transformation. There are many parts of the personality that need to be developed so that the child can separate from the maternal matrix. The serpent or snake is a libidinal image, and can be healing or destructive. This child was dominated and threatened by an over-bearing and over-protective mother. His mother was critical of his masculine interests, and encouraged Howard to join with her interests. This was a gross boundary violation and reflects a lack of separation of mother from her son. His father was aloof and cold. There was no help for the boy's individuation here. For either gender a father needs to help his child separate from mother's world, and be established in his own identity.

Jung (1959) believes that when a snake dream occurs, this indicates that the conscious mind is moving away from the instinctual self. I suspect that his mother failed to develop a positive maternal side as well as a positive relationship to the masculine realm. This left her as a one-dimensional female dependently wanting a girl friend rather than a complex, multi-faceted woman independently raising a son. His mother's lack of boundaries and her narcissistic and libidinal energy were a threat to Howard's incompletely formed and unrealized masculine potential. After the production of this tray, Howard's mother was encouraged to enter psychotherapy with another therapist.

Snakes Alive!

When first seen, Judith was a shy little eight-year-old. Judith's family-life was chaotic and greatly in need of guidance. Her family was referred to a clinic. Her parents were in individual and group therapy with a therapist other than the one who was seeing Judith.

After a month and a half Judith created a tray in which a black infant and a white infant were placed within the center of the tray. The two babies were menaced by four snakes moving toward the helpless figures. The over-filled tray appears chaotic. In this case I would interpret the over-filled tray as representing the child's anxiety in her familial situation.

This tray is a cogent visual description of her psychic situation. It is important for the child's therapist to be aware of the family's process and to take that into consideration when interpreting sandplay imagery. Judith was overwhelmed and threatened by the family's pathology. This powerful material demonstrated the need for family therapy

The snakes were the only frightening images that Judith had ever used in her sand tray work. Snakes are one of several images that may be utilized by a child or adult who is experiencing psychic threat or attack.

Plate 7 Judith's threatened light child/dark child

Dark Child/Light Child

It is important to discuss the image of black infant and a white infant from the last vignette in relation to Nathan Schwartz-Salant's book, Narcissism and Character Transformation (1982). Schwartz-Salant discusses narcissistic patterns from a Jungian perspective. He states that the Narcissistic Character Disorder is the result of the child's parent failing to accept and reflect the child's identity. Equally important, the parent fails to carry the child's projection of the god-like archetype of the Self. The parents have to temporarily accept and carry this archetype, and teach the child that there is such a power, beauty and wholeness available to us. This was the problem with both sets of parents, Judith's and Howard's. They were so caught up in their own unmet nurturance needs that they failed to adequately mirror and affirm their children unique identities.

Narcissistic parents, and their children, have a dual difficulty. They have difficulty in accepting and relating to both the inner world of the archetypes and the outer world of human beings. All of us have experienced some degree of narcissistic wound, or psychic attack, and a subsequent withdrawal of the sense of the divine child of God that every newborn experiences. When this damage is frequent or extreme, a consequence of this process is that the child's Self or guiding center withdraws. A more compliant and masochistic attitude develops. This is the causal process behind the phenomenology of the two children that Judith placed in her sand tray.

Schwartz-Salant gives an example of light and dark children that appear in a dream fragment from an adult patient, "'There are two children lying on a bed, one younger and the other older. A nurse appears and she pours a dark liquid over the older child.' The dark liquid represents a kind of baptism in shadow material: The masochistic child had to integrate its own sadistic nature that was turned back on itself. The only way this could be done was for the patient to integrate her own sadistic energies, imaged by her mother. The dark liquid is her own sadism, and the dream shows this to have redemptive significance. And it did. The masochistic child did become assertive and connected with its divine half" (pp. 167-168).

The snakes and the baby were the only dark images she had ever used as she avoided anything that might look disturbing. The image of the dark child can refer to contaminated, repressed, or split off portions of the personality. Psychological splitting and psychic attack were the two key statements communicated by this eight-year-old who knew nothing of such sophisticated psychological concepts.

Judith's therapist reported that she avoided all of the dark, scary objects. She tried to make everything overly pretty. As the color white does not exist without black, positive feelings cannot exist without hostile or negative impulses in the human experience. Her own sadistic energy is forced back into the unconscious, and there combines with the parent's pathology. Her anxiety is shown in her tendency to over-crowd the tray with nice toys, and to shut out the dark, aggressive, sadistic objects. The masochistic child has what Schwartz-Salant calls a safe territory. He sees this as equivalent to a maternal holding environment. It is important not to attempt to pull the ego away from this territory, i.e. compliance, the known, etc. Rather it is important to take the other side of the child image, the divine child, seriously. Integrating these two inner children is the therapeutic work. The divine inner child often appears in the therapeutic process as a younger, more skittish child. It is frightened by its archetypal connection to joy with its untransformed Oedipal sexuality. Often in these cases the Oedipal complex (Electra) was barely able to form, or it might not have formed at all.

Eight

Roasted In the Fire

> In the last analysis all the complexes attached to
> fire are painful complexes, complexes both conducive
> to the acquiring of a neurosis and to the writing
> of poetry, complexes that are reversible; one can find
> paradise in fire's movement or in its repose, in the
> in the flame or in the ashes. To seize fire or to give
> oneself to fire, to annihilate or be annihilated,
> to follow the Prometheus complex or the Empedocles
> complex, such is the psychological alternation which
> converts all values and which reveals the clash of values.
>
> Bachelard, 1964

Candles can be placed in the sand tray, and lit by the older child. These may only be used in the sand tray or a fire pit and then only with close supervision. The use of fire in the sand tray may quickly become ritualistic play.

One of the most fascinating and secretive young children that I have had the pleasure of working with was eleven-year-old Kevin. Week after week Kevin used the spacemen, spaceships, rocks, and candles. He was secretive about his religious life. He told me that he attended religious meetings every week with his father. His parents were divorced. During our early sessions, he gave me the impression that he believed he was a very wicked person because he had certain thoughts. He alluded to them, but would not disclose them.

Kevin's sessions were conjoint with a boy who made no pretense of hiding his mischievous side. I believed them to be compatible in their play style, yet opposites in their attitudes. Both boys were in the fighting or struggle stage during my initial evaluation. The interaction between these two could be beneficial to both.

Kevin would carefully create an alien planet in nearly every session. First, the sand had to be carefully smoothed and arranged. This is an indicator of high intelligence. This shaping took quite some time and effort. Next, rocks and tracks of men had to be placed in just the right places. The candles, men, and spaceships were usually placed last. Typically, the candles were placed in the upper right corner screening the planet's defenders. When everything was perfect, the candles were lit, and the attack was begun. Kevin narrated the story as he acted-out. The light was under attack by invaders who were determined to extinguish the power source. Kevin came to relish sharing his story of the invasion of the planet, and demonstrating the resulting fight for Mark and me.

Plate 8 Kevin—A trial by fire

Fire is associated with passion, strength, energy, creativity and the masculine principle. It is an important symbol of transformation. Like the unconscious it can be both destructive and healing. A trial by fire (roasting) for some shamans results as their being reborn as men of power. Primitive people think of magico-religious power as burning. The range of meanings is enormous, primitive rage to spiritual purification. Both issues seemed to be important to Kevin. His ambivalence toward whatever was embodied by the fire became increasingly evident during the months that we worked together. During some sessions maintaining the fire in the face of opposition was paramount. Toward the end of therapy, putting out the fire became increasingly important. His negative evaluation of his human nature was also altered during these months.

During their early sessions, Kevin became critical of Mark's murderous scenes. He admired Mark's openness, intensity, and the variety of trays he created. I asked Kevin to stop being openly judgmental. Mark told Kevin that he wasn't such a bad person as he thought. This impressed Kevin, who quickly grasped the truth of the statement.

Kevin assumed that he was intellectually and aesthetically superior to other children. He was certainly intellectually superior to this little roughneck, Mark that he was paired with for sessions. Rivalry occurred because of Kevin's attitude of disdainful superiority. I responded by offering the batakas (encounter bats) to the boys. Kevin assumptions were challenged. Classes were in session and the playground was empty. We stepped outside. Both boys enjoyed the battle at first. Then Kevin began to tire. He was no match for the smaller child's intense energy. I called the battle off. They were delighted to return to their work in my consultation room. This little battle seemed to increase Kevin's respect for Mark, and greatly increased their bonding.

Both boys came to like and appreciate one another from that day forward. They enjoyed sharing their sandplay stories. A few months later Mark moved to another state. Kevin completed his story cycle one on one with me, and may be that was for the best. Several times during our remaining months, Kevin remarked that he missed Mark.

During the last month and a half of the school year, Kevin's fascination with his sand tray theme diminished. It had played itself out. He tried to recapture the old joy. It just was not possible. Kevin created a powerful archetypal tray at this time.

The tray that I have titled, "Search for the Green Stone," featured a female protagonist, an Oriental woman who was on an quest for this special stone. Most children, who reach a point of resolution in the process of working through, create images that relate in some apparent way to the cycle are completing. This tray appears to be enigmatic, yet it relates to the battle on that alien world.

Kevin carefully shaped the sand as a Japanese gardener might. Then he arranged the stones and trees. Finally, everything was ready for his star. The Oriental woman was placed in just the right spot. This was the first occasion he used plant life. The use of trees suggests growth in his inner world. Let's go to the Dictionary of Play Imagery and read the entries for stone and green.

Plate 9 Quest for the green stone

Common associations for stone are durability; imperishability; immortality; unity and strength. Stones are seen to be a symbol of being and reconciliation with self. Immortality is an interesting association since his struggle was spiritual. All the stones are rounded and have been polished by tumbling in rivers.

Green, the color of the thymus and heart chakra, is associated with heart love that is expansive and generous. This center is indicative of our desires, which include our longing to belong to someone. In general it seems to represent attachment. Green is further identified with security or insecurity; i.e. green with envy is a reflection of a feeling of insecurity. Possessiveness and the desire to acquire wealth are associated with green. Vital force and healing are among the more positive associations. Green, the color of growing things, is associated with renewal, youth, hope, and with change. As with other colors, the meaning of green changes greatly according to the particular hue. Bright, verdant green is positive, and this is what the overall look of this tray suggests. The fact that this was his first use of trees adds to this positive association with green.

A highly developed aesthetic sense, harmony and tranquillity characterize this tray. Strength, unity, spirituality, heart's desire, attachment, hope and renewal are the qualities seen in Kevin's quest. I found this meaningful since his initial struggle had to do with fire. Fire is associated with power and spiritual purification.

His transference toward me had been a positive one. He missed having a mother at home and I seemed to represent a loving mother to him. He was freed from his fighting or struggle phase to discover the positive internal female or anima figure within, i.e. the unconscious feminine component within a male. Before he left therapy with me he asked if he could have the plant in an owl-shaped container as a remembrance of me. I explained that I wished I could give it, but could not since I was working with other children at that site.

By this time he was a much more relaxed and down to earth boy than the one I had met eight months earlier. We both agreed it was time to stop. Kevin was sorry that I would be leaving the school. It was obvious that his experience had been a very special one.

Nine

Working Through Posttraumatic Play

> The goal of interrupting posttraumatic play is to generate alternatives that might promote a sense of control, help the child express fragmented thoughts and feelings, and orient the child toward the future. Gil, 1991

Duncan was nine years and three months when he entered therapy. I selected the name, Duncan, for this particular child because it means dark warrior. Duncan appeared to be just that when the process of therapy began. He was dark complexioned, and his sandplay themes were warlike and violent.

During his first five years, he and his sister were witnesses to domestic violence on many occasions. Their mother so feared for her safety and that of her son and daughter that she gladly allowed them to be adopted and brought to this country from Mexico. By the time I met him, Duncan had made a positive identification with his adoptive father, a warm, caring person in contrast to Duncan's natural father.

Duncan's Full Scale I.Q. was 144. Accept for occasional slight learning difficulties, his schoolwork was excellent. His Human Figure Drawing indicated identification either with his adoptive father or his natural father. When asked to draw a person, he drew an older male with a mustache. His mother reported that at times he had difficulty being accepted by his peers. Sometimes his behaviors were disruptive, and at other times he was unresponsive to management efforts. He needed more maturity, and self-control. There were times he would withdraw from teachers or peers. Generally, his adoptive parents were pleased with him, and thought he was remarkably creative youngster.

The first time we met, Duncan commented that he did not like to work in the sand tray as he had been to the counseling center before. I assured him that there would be no judgment, such as grades. He seemed eager to work in spite of his negative comment. He knew exactly what he wanted. He created a variant of the same theme each session for months. His sand trays were much more repetitive than those of other males of his age and intelligence. It was clear that his repetitive play was the result of the early trauma of watching as his biological father batter his mother.

Lenore Terr's (1981) found that patterns of repetitive play may occur after a severe trauma, and do not dissipate of themselves. Because of this severe impasse characterized by the compulsion to repeat the theme of violence along with rigid defenses, my primary therapeutic goal was to support this process until the block began to open up. In time I would expect the themes to became more elaborated, and the violence to be neutralized.

Many indicators of pathology were evident in his trays. These indicators are based on Buhler's (1941) findings: rigidly fenced worlds without gates, dinosaurs devouring people and other animals; burying of objects.

Duncan was afraid of his own aggressive impulses, and was morbidly preoccupied with the power and destructive potentialities of primitive rage. Like many young boys, who see their mother battered, he felt endangered as his mother was, but could not fully identify with her, as his developmental need was to differentiate from the feminine realm. It also seems to be a psychologically stronger position to identify with the perpetrator than the victim. The identification with power then implied he might hurt mother as his father had. To find the strength in anger and not to be overcome by it is a difficult quest for anyone. This is all the more difficult for those who have been psychically seared by scenes of violence their formative years.

The siblings were seen in conjoint sessions. Duncan aggressively invaded his sister's space. He would tell her what to do and how to do it. He pushed toys at her and tried to control her work. While there is little that this therapist does not accept in terms of expression of violence, sexuality, and so forth, intrusions into another child's play space, and manipulative behaviors with another child are discouraged in a firm but gentle manner. Whenever possible I prefer to work with children as pairs in conjoint sessions so that I may deal with these boundary issues.

Duncan's initial tray began by a dumping of soldiers, weapons and dinosaurs into the center of the tray. He set up fences immediately. He placed two fences in the tray from one side to another, completely dividing the tray into three sectors. These fences were without gates or openings, one of Buhler's (1941) indicators of disturbance in an older child. Duncan sorted toys into both the right and left thirds of the tray. The middle sector was the fighting arena. Hand to hand combat was acted out in this section. Toward the end of this highly dramatized play filled with mayhem, a tyrannosaurus rex appeared. This monster proceeded to devour a man. Following this slaughter, a second tyrannosaurus appears. A battle ensues in which one of the two is eaten by the victor. At the end of this initial tray, Duncan introduced volcanoes into the left and right sectors. The resulting eruptions totally destroyed everything and everyone. Clearly, Duncan was filled with violent imagery that was weakly controlled by the obsessive fencing motif. This type of play continued for months.

Plate 10 Duncan's battle scene

Later a sand tray showed a further evolution of this original theme. Duncan separated the world of men from the world of the primitive dinosaurs. The men eventually emerged victorious against the dinosaurs. It is interesting that Duncan placed the dinosaurs on the right side of the tray and the men on the left. It is usually the more conscious material that appears on the right hand side of the trays while more unconscious material is placed on the left. Possibly Duncan needed to acknowledge his own angry, sadistic impulses while continuing to bring them under control.

Violent play, with total fencing off of the pocket of violence, persisted with only partial dissolution's of this rigid form, throughout the first three months of therapy. As therapy progressed he began to create some open battle scenes. The obsessive fear that demanded total blocks would then occur at odd moments. In the middle of an open battle between cowboys and Indians, Duncan's anxiety level became too high and he introduced fences adding a strange, illogical appearance to the typical Western scene. Again, these fences appeared as total blocks. When Duncan's anxiety began to drop he removed the fences.

Plate 11 Open battle

Duncan's religious education class preceded the next few sessions after this ambivalent session. The content from this class and from Halloween tended to temporarily obscure and block his struggle with the issues of violence and death. When child is threatened by the contents of his inner world it is often easier to follow the course of least resistance and create banal pictures that reflect the outer world. He may have been genuinely affected by these classes. Just the fact that he was able to abandon this battle and mayhem theme shows movement. Duncan's Noah's ark tray appeared trite. It is difficult to interpret this material, but it seemed this was an attempt to reconcile his inner turmoil with his developing spiritual values. .

Finally, Duncan created a sand tray that clearly demonstrated a positive shift. This was the breakthrough I was looking for. Duncan's story was that a couple, toward the rear of the tray, and a boy, seen on the bridge, were visiting an amusement park. The dinosaurs, which had wrecked so much havoc in earlier trays, were now entombed in a tar pit; an amusing resolution. This tray was clearly characteristic of the community stage described by Kalff (1980).

This tray contains the circular, centering motif characteristic of the psyche. It often takes many cycles of destruction followed by such positive trays, to work through so much pathology. Duncan has taken the first steps in coming to respect and value the feminine in him, in his sister, and in the world.

If this breakthrough had not occurred I agree with Terr (1981) and Gil (1991) that the child is in danger of being re-wounded by the compulsive posttraumatic play. If this repetition compulsion continued I would have asked Duncan how his figures might be helped. I would not reach into the sand tray to move a toy for this would be the very boundary violation I had discouraged. Discouraging domination of his sister, while Duncan was symbolically reenacting the family's trauma, planted additional seeds for his healing.

One Down, One Up

I was not aware that Kate Amatruda and Phoenix Helm Simpson (1997) cautioned against using sandplay with psychotic or alcoholic individuals who are not in recovery since it is such a powerfully evocative medium. These clients can be seen in residential settings if the facility or recovery program forms a good container. The director of a group home where I was to work thought that sandplay would be a great addition her facility. This particular group home was a level 14. Most of boys were on psychotropic medications.

Ten-year-old Geoffrey had spent most of his life in a group home. Geoffrey was the youngest resident. Twelve-year-old Brian was also heavily medicated. Most of the teen-aged young men created traditional looking trays using houses, soldiers, Indians and trees. The two youngest, Geoffrey and Brian were different. Even though I saw each of the boys separately both Geoffrey and Brian spent most of our time together burying objects in the sand. Despite this similarity there was a qualitative difference in their play behaviors.

Of the two boys Brian was the more severely disturbed. Eventually everything was pushed under the sand. His worlds were continuously disordered, dark, chthonic and vegetative. He appeared to be a masculine fighting stage within an Infancy II context. He always selected robots, cars, monster trucks, dinosaurs, burly fighting men, Batman, one typical adult female woman, and Cat Woman. The Cat Woman figure was one of his more important figures, but he primarily played with the masculine figures.

He focused intensely on having his objects fight, and as they fought he buried them. Sometimes the battles would continue under the sand. This child's regressed ego was continually overwhelmed. Like John Perry's view of psychosis as a crisis/opportunity, burial gives the personality an opportunity to reconstitute. His public school experience combined with being a younger male resident in a predominately adolescent facility was stressful for this child. Frustration with his school and group home environments added to his underlying rage at his abandonment. To all this was added the constellation of the Terrible Mother archetype since his mother was not at all maternal. Even before I came to the facility with my sandplay materials Brian had cycles of disruptive behavior which would escalate ending in another hospitalization. Brain enjoyed all the positive attention he received in the hospital. He was hospitalized several times during that year. As hard as Brian was to handle he had a sweet side and he was genuinely sorry to see me leave the facility.

Geoffrey's burials had more of the character I had seen in Bertha's sandplay. He often asked me to turn my back so he could bury an object usually a car. The game was whether I would be able to guess it was quickly, or whether he would be able to stump me. Was this a case of an early difficulty with object constancy? Peek-A-Boo, the mother hiding and reappearing, is a universal game of Infancy I. Bertha's and Geoffrey's game of hiding objects seemed to echo this.

Looking at the possible etiology associated with Bertha, Brian and Geoffrey's burials, Bertha's family was damaged, but intact. Geoffrey's family seemed to consist of his uncle and cousins. His parents were incarcerated. Brian's mother was a prostitute. His father was unknown. When Brian's mother would visit occasionally she would be inappropriately dressed, and this caused him a great deal of embarrassment as well as being sexually provocative for the boys.

A Breakthrough

This hide-and-seek type of play seemed to fascinate Geoffrey for months. With the wealth of play objects I brought each week, and the interesting variety of objects supplied by the psychologist who owned the group home, I kept waiting for Geoffrey to leave the regressive burials and move on to the typical, age-appropriate fighting stage. He was wounded but not psychotic, and he clearly had the intelligence.

After our initial two months together when our relationship was strong I made a bold move to bring Geoffrey forward. Before I brought him into the sandplay room I created a sand tray. It was a peaceful scene, yet the villagers were menaced by evil figures. As I often ask my clients to do I told Geoffrey the story the tray pictured.

From that intervention onward Geoffrey created a wide variety of trays. He created the usual battles with soldiers, and racing car scenes. What were interesting were the desert ranches he created. As he made these scenes he began talking about his family. This led to his resolution to return home. He began to talk of this often and contacted his relatives. Eventually his uncle agreed to weekend passes with the plan of Geoffrey living there.

Occasionally he would return to the guessing game. More often when he did not create a tray right away he would ask me to make a tray and tell him a story. Our communication had changed radically, and he had developed a vision of where he wanted to go and how he wanted to live. Geoffrey was changing and growing into a more confident child.

Ten

Gifts From the Unconscious

> Dream is the depersonalized myth, myth the depersonalized dream; both myth and dream are symbolic in the same general way of dynamics of the psyche. But in the dream the forms are quirked by the peculiar troubles of the dreamer, whereas in myth the problems and solutions shown are directly valid for all mankind.
>
> Joseph Campbell, 1949

Ten-year-old Sharon was the most introverted and secretive child that I worked with. At first when she was questioned she shared some of her stories. As she got into deeper work she became silent. A child who frequently refuses to talk increases the value of non-verbal approaches in psychotherapy.

Sharon was a middle child of six children. Her mother was a single parent over-burdened with responsibility. Sharon's teen-aged brothers liked to stir-up trouble for the younger children.

Sharon buried many toys and figures during the time we worked together. It was not always clear as to whether this burying was pathological, or an acceptance into unconscious as Eve Lewis Bowyer

(1971) observed. Most of these burials had a powerful, ritualistic quality. Something was happening that was terribly important for Sharon.

First trays are important in that they usually indicate the chief concerns, the psyche's situation, and a possible solution. Sharon's first tray portrayed a war scene that included family figures. When I asked, Sharon told me that the soldier under the truck was not hiding but was dead.

During this session she created a second tray that featured a large hill. Animals streamed down the hill on all sides—psychic movement around a center point. At the bottom of the hill a hunter was pointing his gun. I mentioned the animals that were coming down the hill. Sharon pointed out that a few were going uphill. I asked about the man with the gun. Sharon said that he was going to kill them. This is not an image most girls in the city portray. Was her father a hunter, or does the threat speak to her instincts?

One could postulate that a war was going on between various members of her family. My sense was that she was threatened by and angry with her teen-aged brothers. Her sense of security was threatened by her father's abandoning the family through divorce. Animals are usually interpreted as representing the instincts. This would led one to believe that her instinctual feelings were threatened by her family situation, and by her father's leaving the home. The father's abandonment is especially damaging to a young girl's sense of her self-worth. That she created a scene in which some of the animals were moving away from the hunter improves the situation. There was a solution suggested in moving to the center. During her second session Sharon drew the head of a little girl with tears streaming down her cheeks. This image affected me deeply and I quietly put it aside.

80 • *Sandplay*

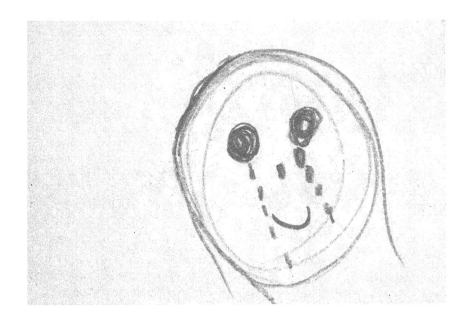

Plate 12 Sharon—Smiling while crying

Her first sand trays described her family situation. Then she moved to a deeper level that one does not always see, the archetypal level Jung studied for so many years. She created an enigmatic tray, which can only be understood by interpreting it as archetypal. A large stone was placed in each of the two upper corners of the tray and in the lower left corner. Standing stones are associated with the sacred, and the life force. In the fourth corner, the lower right, or ego consciousness sector, an elderly couple was placed. I asked whether the figures represented grandparents. Sharon replied that they did not. There it was the fourfold personality structure, with male and female representatives of inner a positive indicator. The presence of inner archetypal parents, or Wise Old Man and Woman is unusual so early in sand tray work.

Plate 13 Archetypal parents/fourfold structure.

Sharon gave herself a gift with the creation of the next session's tray. A boy's house and his parents were placed in the upper left side of the tray. A girl's house and her parents were placed in the lower right hand corner. The containers held food. A female, Japanese figure represented the girl's doll. The slender, Oriental male figure represented the boy's doll. I asked if there was a story. Sharon replied that there was a contest between the boy's doll, and the girl's doll. The girl's doll was given first prize. This was a big step toward resolving the problem with her brothers.

Looking at the objects it was apparent that the masculine realm takes up a great deal of the physical space in her tray, just as the masculine realm takes up a great deal of space in her consciousness and life. The theme was competitive; masculine energy and creativity against feminine—Sharon's teenage brothers against little Sharon. Here was a positive variation on the theme of sibling rivalry that was dealt with angrily and destructively in her first tray.

Sharon explained her use of the elephant. She moved the girl, the containers of food and the elephant together. The girl fed the elephant. In turn he served as her protector. The threat of the hunter killing the animals in her second tray appeared to be overcome at least for the moment. Sharon was protected by no small instinctual power.

Sharon moved to the art table next. She created a mandalic design that she painted, cut out, and pasted on a card. Underneath the design she painted the words, "I love you Mommy." Sharon was thrilled and eager to take it home.

A brief tray followed in which the theme of rebirth emerged. Sharon explained, "A dragon and a dog were friends. The dragon was the dog's protector. Together they saved a woman who fell into a river, and had been buried. This sounded like a drowning. The instinctive, non-verbal portions of the mind serve to help the endangered woman. Together the R-complex (dragon) and affective brain (dog) work together to rescue and protect the woman (ego) who was destroyed (by the divorce) and rescued by the instinctual level (reborn).

The next tray was complex. A bride and groom were separated by a tree near the center of the tray. This image seemed to represent her parent's divorce, or may speak to the separation of masculine and feminine characteristics, or both events, as in Freud's concept of condensation. A tree is often used as a symbol of the Self. Does Sharon feel responsible for her parent's divorce? Many children take on this burden.

Two sets of fighting men threatened the tranquillity of her feminine world. One set was placed in the upper right portion of the tray. The other set was placed in the lower left—the tension was absolute. Animals were placed throughout the right side of tray. Most of the animals were gathered around the pond. The bears, owls and fowl were placed closest to the cave. Here ego and instincts seem joined. Looking at the tray as a whole it seems to picture her unconscious with the animals, dwarves and cave on the right.

The Oriental world stood in the upper left of the tray. This is generally interpreted as least conscious portion of a sand tray or piece of art. The Oriental way of handling aggression is to use the opponent's force against him. This philosophy is a careful following of the feminine principle. The Western way of competition and direct conflict was apparent in the first few trays. This element introduces the feminine principle into her conflict-filled psychological situation. The dragon stood directly behind the house. This adds additional energy and power.

Plate 14 Sharon's separated bride and groom

Two areas call for special attention. The group of eggs with birds sitting upon them was placed next to the little girl. The cave in the lower right portion contained a baby bear and adult bear. The adult bear represents the child's mother. The mother and child theme, the image of eggs, which would recur in future trays, and the unusual placement of the powerful cave symbol are all of great interest, as are the trio of dwarves (animus figures) that stand between the girl and the animals.

Eggs, as libidinal potential, represent an unformed portion of the personality. It is notable that they were placed next to the little girl. The mother and child in the cave may speak of the need to transform the mother-child relationship. The owls suggest instinctual wisdom; the pond and cave, sources of renewal. The dwarves are early animus figures.

The boy going up a ladder that rests on the Oriental house is another striking feature of this tray. Stairs are symbols of ascension, and passage from one state of consciousness into another. Threshold symbols such as stairs, doors, bridges, etc. are important indicators of psychic movement. As a threshold symbol the ladder suggests a change of state or consciousness different from that obtained from exploration of the cave. Personalities with such a rich variety of symbols in their dreams, fantasies, or sand trays usually demonstrate great capacity for inner work and exploration.

Two weeks later Sharon placed eggs in the mouth of a volcano. Sharon used the spaceship captain to rescue the eggs. A positive image of an adult male was wonderful to see in the face of abandonment by Sharon's father. Opposite the captain, an octopus threatened the eggs. This seemed curious since the octopus is closely associated with the negative mother-complex. Jung believed that as we touch upon the archetypes both dark and light sides of the archetype will emerge. Another explanation is that even though Sharon seeks to find additional security by courting her mother, the maternal realm can thwart a child's individuation. The white horse behind the octopus is a positive spiritual image.

Plate 15 Eggs in a volcano

It was obvious that Sharon felt a strong connection to her mother. She spent a great deal of time creating gifts for her mother. Excessive attachment could be unconsciously perceived as a regressive threat to the unfolding of new, unformed portions of her personality and creativity.

The white horse is an extremely positive symbol that carries spiritual implications. This contrasts with the pond that contains a fish, a scorpion and a centipede. These images are associated with evil. This child accepts the dark side of life and does not hysterically deny the dark, dangerous side of life. Again, there was a great capacity for conscious development shown by the variety of symbols, especially masculine images. My supervisor walked into the room at this moment. Immediately Sharon abandoned this tray in favor of cutting shapes out construction paper.

Two weeks later the theme of burial, the images of the mother bear and baby bear reappeared. Sharon selecting the figure of Mickey Mouse as the Sorcerer's Apprentice, Pluto, Goofy, a mother bear, a baby bear, and miniature flags. Sharon created a circle of flags with the figures placed to the right of center in the tray. These flags appeared to indicate a celebration.

Sharon began a second version of this tray. Her partial burial of the mother and baby bear seemed puzzling. Does this continue the process indicated by the presence of the mother and baby bears in the cave? This seems likely. She placed flags in a spiral toward the right. She created more separation between the mother bear and baby bear. This movement away from mother seemed to have a positive quality, as a toddler during the reproachmont stage is able to venture away from mother and return to her safety. The theme of burial returned a month later.

Sharon used tiny Japanese umbrellas in creating what appeared to be a beach scene. When I asked if it was a beach scene she failed to reply. During the early weeks of our work together she answered my questions. Now she was silent. Sharon selected family figures and seemed to be involved with a ritualistic burial of these figures. Was this a struggle to transform her relationship to her family through the power of the unconscious? Was she angry?

She exuded a powerful aura of secrecy that indicated how intense this process was for Sharon. This child's need for privacy during her play was extremely important now. I remained silent most of the time.

Plate 16 Finding Sharon's buried eggs

For her next tray she placed all the white doves in a circle. A duck and a dog were placed in the center of the circle. I cleaned out the tray after Sharon ran off to class, and found a clutch of eggs buried in the sand under the spot where the animals stood. Sharon was so secretive that I had not seen the eggs being deposited in the sand. I felt wonder and awe. Here was Sharon's image of centering that included her coming to terms with the instinctual realm. Like the psyche, this image was multi-layered with hidden potential developing below the surface.

Here we have a Hero's journey. The eggs were moved through a heroic journey from a safe place next to the girl. Next they were called to adventure which resulted in their being threatened in the mouth of a volcano. A magic helper rescued them. Finally they underwent a symbolic death in burial. All that seemed to be lacking was the receiving of a boon.

This receiving of the boon might have occurred when Sharon's girl received an award for the best doll, or in the improved relationship with self/Self and with her mother. Of course, all of these might have been the reward or blessing, but these important symbolic events happened prior to the ultimate burial of the eggs.

The burial was an acceptance into the unconscious of what the eggs symbolized as Eve Lewis (Bowyer, 1971) suggested. It is inaccurate to label all of these burying behaviors of Sharon's as pathological. That negative judgment would be doing the child and her psyche a grave injustice.

Material flows from the conscious to the unconscious in a steady stream. It is equally true that the unconscious thrusts material into our conscious awareness, as we need it. Material that flows from conscious to unconscious usually returns transformed in some way. I object to the blanket label of pathological to every act of burial. Pathological refers to disease contrasted with the notion of mental health. Wounds to the psyche may cause discomfort or dis-ease. The psyche, like the body, will move toward self-healing or psychological wholeness. This wounding often causes a mixing of archetypal and personal material. The dark side of any archetypal image is likely to be branded as pathological by individuals who have not studied the dualities inherent in psychological symbolism. Anyone who has been psychologically wounded will be in need of the healing that comes from the unconscious or superconscious. A therapist is simply the facilitator of psychological self-healing.

Mental health professionals who have not experienced narcissistic must be careful not to become smug. As Jung so aptly pointed out in his development of typology, we are all out of balance, and to some extent we all need psychological work. This propensity toward psychological imbalance creates a sense of discomfort, or dis-ease, in most of us sooner or later.

Sharon's major themes were complex. The need to be seen as better than her brother(s) was a primary theme, as was abandonment by her father. Animals (instincts) that were going to be killed (loss of father) was a key motif. This created a damaged sense of self. Animals later appeared as helpful. The mother bear, the elephant, the dog and duck, and the doves, all helped.

The emergence of the Self was seen in the four-fold personality structure with the Wise Old Man and Wise Old Woman figures, and in swirling circular sand tray designs, and in the mandalic design that she eagerly took home to mother.

Initially, the male figures were all threatening. This demonstrated an encounter with a negative animus. After the girl's doll received the prize, males appeared as helpful figures.

Considering the image of a bride and groom separated by a tree, might the tree be symbolic of Sharon? Children often feel guilt when their parents separate. Her parent's divorce might have threatened to split her inner masculine and feminine components. Sharon's hard work and creativity prevailed. She created both positive female and positive male imagery.

Since her father was no longer available, her mother needed to be courted, but that created another psychological difficulty. The octopus, which is closely associated with a mother-complex, was not able to destroy the libidinal potential of the eggs for a magic helper, an animus figure, came to our heroine's aid.

Finally, the eggs, symbolic of growth and renewal, were threatened, rescued, and finally accepted into the unconscious. What she accomplished is striking.

Soon school would end for the year. I had a good-bye party for the children. Most of the children told me that they were going to miss me, my toys, and the work we had done together. Sharon was a notable exception. She quietly walked around the room, looking sadly, yet intently, at the toys, as if she were silently saying her good-byes to each of them.

I asked the teachers and aides whether they had noticed any changes in her behavior. They all had. She spoke up for her own rights now, and had friends. No one had to tell me that her sadness had diminished as I had seen that in her artwork, but they told me just that.

Gifts from the Unconscious

James was twelve years and seven months when he was first seen. According to Machover's interpretations, James' Human Figure Drawing showed signs of nurturance needs, and desire for affection in the overextended arms. James' performance score on the WISC was considerably above his verbal score, 131 as compared to 92.

James appeared to be a relatively happy and self-contained young man. He was quiet with me. Observing his behaviors before and at the end of the session it was evident that he loved to play, and tended to be a bit mischievous with other children at the counseling center. This seemed to be a healthy situation.

James created a wide variety of sand trays. As therapy progressed his themes became increasingly complex, and touched on deeper levels. Humor, the problem of evil overtaking innocent people, being taught and nurtured by inner figures, and sports and games were among his common themes. One specific theme was elaborated over a three-week period. I titled this series "Gifts from the Unconscious."

"Gifts from the Unconscious" is a peaceful cycle. James story was that an infant male was given to some spacemen by space travelers from our planet. When our space travelers came back to see how he was doing, they found that he had learned to play. He was playing in a fantastic amusement park with whimsical rabbits as his teachers. Here was an answer to his need for nurturance.

The spacemen appear to be the helping, and accepting intrapsychic factors or inner parents that James had not fully experienced in the outer world. The rabbits, which helped and taught him, are symbolic of his inner nature that is sensitive, skittish, and could easily be prey for aggressive personalities. The space travelers were placed on the right side of the tray, while the positive development of gifts were elaborated on the left.

The theme of evil menacing or overtaking innocent people occurred most strongly in two very different trays that he created several weeks apart. He placed a man, a woman and a skeleton on a small tropical island in the middle of an ocean. A wrecked ship rested on the shore. A gigantic water snake inhabited the upper left corner of the tray. Below the snake was a ship with an octopus reaching into it. A dragon stood in the rear of the tray. Sharks circled in the lower center of the tray. No help is evident. To top everything off, an alligator was walking up the shore toward the people. The couple appeared totally vulnerable and incapable of defending themselves.

These images, the shark, octopus, and alligator are associated with the mother-complex. The overall look of the tray may indicate anger at his parents. Mother may have nurtured his sensitivity, and father is pushing him to excel in what may feel like a difficult manner.

Plate 17 James' couple in danger

The second tray was a soccer game in which the players on the right side of the tray were vulnerable innocents—ballet dancers, an elf, a clown, a rabbit, a woman, a man, an infant, a little boy, and a dog. To the left were their opponents: Darth Vader, soldiers, cowboys and Indians, a Turk with a sword, a conquistador, and a snake. The good side was forced to "play soccer or die!"

James was under pressure from his father to make the football team at school. Since the menace was coming from the left toward the right in these trays, the unconscious would be viewed as being disturbed and threatening. James' seemed to be identifying with both victim and aggressor. This ambivalence about using aggressive power was causing him deep distress.

Plate 18 Play soccer or die!

James, an unusually sensitive young man, was pushed by his father to be an achiever in sports and other masculine pursuits. This is not a problem for aggressive sensation type males, but was excessive for this particular boy. He was outwardly compliant, yet passive-aggressive in his behaviors. More than his father realized James' needed to deal with his sensitivity and his feminine side (creativity and Eros). Males need to separate from the world of the mothers without loosing their sensitivity. A sensitive father, or father figure, would be a boon. James had to provide his own supportive inner figures.

Self-Disclosure in Sand Tray Work

One of the most influential books that I read in graduate school that affected the development of my therapeutic style was *The Transparent Self*. Sidney Jourard (1964) discussed the value of occasional, topic appropriate self-disclosure. There are times when relating a key experience or dream will illuminate a client's current situation. The whole idea is to help bring the client forward. A few years ago I worked with a seventeen-year-old young woman who wrote poetry. She shared her poems with me and I shared a few of mine with her. Sonia found this to be rewarding. As a rule I use this technique with the more verbal teens and adults, not with young children. Since my positive experience with making a sand tray for Geoffrey I have on occasion done a sand tray to speak to a child's unconscious, and hopefully to facilitate the unblocking of repressed shadow material.

Shadow material can vary greatly amongst different individuals. A girl who is all sweetness and light would have dark, aggressive shadow material that may be projected onto another person, or come out as frightening nightmares. A boy who has been identified as "a bad boy" may be aggressive, physical, have difficulty verbalizing his emotions and be prone to fighting. This child might have shadow material that is gentle, beautiful, and peaceful. In either case, extreme rage or murderous feelings may be repressed and appear as shadow material. Giant snakes, the tyrannosaurus rex, and sharks get a lot of play. For some individuals this material may feel totally foreign to the conscious personality.

When I do a sand tray to speak to a child's unconscious or preconscious mind I use imagery that accurately reflects my psyche. My worlds have a distinctly feminine character that does not shun dark and aggressive elements.

Oh, Danny Boy

Six-year-old Danny was an only child living an acutely lonely life in rural Texas. He was on medication because his mother, grandmother and teachers believed he was hyperactive. Danny was desperately hungry for a playmate. During one of the hours we spent together each week at his school he said, "You are my best friend." I felt awful for this child. It is important to encourage parents to play with their children and to arrange opportunities for play with other youngsters.

Danny's sand trays were typical of those made by many of his peers in the five to seven-year-old age range. The trays were not as disorganized as Andrew's, but were poorly organized. His object choices were typical for his age, for example: the castle which contained rocket ships, a few dinosaurs, a volcano, Jabba the Hut, a space ship, a house, a bridge and "water." It would be difficult to organize this hodge-podge into a coherent whole. This is typical of many of the kindergarten and first grade children who are referred for counseling. What was both interesting and different in his early tray was that he buried "Aladdin's lamp" in one part of the tray and a skull that called "a fossil" in another part of the tray. He had a man with a shovel digging up the fossil. He also told me that the tyrannosaurus. rex was the pet in the castle. I found promise of self-control and self-discovery in these images.

Since there were two trays I made a tray that featured a river running diagonally around the tray. A canoe was navigating down the river. A Native American village was in the upper portion of the tray and cowboys and a house in the lower right. A bridge connected the Native world with the Euro-American world. I used trees and flowers to soften the landscape. My Native American villages are usually placed on the edge of a forest.

Danny was delighted by this scene and threw himself into creating an elaborate, well-organized tray of his own. He borrowed freely from my tray, but created a unique world of his own. A river ran diagonally though the tray, and on it he placed a canoe and a bridge. In the right portion of tray he place a giant tree that he worked on assembling as the branches and large leafy portions can be removed. Circling the giant tree he created a dense forest. To the right of the giant tree he placed a bear family—father, mother and baby bear. At about eleven o'clock on the tree he placed every small pinecone in my collection. At the extreme upper right he placed a Western storefront. By the end of the bridge on the right side he placed a small, flat piece of driftwood.

On the left side of the tray at the top he placed a woolly mammoth. Just below the mammoth he placed, and half-buried a millipede. To the right of the millipede he placed a house. To the right and the back of the tray about in the middle back section he placed another Western building front and a cluster of flowers. In the lower left corner of the tray he placed a third Western building front with a Victorian house and a cluster of flowers to the right of the storefront. Below the millipede and above the Victorian house he placed the three pots with cactus plants. To the right of that he placed another cluster of flowers. Danny looked over the tray, very pleased with his creation. He scanned the table for another item. Danny's eyes lit-up when he saw two nests filled with eggs. He carefully placed one nest just north of the dense forest and one to the south of the forest. The tray was finished, and it was perfect. He beamed with pleasure. The feeling of joy in that room was tangible. From that session forward Danny's trays were much more coherent.

Eleven

Free the Maidens!

"Now really, what are you about? You are building a small town, and doing it as if it were a rite." I had no answer to my question, only the inner certainty that I was on the way to discovering my own myth. Jung, 1961

Seven and a half-year-old Ruth had lost her mother after a lingering illness, and now her grandfather was dying. Her first session was awkward. She placed too many toys in the tray. This created difficulty creating a story. Ruth's initial tray looked like an anxiety reaction in the awkward placement of the figures and the multiplicity of objects without design or censorship. All the figures were placed facing forward. There was no interaction between figures. Everything chosen reflected an ultra-feminine, overly nice world-view. Every female had to have a mate, and all the couples must have a wedding. Ruth appeared to have a rigid personality.

Ruth's second session was more productive. She seemed to be more relaxed. At first she was scattered. She started and abandoned many ideas. Ruth selected a female figure and then abandoned it for another, which was eventually rejected. Her rationale was that one was dressed too rich, while the other was dressed too poor. She said she wanted a castle and a rich person's home (she seemed to mean a mansion). Then she spent her time with two humble cottages. She placed the gingerbread house in the upper right hand corner with a witch standing next to it. The Smurf cottage contained the sweet-faced, smiling Pilgrim lady.

Approximately twenty minutes into the session she began to focus intently. Ruth created a fairy tale, out of bits and pieces of those she had heard, and out of her own fertile imagination that was stimulated by the toys.

A mountain stood in the upper left-hand corner. She placed a castle tower on top. A forest surrounded the tower, hiding it from the world below. The forest was so dense that no one could get through it. The swan was placed next to the tower, then replaced with a princess.

Eventually the swan was moved to the base of the mountain, and placed in a pond. In front of the pond, some distance away (using one's imagination) was a meadow filled with horses. A unicorn, that has magical powers, was master over the horses. The story took place on an enchanted island. The cottages were summarily swept away as Ruth informed me that the right edge of the tray was the sea. Ruth narrated as she played out her story.

Prince Ivan was magically transported to this island. He was not sure where he was. Ivan approached the unicorn, and asked him where he might be. The unicorn informed the poor Prince that there is no return from this island. The unicorn called Ivan closer, and said that he just might be able to leave through magic.

The unicorn told the Prince that a beautiful Princess was held captive upon a high mountain on this island. If the Prince frees this maiden, he would be able to leave the island and return to his land and his family. If Prince Ivan was going to be able to free the Princess, he would first have to ask for additional help from the swan.

Prince Ivan traveled north to the land of the swan, and found the swan floating upon a pond.

"How may I help you?" asked the swan.

"I want to free the captive Princess and return to my home," replied Prince Ivan.

"First you must walk around this pond three times. Then you will be able to get through the forest that no one can go through," said the swan. After the Prince circles the pond three times, he was given a magical rope ladder by the swan.

"Climb the mountain. At the top you will find the enchanted forest," said the swan.

When Prince Ivan reached the top of the mountain he found a forest so dense that no one could pass through it. Since the Prince believed the swan and was wise enough to do exactly what he was asked, the trees of the forest moved out of his way, as if they were his servants.

As Prince Ivan walked into the clearing he saw a beautiful Princess standing next to strange tower. The tower had a window way up high, but no door.

"Oh, I am so glad to see you," said Princess Anne. "I've been alone here for a million years! If we can get the treasure that is locked up in this tower, we will be able to leave this island."

"I was given a magical rope ladder by the swan, I'll throw it up to the window," the Prince said.

Ivan threw the magical rope and it fastened itself to the windowsill. He helped Princess Anne climb the ladder and he followed. The ladder also served to let them down into the doorless tower. Inside they found a very old trunk. Prince Ivan opened it up. They saw an enormous gold nugget. Since it was so dusty, Ivan found a cloth and began to wipe the dust off.

Poof! "I am the Genie of the Tower. You have two wishes," said the Genie.

"Please, Genie, we would like to leave this forbidden forest with our gold treasure, and return to my home," replied the Prince.

And so it was.

"What is your second wish?" asked the Genie.

The Prince and Princess asked for a beautiful castle to live in. And so it was!

I have retold this story from my notes since I did not tape record the session. Small details have been lost, and I have, in my adult fashion, added a few larger words. The essence of the story is Ruth's very personal fairy tale. Based upon our first session this tale was far more than I would have guessed would emerge, and was a far more complex fairy tale than I have heard from any other child of her age.

Fairy tales are psychological tales of the inner world of the psyche, not simply the outer world of the ego.. The tower without a door sounds like Rapunzel's tower, yet our heroine is standing next to the tower rather than imprisoned inside. She still remained a prisoner. The ability to focus and develop strengths (animus development), and the development of trust in one's instincts were the solution to this child's psychological imprisonment I am struck by the obvious difference between this gentle tale and the masculine mode of battle. A sword was not used to penetrate the forest. A dragon did not need to be conquered. The task here was one of cooperation, obedience and trust in the inner, instinctual process symbolized by the unicorn and swan. In this age of minds dulled by television and video games, this creation demonstrates the power of the psyche to work out its difficulties when it is stimulated and permitted sufficient freedom.

Mother's Little Captive

Jung says of complexes, that the individual does not have a complex, the complex has him. Jennifer was bossy with other children. She was an extremely bright, creative, twelve-year-old with low self-esteem. Jennifer was tall, red-haired, and moderately overweight. She expressed her poor self-image through negative and competitive attitudes toward others.

Her alcoholic father neglected his wife and children. Since father was neglectful and a poor provider, mother ran the household and attempted to be both mother and father to the children. Jennifer was the youngest of four children. This family should be referred to Alanon, Alateen, and AA, and treated. In this school setting I worked with the one child

Jen spent most of her session drawing, playing in the sand, and talking. She talked about her father while she created a doodle-like drawing using two crayons. The theme was "dad-a-dog," words she wrote over and over.

Her anger father was totally laid bare in this drawing, and is one of her primary issues. There are other issues that will come before her intense father-complex.

Jen described herself as a scapegoat. Her teenage brother and sisters dominate and overshadow her life and activities. Jen felt threatened by them. As she spoke of this feeling she created a sand tray depicts herself as a young girl surrounded by her brother and sisters who were depicted as dinosaurs. So far she presented two important issues in this first session. More than the threat of a negative father, and bullying siblings, was the difficulty she has with still another person in the family. This next theme will emerge as her primary theme.

Jen described herself as accident and illness prone. I suggested that she might find other ways of expressing her feelings other than in having accidents and becoming ill. While I do not interpret to children, I try to introduce consciousness to individuals who are accident-prone.

Next she spoke of expecting to die early. Her anger alternated between flowing inward and outward. This seemed to be a histrionic attention-getting device, not a genuine suicidal threat. While she was talking, Jennifer picked up the Rapunzel tower. Jen commented that if she filled the hollow tower with enough sand the girl would drown. She asked me if she can do this. I replied that she might. Jen proceeded to bury the Rapunzel girl in her tower.

Plate 19 The Rapunzel tower
Plate 20 Rapunzel drowned in sand

In the fairy tale an older woman, a type of mother figure, holds the Rapunzel girl captive in a tower. Even though she was angry with her father, and her siblings, the theme of drowning relates to her mother-complex, which was Jen's primary psychological problem. This mother-complex/drowning theme would re-emerge in subsequent sessions.

During her next session Jen worked in the sand tray while she described her neighborhood, and the behavior of her brother and sisters. Jen alternated between creating peaceful, realistic trays, such as a tray, which pictured the apartments and streets where she lived, and hostile, aggressive trays. Next she created an airplane that crashed in the ocean. Sharks and an octopus menaced the survivors. Jen's related that the passengers were being attacked. It was obvious that this young pre-adolescent was filled with rage. Her work evidenced a sadomasochistic flavor. She stated that she was the victim at home. Here she seemed to be identifying with the aggressor. Psychic attack was the second of Jen's leitmotifs.

The octopus is often used when the individual is in the grip of a mother-complex. The engulfing octopus image emerged again during our next session. One of Jen's powerful sand trays featured a Disneyland-type submarine ride. As she moves the vehicles she created a beautiful tray while talking about the submarine ride at Disneyland. This process of moving toys while telling a story is more frequently found in much younger children. Jen is one of the few children in her age bracket that I have observed intensely playing out sand tray stories rather than making a picture in the sand. This indicates the early age of her wound.

Her rage emerged once more when she shared the story of the octopus coming to life and killing all the riders in one of the submarines. Here the anger that expressed itself in the form of being accident prone; in the fear of an early death and was turned outward in her bullying, manifests as her fantasy desire to see others die. Sharing this fantasy may not sound like progress to some, but in a very real sense it is. She has shared her anger with another person that provided a safe container for the discharge of her feelings. Neutralizing aggression is one of the key benefits to this type of non-directive play therapy.

New imagery emerges in her next tray. Jen placed "The Pink Lady," an Oriental lady dressed in a pink kimono on a bridge. She identified the fat sage and the slender Oriental male figure as two suitors who want to marry the young woman. The woman's mother wants her to marry the rich, old man (fat sage). The young woman prefers the poor, young man. She was immobilized by the conflict between her desires and those of her mother. She stayed in one position, undecided, "forever." Jennifer then offered an alternate ending, "She picks the poor man."

Jen felt trapped by an immobilizing mother-complex. She was angry with her powerful and controlling mother, yet she was paralyzed by her fear of mother. The alternate ending sounded like a move toward greater autonomy. That may not be altogether true. There was a self-destructive element since the young suitor was simply identified as a poor man. Jen's father and male role model does not make a good living. The trapped feeling may include the fear of becoming just like her mother.

Adolescence is a challenging time. The onset of adolescence brings a flood of feelings a desire for more independence alternates with a desire to return to the dependency upon the parental figures that one felt as a small child. Most adolescents fight against their regressive urges and begin to look for an object of affection outside the family. Jen wants to be able to make this break with her mother, but the strength of the complex makes it difficult. Her father does not provide her with a positive image of an adult male and male-female relationship, which would have helped free her from the grip of the mother-complex.

Fathers need to impart an affirmation of identity and destiny to their children. A rite of passage is needed at this time of life. Jen struggled to provide her own rite of passage to womanhood. She created a giant forest filling the tray. A forest is symbolic of the unknown in the individual's psyche. A group of animals gathered in the middle—the instinctual part of Jen's personality. The "rainbow girl," as she called the girl with a paintbrush, was symbolic of her creativity. Jen narrated the story as she played it out. "The rainbow girl paints the trees. At night she sleeps in the giant clamshell. Since clams dig, it buries itself in the sand. This happens once a month." Traditionally the shell is a symbol of the feminine principle. Clearly, Jen was referring to the onset of puberty, and to the menstrual cycle.

Plate 21 Rainbow girl in the forest

Jennifer's creativity is admirable. I had not administered psychometric tests, I had no doubt that she was highly gifted albeit emotionally immature.

Next, Jen creates a tropical island. Here food was the main focus, as in the fairy tale *Hansel and Gretel*. Bettelheim interprets *Hansel and Gretel* as being indicative of the child's need to overcome infantile oral incorporative drives during the early phase of the separation-individuation process. As Jen created this tray, she looked for every food item possible and carefully placed them in the containers. Bettelheim states: "The mother represents the source of all food to the children." (1977, p. 159). Again this points to a mother problem, or complex. As she created this tray, Jen spoke as if a male figure would consume this gargantuan meal. At the last moment she abruptly chose a female figure that greedily ate everything.

The male figure who was originally to consume the meal was an emergence of an animus figure, i.e. the unconscious masculine component within a female. Here her feminine ego is identified with oral greed.

Plate 22 A gargantuan meal

The Freudian notion of oral greed has great validity here. One may interpret this imagery as being symbolic of wanting more in a larger sense, such as a hunger for attention, love, unmet dependency needs and so forth. Jennifer is emotionally starved. Alcoholic and co-dependent parents are often so narcissistic and self-involved that a child receives little or no positive mirroring and acceptance.

During our next session Jen recreated The Pink Lady with the two suitors theme. This time the woman quickly chose her preferred suitor. Jennifer was less blocked than she was weeks earlier, but some resistance was apparent in the amount of time she spent in unproductive play during the session. It appeared that she was angry with me because I refused to let her add water to the single sand tray. At the end of this session, Jen asks me to provide a wet tray next time. I agree.

The next time we met, Jen was delighted to see that a second wet tray had been added to the consultation room. She busied herself creating drip castles, i.e. wet sand dripped into crude tower shapes. She explained that she liked to create these at the beach. Sometimes play is just play. It can also be a stalling technique—a holding pattern while psychic energy accumulates. This period of unproductive play was followed by the creation of a sandcastle. She used the sandcastle mold and then scooped out a moat around the castle. She placed a woman next to the edge of the moat. Jen narrated, "And when the tide comes in," she said menacingly. With rapid gestures she buried the figure.

Here Jen's rage has re-emerged. It would be facile to say that this burial represents her anger at her mother. The figure may also represent Jen, her sisters and brother, her transference, (jealously and competitive feelings) toward her female therapist, or a combination of these feelings toward mother and others.

During our next session Jen created a jungle river scene that featured The Pink Lady trapped upon the bridge. Here we see many hostile, aggressive symbols. An octopus and alligators savagely block the young woman's movement in any direction. Jen's anger at her father serves to block her movement toward a healthy male-female relationship and serves to strengthen the mother-complex since father was not available to affirm her identity and help free her from mother's grasp. The alligators, octopus and dragon are symbolic of primitive instincts, devouring, enmeshment, and oral-sadistic rage.

Jen identified the area in the upper left of the tray as quicksand. Quicksand may be interpreted as a further downward pull into the unconscious, and a further entrapment in the mother-complex.

A river is associated with the passage of life, or a change of state. Both the diver and cave symbolize going deeper into the unconscious. A cave is a symbol of transformation. Going into the unconscious can be either destructive or healing. Although Jen had characterlogical problems, she had a fairly strong ego. Moving into the unconscious offers her the possibility of transformation of her marred self-concept.

The Pink Lady was trapped upon the bridge. In her desperation she dove into river to commit suicide. At the same time the dragon slipped into the water near the cave. A female diver dove into the water to help The Pink Lady.

Plate 23 The day the dragon died

The diver emerged saying, "Yum, yum, that dragon was tasty." Here the concept of oral, sadistic rage was clearly illustrated and fully satisfied as it was with Jeff's cannibal. How many heroes, let alone heroines, have you ever heard of that eat their enemies? The spontaneous expression of primitive rage that sandplay allows is amazing.

Jen has produced a number of important symbols. The alligators and octopus can represent the negative parental introjects and the dark side of the archetypal Mother, the Terrible Mother. The bridge is a connecting link between the left side of the tray that indicates the unconscious portion of the personality, and the right side of the tray that is indicative of the ego. The movement is blocked, and Jen appeared caught between her inner world of unconscious forces and the outer world. Even when the imagery appears static the presence of a bridge indicates a flow of energy from one sector to another.

The cave is a place of union of the Self and the ego; the meeting place of the spirit and the human; a place of initiation; of burial and rebirth; a cosmic center that is hidden and closed. It is associated with the feminine principle. In myth the cave is often guarded by some monster, such as Jen's dragon, or supernatural person. Entry can only be gained by overcoming the opposing force. Passing through the cave represents a change of state.

Since Jen gives the Oriental woman the name "the pink lady" for the color of her kimono, let's analyze the color pink. Red is the color of rage and of sexual passion. Pink is a soft, warm, more delicate variant of red. People who like to be pampered and sheltered from the world usually select pink. Many girls and women want and need a certain amount of protection. This color is rightly associated with the more tender aspects of the feminine principle. This is further reinforced by the use of the word "lady," rather than woman or girl. In Jen's case the more delicate aspects of her feminine ego fell victim to the immobilizing mother-complex that held her captive. .My sense was that mother was an animus-dominated female. Women who take on male roles and attributes are often dominated by animus figures. When an archetype dominates a personality the individual's personality and human warmth will be eclipsed. In addition, great damage was done her sense of femininity by a negative, rejecting father. The female diver represented a stronger, animus-dominated portion of Jen's Self that was called upon to act-out a feminine version of the Hero myth. Dragons are typical monsters to be mastered by the Hero.

> "Dragons, as monsters, are autochthonous 'masters of the ground', against which Heroes, conquerors and creators must fight for mastery or occupation of the land; they are also guardians of treasures and the portals of esoteric knowledge. The struggle with the dragon symbolizes the difficulties to be overcome in gaining the treasures of inner know ledge. Killing the dragon is the slaying of the destructive forces of evil, or man overcoming his own dark nature and attaining self mastery. Rescuing the maiden from the dragon is the releasing of pure forces after killing evil powers" (Cooper, 1978, pp. 55-56)

Mythological beasts like the dragon, that must be either tamed or slain in myth and legend, are symbolic of man's animal instincts that are mastered and brought under control. Rescuing a maiden from the dragon is a releasing of pure forces after subduing evil powers. In Jen's case evil was destroyed in a cruel, regressive manner. One might presume it was not totally overcome. The delicate aspect of the larger Self, which might have been integrated into the ego, was not rescued but appeared to be drowned in the cave. Was she forgotten?

As we recall, the theme of drowning was introduced during her initial session with the drowning of the Rapunzel girl who was imprisoned by the witch-mother. Drowning can be a symbol for the loss of the self or ego in the ocean of non-differentiated unity. Since the cave represents a place of burial and rebirth, we can assume that given enough time in this form of depth therapy that the maiden will be saved.

Plate 24 The Pink Lady with fawns

Next week Jen created a tray I named, " The Pink Lady with fawns." This tray was a surprise coming so quickly after the drowning of The Pink Lady. It was heartening to see her restoration, along with the gentle fawns nestled together under the tree. The young suitor was separated from the maiden, and placed in the right side of the tray seemed to be a positive animus figure. This scene was a touchingly beautiful one, and clearly shows the feminine potential that Jennifer struggled to integrate. As she reached a sense of resolution she created a tray that elegantly embodied the community stage that Kalff described. This resolution came after seven months.

Following this beautiful tray Jen returned to the vegetative stage with a new theme. Jen's anger at her father, evident in her initial session, was the next theme that she took up. Since there was so much pathology, many cycles such as this would be necessary in order to restore this child's intrapsychic balance. She returned to the vegetative stage with a new theme and new imagery. During subsequent sessions, Jennifer continued to work on themes that seemed to represent her father, usually in a very destructive manner. She choose a male Native American figure to represent her father, and a white horse. During this next cycle there was much anger, destruction and burial of key images, but that is another tale.

It is vital to understand the theme of death and rebirth. Jennifer described herself as accident and illness prone. She started therapy by introducing the fantasy of a possible early death. She buried the Rapunzel tower where the witch-mother held a young girl captive. She needed to deal with the regressive, primitive, and often destructive aspects of the psyche. As the work progressed she elaborated this theme of death by drowning. Finally the image of drowning was transformed into one of rebirth of The Pink Lady.

Rebirth is synonymous with the transformation of intrapsychic processes. Jung (1959) says that, although we cannot observe the notion of rebirth, it is a reality to the psyche. What Jennifer had done was healing for her, and illustrative for us. We have had an opportunity to travel with her along her inner journey and actually see one individual's intrapsychic rebirth.

Jen's journey started with the burial of the Rapunzel girl. She moved on to the image of The Pink Lady paralyzed on the bridge, caught between her mother's will and her own, and between the outer world and the inner world since a bridge is seen as a link to the unconscious. Jennifer created a more positive image of burial with the rainbow girl sleeping in the clam. The clam may refer to the original symbiotic mother and child unity. In this case it also was used in conjunction with her emerging womanhood, and bodily processes, since this scene is enacted "once a month." The burying of the dark woman in the moat during high tide, like the airplane crash in the ocean and the Disneyland-type submarine ride, seemed to be a turning of her rage outward. Once again, her imagery returned to her pink lady immobilized upon the bridge. Again, she referred to suicide, but since she created a heroine and destroyed the monster, death became rebirth.

As Campbell (1949) noted in *The Hero with a Thousand Faces*, certain individuals' dreams will sometimes be similar to traditional myths. Clearly, Jen's tale has striking similarities to the archetypal Hero's journey, and very personal differences from the archetypal stories. Archetypal psychology offers a method for deepening our therapeutic knowledge of the human condition by offering us a broad view of these very human processes.

Twelve

When Ends Meet

> But gradually it got better for the teachers.
> We began to notice that about two-thirds of the
> way through a problem-solution sequence, the
> right-handed knowing began to dominate. That is,
> the closer the children got to rational solution,
> *the more difficult it was for them to return
> to metaphor.* Bob Samples, 1976

In *The Metaphoric Mind*, Bob Samples demonstrates that children learn through playful exploration, or what he calls "left-handed knowing." "When the inventive mode is functioning, a total synergetic kind of knowing evolves. Exploration has the quality of dream." (Samples, 1976) This synergetic, dreamlike thinking has been exactly what you have been privy to in the stories of Jennifer, Duncan, Sharon and the other children whose lives have touched yours and mine. Having read this far I expect that you have developed a good working understanding of what imagery in children's play therapy might mean. Let's review what we have covered.

In my opening chapter, I present bits and pieces from many different theorists. Let's briefly review some of these theories in the light of the case material. In Axline's (1947, 1964) view the parent(s), and possibly others, have rejected some part of the child. The therapist serves to facilitate healing by accepting the entire child. When I think of this theory I remember Kevin. He was secretive about his life, most particularly about his religious life. When we met, he gave me the impression that because of certain thoughts he had he believed he was a wicked person. After Mark challenged Kevin saying, "You're not so bad as you think," and after he played through his obsessive fighting stage, Kevin found peace. A serene picture that featured a woman on a quest was surprising and sophisticated resolution. Mark and I accepted both the spiritual and the aggressive sides of Kevin. This allowed him to reintegrate each part on a higher level.

Anna Freud (1927) maintains that small children cannot verbalize their conflicts, but can demonstrate them in the process of play. This non-verbal communication seems to be particularly true of children filled with rage who alternate between impulses to hurt themselves or attack others, such as Ken, who buried a house surrounded by weapons. Months later, Ken placed the Oriental house in the middle of the tray. Weapons stood on either end of the tray facing the house.

Ken stood still and looked at the tray.

"What happens to the house?"

He replied, "It's all right, it isn't destroyed."

I spoke with the aides on the playground and found that the destructive boy's games in which Ken had been the victim stopped during the time we worked together. Acceptance of the whole child by the therapist was a factor in healing.

Bruno Bettelheim (1975) states that when the unconscious comes to the fore in a child, it overwhelms rather than strengthens the total personality. For this reason a child must externalize his or her inner processes. The child uses play objects, such as dolls and toy animals, to embody various aspects of his personality which are too complex, contradictory and unacceptable to handle. This substitution helps the child gain an intuitive sense of mastery. When I think of complex, contradictory and unacceptable aspects of the personality, I think of

Sharon whose drawing of a crying girl and war scene startled me when I first saw them. Her statement that a man with a gun was going to kill the animals was additionally troubling. Dundas points out that girls often use animals, symbolizing the instincts, and alternate between penning them up and loosing them to gain a sense of mastery over the instinctual realm. Sharon clearly had contradictory and unacceptable feelings about her family life that were disrupting the development of a healthy ego. In the eight months she worked with me she was able to find release from the overwhelming burden that she felt without my intruding upon a sensitive and private process. Again, as Bettelheim said, "It is always intrusive to interpret a person's unconscious thoughts, to make conscious what he wishes to keep preconscious. This is especially true in the case of a child" (1975, p. 18). If I had attempted to share my interpretations with such a sensitive child as Sharon she would have shut down.

Dora Kalff (1966b) believes the emergence of the archetype of the Self serves as a healing factor in sandplay. Several of the case studies show numerous examples of this, for example, Sharon's enigmatic tray in which she placed a large stone in the two upper corners of the tray and in the lower left corner; in the fourth corner she placed an elderly couple. When I asked, Sharon told me that these figures do not represent her grandparents. There it was, the archetype of the Self in the fourfold personality structure, and male and female representatives of inner wisdom. This was a benchmark in her work. When Sharon touched this deep and powerful archetypal reservoir within her psyche, this seemed to strengthen her.

Jennifer created a giant forest, the unknown portion of her psyche, where she met a group of animals, the instinctual part of her personality, and the "rainbow girl" symbolic of her creativity. New energy coming from the unconscious may be indicated by the image of a forest. It was after she touched upon some of her strengths that she was able to break free of her mother-complex and assert her individuality.

While making one of her last trays Camellia asked me to help her search for the "right" little girl whom she described as being four or five years old. This younger inner self or divine child was quite a contrast from eight-year-old Camellia's real life responsibility of being the second mother in an over-burdened household. It seemed that finding her archetypal Self in the form of her inner child was the lost treasure. In each of the cases I have described I learned from the children as well as providing a stimulus filled container for their process. You can do the same.

Begin where you are; a neglected area in your counseling center that can be turned into a playroom, a drawing pad and markers, clay, a few games, a few dozen toys, or what have you. You do not have to create an ideal playroom. Most children are receptive to caring, interest and private time with an adult and with non-structured materials. As you grow with the children, I hope that you will feel freer to facilitate transformational play. The wounded children await you....

About the Author

Susan Perkins McNally, Ph.D. received her Master's degree in Counseling Psychology from California State University Northridge, and her Ph.D. from International College, Westwood, CA. She is a specialist in Chemical Dependency Counseling from Mission College, as well as a specialist in sandplay therapy. In addition to her psychology background, she has a Bachelors degree in Art. Multifaceted, Susan is an accomplished artist who has exhibited and sold her paintings, prints and sculpture. Susan's artwork is in collections in California, Washington, Oregon, and Texas.

Dr. McNally has worked in various settings including clinics, schools and private practice. In California she was licensed as a Marriage, Family and Child Counselor (M.F.C.C.), and she is currently licensed as Licensed Professional Counselor (L.P.C.) in Texas where she is employed by Buckner Community Services. She was a member of the San Fernando Valley Child Abuse Council in Southern California, and has been a speaker at many children abuse prevention conferences.

Dr, McNally has spoken for numerous professional organizations including: The California Association of Children's Homes, Bienvenidos Foster Family Agency, Walden Environment, the San Fernando Valley Child Abuse Council, and A Creative Change Place.

She is married, has three grown sons and three grandchildren. Her hobbies include painting, sculpture, reading, writing, cooking, traveling, teaching, and when the climate allows, gardening.

Dr. McNally is available for lectures and workshops in sandplay therapy.

Appendix A

Dictionary of Play Therapy Imagery

> The symbol is not a sign that disguises something generally known. Its meaning resides in the fact that it is an attempt to elucidate, by more or less apt analogy, something that is entirely unknown or in the process of formation. C.G. Jung, 1953

Jung developed the technique of symbol amplification. It consists of adding to the client's associations to a symbol by looking into mythological, religious, and folk tale representations of similar material. With highly functional adults, this can be explored consciously, both therapist and client delving into the material in depth. With a child, or an adult with a weak ego, the therapist delves into the material, and contains it within his consciousness. The transpersonal bond between therapist and patient is the foundation of the therapeutic process. This transpersonal bond, or interpsychic bridge, is the heart of any truly strong and effective therapeutic alliance. Many of my observations, and those of other sandplay therapists, are included in the commentaries.

The discussion of specific symbols that follows is not meant to be used in an absolute or reductive way, but as an aid in seeing some of the potential meanings that occur in the process of sand tray work or art work. The power of the object to attract the attention of the patient's consciousness must not be diluted by an absolute interpretation. The process seems to be best served by not speaking of these meanings, but rather just containing this awareness.

AIRCRAFT

Airborne methods of transportation, such as airplanes, helicopters, and spaceships are indicative of mobility that is not attached to the earth (mother). They are associated with power, speed and freedom. Males use aircraft, such as military planes, helicopters, transport planes, and spaceships more frequently than do females.

Air has a wealth of associated meanings that may relate to a child's symbolic play. The ancients considered air an active, masculine element. It is associated with the spiritual, with creativity, and with the life force as in the "breath of life." Thoughts, ideas, communication, and imagination are common associations.

During active sandplay, the sphere of combat may be in the air above the tray. This might indicate mental conflicts that relate to thought or communication, or spiritual conflicts, or just a tendency to be intuitive or ungrounded. Personalities who continually favor this realm may not be realistic, may have poor body consciousness, or be "flighty," or they just might be future pilots.

Young men who are engulfed by a mother-complex often become pilots. This may be an attempt to escape from an over-powering and destructive mother. Escaping from the earth may be thought of as tantamount to escaping from the grasp of a destructive mother. See Marie Louise von Franz's (1970) book on the archetype of the Eternal Youth or Puer, for an in depth explanation of this personality type.

Aircraft are known to crash. Crashes, like the downfall of block towers, occur more frequently in the play of young males. The phenomenon of aircraft crashes has also been seen in certain girl's sand trays, but is less frequent. This image suggests a loss of power and control. The narcissistic phenomenon of over inflation may be suggested. A crash may depict the depression that tends to follow such inflation. See Earth and Earth Mother.

ALLIGATOR

Evocative of the reptilian complex or R-complex, this beast is frequently used with the octopus, dragon, and crab. The alligator or crocodile is thought of as bearing a similarity to the dragon and the serpent.

Like the shark and the tyrannosaurus Rex, this beast is notable for its large mouth and multiplicity of teeth. Oral aggression as they devour their prey is an essential aspect of this creature's instinctive nature. The alligator represents rage, viciousness, greed, and evil. he closely related crocodile was thought to represent the fertility and destructiveness of the watery world. Other associations are deceit and dishonesty. See Crocodile.

ANGEL

An angel is a winged supernatural being. Powers greater than those possessed by a mere human are attributed to these beings. The word for angel in Hebrew means messenger. A good angel is a spirit messenger, intermediary or helper, sent from God. Angels have been described as guardians and as warriors. Helpful angels appear in dreams, fantasies, and in sand trays). Many children believe they are protected by a guardian angel. The Bible says "some have entertained angels unawares." (Heb. 13:2)

Associated symbols are stars, trumpets, heavenly chariots, flaming swords, scepters, musical instruments, censers, and the lily. An angel is also associated with a person who is considered good, innocent, or beautiful. See Demon.

ANIMALS

Animals are interpreted as being representative of instinctual and emotional urges. Jung (1956) believes that animals are representative of non-human aspects of the psyche. These interpretations anticipated research findings on the triune nature of the brain. Animals can also represent poorly integrated aspects of the Self, old memories.

There are a world of difference between mammals, who possess an affective or emotional brain, and the world of the reptiles and amphibians. Mammals care for their young, nursing them and training them. In contrast, some reptiles will unemotionally feed on their own offspring.

Some older children are aware of this, and will include this dimension in their play.

Generally we think of dinosaurs as embodiments of primal urges. New research seems to indicate that some dinosaurs cared for their young. Many children make a sharp distinction between dinosaurs that are predators and those that are herbivores. Usually an aggressor/victim relationship is observed. This is an important dynamic as the case material demonstrates.

Among the mammals there is a tremendous difference between predator and prey animals. Animals may be roughly divided into those who are governed by the impulse to fight and those governed by the impulse toward flight—the predator animals and the prey animals. "Mean as a bear," and "scaredy cat" are accurate observations. Just as animals may be divided into those who react with a fight or flight response, so may many humans. Generally, we associate fight with males and flight with females. This tendency is reflected in the objects and types of scenes created by the two sexes. Individual differences and parental introjects may contradict this in certain individuals.

Animals that are used with great intensity are indicative of certain characteristics that the child may possess, or may picture a survival need in her situation. Make a careful note of this phenomenon when a child places her "totemic" animal in nearly every tray. Ponder the nature of the particular animal chosen. The child is saying, "This is important."

Many cultures have revered animals for their extraordinary perceptions, such as keen sight or sense of smell, and associated them with unseen cosmic forces. Animals may represent a paradisiacal state of consciousness that includes an understanding of instinctual wisdom, and access to an animal's perception of the world.

The theme of the abandoned child is noteworthy. The abandoned child is cared for by nature in the form of helpful animals. The animals in Disney's Cinderella, who helped dress the maiden are typical of this archetypal association. Helpful animals are associated with the feminine principle.

Animals, or mythological beasts, that must be either tamed or slain in myth and legend, are symbolic of man's animal instincts that are mastered and brought under control. When a higher animal is victorious over a lower animal, such as an eagle vanquishing a snake, as is found in pre-Columbian art, this represents a hierarchy of instincts. Higher life has emerged victorious over the base instincts. Combat between man and animal can have a healing significance. Reconnecting to the instincts blocked by neurotic defenses is required in some cases.

Creatures, such as the frog, fish, and water fowl, are associated with water and represent life's origins or rebirth.

A domesticated animals that is a pet. such as a dog or cat, may be seen as an aspect of the instinctual life that has become related to ego consciousness. Additional information is listed under the name of the specific animal. See individual animals: Bear, Lion, etc.

APE

Eastern associations to the ape tend to be positive while Occidental associations tend to be negative. Associations range from gentleness, mischievous, cunning. The ape with an apple in its mouth is associated with Adam's fall. See Monkey.

ARK

At times children will create trite appearing sand trays using the Noah's ark and animals two by two. This usage may simply refer to the child's religious education. An ark is potentially a potent symbol of protection and refuge, salvation and regeneration. Since the Biblical ark protected both man and animals, it might be interpreted as a refuge for both ego and instincts from overwhelming forces. The ark symbolizes trial and spiritual purification. See Whale, Flood.

AVALANCHE

An avalanche can represent a sudden overwhelming, such as the ego overwhelmed by unconscious, libidinal energies. This is typical situation when there are severe psychic wounds in a child. A personal or family situation that is overwhelming to the child may be indicated by this imagery.

Overwhelming fear of family members or anger at family members, may be suggested. See Burial and Flood.

BABY

An infant is a potent symbol of transformation. This image may carry many levels of meaning. An image is especially potent when it carries meanings at several levels of the psyche. A baby may refer to the undeveloped portion of the personality; feelings of helplessness and weakness; narcissistic needs that have not been filled; the archetype of the Self, i.e. the "child divine," a new development in the individual. See Child, also Dark Man, Woman, Child.

BAG

A bag is a secret container. It is associated with the feminine principle.

BASKET

The basket has numerous associations with fruitfulness or abundance; the feminine principle. See Containers.

BATTLE

Battles are typical subjects in the sand trays of boys from ages four to twelve, and occur in the trays of adolescent boys. A battle is a struggle or conflict and indicates opposition to powerful forces. Battles may refer to a male's struggle to establish a strong ego, particularly his need to separate from the maternal matrix.

The battles of Star Trek and Star Wars are popular precisely because of their clear archetypal content. The struggle of good against evil may be seen as a type of the inner struggle to develop one's ego and moral strength against one's lower nature. When a battle occurs in a female's tray, her family situation is likely to be the stimulus. See War.

BEACH

A beach is usually thought of as a place for swimming and sunbathing. Symbolically it is a transitional area where land and water meet, and may denote a movement to or away from the unconscious, to or away from one's feelings. The preconscious may be suggested.

BEAR

Bears are large, omnivorous mammals notable for their strength, toughness, ruggedness, determination, and stubbornness. For the Japanese they represent wisdom, strength and benevolence. Native American tribes often had similar associations. In China the bear was a masculine emblem. In early Christians and Islamic traditions the bear was associated with the devil, cruelty, evil, greed, vengefulness, and lust. Bears have been associated with individuals who are clumsy, gruff, and rude. In the West the bear has been used to represent gluttony.

She bears are generally thought of as good parents who look after their young. Ancient imagery associates the bear with primeval birth-giver, pregnant woman and mother.

Dundas (1978, p. 94), says: "The bear often stands for a primitive and perilous part of the unconscious that needs healing, yet it is a symbol of bravery, endurance and strength." She suggests that these creatures represent instinctual wisdom and teach us to think from the inside. Even though this is considered to be true of animals as a whole, Dundas found that the bear and the owl were used more frequently than other animals or birds. These creatures are associated with caves and secret places. Since the bear becomes dormant each year within the protection of the earth and then emerges in the spring it is associated with the notion of rebirth or resurrection. Other associations are leadership, introspection, stability, durability, caution, bravery, fairness, curiosity, organization, maturity and healing. See Rebirth.

BEAVER

The beaver is an animal that functions well on land and in the water. In moving from one realm to another it symbolizes moving into the depths of the psyche. Native Americans associate the beaver with security, industry, contentment, patience, affection, and balance. See Frog.

BEE

We find bees fascinating since they engage in a harmonious collective effort. Peoples throughout the world value the honey they produce. There are many associations to bees: industry; order; purity; prudence; winged or heavenly messengers. Their fierceness in defense of their hive is renown. Bees are thought to symbolize regeneration.

BELL

Ringing bells represents a summons or a warning; a charm against destructive powers; the sounds associated with Paradise; respect; veneration; harmony between man and heaven; virginity; the deity's presence.

BIRD

Like thoughts and imaginings, birds inhabit the sky. Birds are associated with the transcendent and the spiritual, goodness and joy. They are thought of as representations of good and bad spirits.

In fairy tales birds represent helpful spirits that convey useful secrets to a Hero, or take important information from one person to another. These light, airborne creatures may represent entering into a different or altered state of consciousness. Dark and light birds seen together represent the dualism of dark and light, good and evil. Mythical winged creatures represent celestial realms, and like the eagle may oppose the snake or serpent.

Waterfowl, swans, duck, geese, are associated with positive emotions and experiences: nourishment; wealth; happiness. The owl and the cuckoo are associated with spring, marriage, prophecy and death. Birds of prey, owls, vultures, ravens, are associated with death.. Many cultures see them as omens of death. Native Americans associate the raven with wisdom, spirituality, intelligence, duality, community, and balance The dove, cuckoo and other small birds are associated with the soul. See Angels, Dove, Feathers, Eagle, and Owl.

BLACK

Black, in this culture, is symbolic of the unknown, of evil, and of the unconscious. It is representative of nothingness or extinction, void, death, destruction, and chaos. It stands for ignorance, disaster, and mourning. The emotions associated with black are: sadness, grief and mourning, humiliation and shame, despair and deep depression. Spiritual corruption and darkness are also represented by blackness.

A positive association is the initial or germinal stages of any creative process. Lusher (1969) associates black with renunciation. Traditionally, black was associated with the dark side of the Great Mother archetype, i.e. the Terrible Mother. The Hindu goddess, Kali, is an image of the Terrible Mother. Psychologically she is a death mother—a mother who wishes death upon her child.

Black was worn only by European nobility and priests and has long associations with power. As the color worn by Christian priests and nuns and Islamic clerics it is associated with renunciation of worldly pleasures. Satan, the Prince of Darkness, is associated with black. It is a popular color for youth that identify with rebellion of society's values.

In other cultures black may be associated with the earth and the maternal.

BLACK PERSON

See Dark Man, Woman or Child.

BLOOD

Blood is symbolic of life force potency, and divine energy. It is associated with emotions and inherited tendencies. A further association is rejuvenating force.

More males than females have mentioned spilling blood during their sandplay. Males have a greater interest in both combat and bloodshed. The most primitive blood related ritual is the drinking of an adversary's blood in order to absorb his potency. One child I worked with created a sand tray that utilized drinking of the enemy's blood.

Children who are extremely fascinated with or disturbed by this image may need to be assessed for exposure to Satanic or ritual abuse. Catherine Gould Ph.D. (see Appendix) has developed an excellent four-page questionnaire to assess ritualistic abuse in children.

Covenants are marked or sealed by blood, or the mingling of blood.

BLUE

Blue is the fifth color of the rainbow. Blue is the color of the thyroid and throat, chakra. Like yellow, blue is associated with the intellect. It represents holistic, or intuitive, thought. This chakra is associated with the element AIR and communication. Since it is more holistic than the thought processes associated with yellow, it would be associated with right brain processes. Interestingly, this is consistent with the research findings that associate depressive tendencies with right brain processes, i.e. being depressed is "having the blues." The emphasis is upon mental ideals, concepts, devotion to God, tradition and authority, respect for the past, and memory. Hills (Hills and Rozman, 1978) believes that abhorrence for war and the willingness to settle for peace at any price are also indicative of this center. Music and wind instruments are associated with this center.

Other associations are spiritual life, truth, piety, loyalty, chastity, prudence, contemplation, devotion, peace, infinity, and coolness, or introversion. Hebrew tradition links blue to wisdom, and to the color of a Hebrew man's shirt tassels that remind him to be mindful of God. Blue is considered a heavenly color. Hindu representations of the god Vishnu depict him as blue-skinned.

BRIDGE

A bridge is a threshold symbol—a connection between poles. It usually appears when there is linking between consciousness and the unconscious. A bridge may serve to connect opposing parts of the psyche, for example the passive and the aggressive, the good and the bad. Is it a connecting link between the left side of the tray that often indicates the unconscious portion of the personality, and the right side of the tray that is indicative of the conscious personality? Even when it is not clear what the bridge is connecting its value as a connector is remains valid. Is there much traffic over the bridge, or is the movement blocked? Even if the imagery appears static the presence of a bridge indicates a flow of energy from one sector to another.

In mythology the bridge is a connecting link between the world of mortals and the realm of spirits. The symbol of the bridge includes man as a mediator or midpoint between heaven and earth. Narrow bridges may represent of the slim separation of opposites. Extremely slender bridges offer a challenge to the hero so that he gains enlightenment, and victory over death.

BROWN

Brown is associated with the color of the earth; earthiness. Lusher (1969) believes that brown, especially red-brown, represents the body's sensory condition. If it is an important color for an individual, there is an indication of physical discomfort or dis-ease. He found that individuals who were dispossessed and homeless during the Second World War placed brown as the first in the series of colors in his test. Lusher attributed this finding as being indicative of their having no place in which they could be at ease. He believes that brown indicates an emphasis on roots, hearth, home, and familial security.

BROKEN DOLLS

Abused children who feel broken or damaged often use broken dolls.

BUFFALO

Native Americans associate the buffalo with spirituality, ancient wisdom, generosity, hope, and selflessness.

BULL

Bulls are symbols of vital energy and sexuality. Bulls denote masculine powers and attributes. In ancient times this was extended to the powers of the heavens, and its elements.

Bulls were sacrificial animals. To the Romans the bull was seen as symbolic of regeneration and of the source of life in Mithraism.

The horns of a bull have been associated with the crescent moon in India.

The term bull is not only applied to males of the bovine family, but to males of certain other large animals, such as the bull elephant. The bull is associated with royalty, specifically with the king.

BURIAL

Buhler stated that burying objects by children over the age of four is an indicator of pathology. Much of my clinical experience bears this out. By contrast, Eve Lewis (Bowyer, 1971) observes a very different phenomenon and suggests that the careful burying of an object seems to indicate acceptance into the unconscious of whatever the object symbolizes.

Burial may be seen as an overwhelming of the ego by unconscious forces, primitive rage, masochistic tendencies, self-destructive tendencies, or the potential for transformation of psychic energy.

Burial, like baptism, can be a type of death and rebirth; initiation; renewal. Burial can be seen as an opportunity for intrapsychic transformation.

BUS

All modes of transportation relate to energy. A bus is a collective form of conveyance, rather than a personal form, such as a bicycle or motorcycle.

As anyone who works with children knows, teasing, arguments, drug use, conversations about sexual behaviors, bullying and fights on school buses are common. Negative experiences on school buses are a source of much upset to many children. School buses often represent an out of control situation. Often the adult in charge cannot take the time, nor does she have the skills, to stop conflict between children.

BUTTERFLY

A butterfly symbolizes miraculous powers of transformation, change, joy, and immortality. The lowly caterpillar is transformed into a graceful winged creature that, like birds, inhabits the air. Associations are with spiritual transformation; resurrection; the spirit in man; rebirth. See Rebirth.

CANDLES

See Fire.

CAR

All modes of transportation relate to energy. Cars provide mobility and power and can be seen as indicators of ego strength. Cars are popular with little boys. Various types of cars are seen as reflective of a person's personality type. A child who is feeling weak may use a powerful car or truck as compensation for these feelings.

CASTLE

A castle is a fortified residence built by people of means. A castle may be used as a symbol for the Self. It is particularly associated with the ego strength and will. The castle and the tower symbolize the masculine realm of accomplishment, authority, power, rulership, and respect from others.

The home of the king and queen is the seat of rulership and power. This may represent the home of the old (archaic) ruling order, i.e. parental authority, that needs to be overthrown in order that the individual establishes his own authority, i.e. the process of separation and individuation.

Castles of old were both positive and negative. Castles serve as protection against invaders, and are characterized by strong defenses. Walls several feet thick, battlements, men in armor poised upon the walls, and a deep moat completely surrounding the structure suggests the child is protecting himself from the frightening world of adults, the frightening world of other children, and possibly from his inner world as well. Much good might be found there, but they also contained dungeons, mysterious rooms, and lonely towers.

A castle may symbolize the goal of Hero's quest Castles may contain treasures. In Hero myths the heavily walled castle may be seen as something difficult to attain and is representative of spiritual testing. A wicked person may live there who must be overcome before the treasure is gained. For a child the wicked person may well be an introjected negative parent, and/or the perpetrator in his life. The castle, like Rapunzel's tower, may be a prison. Walt Disney's castle at Disneyland is a positive symbol of the magic of childhood. See Tower

CAT

Cats, whether domesticated house cats or large wild animals, have an elegantly independent air. Associations for house cats are softness, affection, independence, sensual beauty, slyness, deceit, aloofness, or witchcraft. Ancient traditions associate cats with clairvoyance, watchfulness, transformation, protective forces, mystery, fertility. The Celts associated black cats with death.

The context and type of cat are important. It is notable that some males may resent a cat's independence. Cats are not easily coerced, but may be teased. Girls usually do not try to dominate house cats, but more often find them affectionate pets. The negative reaction to small cats may be indicative of an aggressive personality style, or simply a person who dislikes being scratched. See Lion and Tiger.

CAVE

A cave is hollowness within the earth and as such provides one of the richest symbols available to the play therapist. It can be thought of as womb-like, and symbolic of the early symbiotic stage of development. Entering a cave relates to the feminine principle, the womb, or mother earth. This image is associated with the cosmic egg, also a place of possible rebirth and transformation. Passing through the cave represents a change of state.

The cave is an entrance into a deeper world. It can be thought of as an omphalos, centerpoint or navel that permits entrance into this deeper world. Going into a cave can symbolize going into the unconscious.

The cave may be a temenos, that is, a magic or secret place. One of the many interpretations of the cave is the universe or the world center. Caves or grottoes on mountains or hills were used as axial symbols connecting earth to sky. In archaic belief systems it was the meeting place of the human and the divine; the conscious personality and images that represent the archetypes, or the unconscious personality and spirit beings, as in shamanistic religious systems. These images need to be understood psychologically. A cave is place of meeting and union between the ego and the Self.

The cave image is a potent symbol of transformation associated with both initiation and rebirth. The cycle of death, rebirth and illumination are frequent occurrences within the containment of a cave. Caves were places of initiation. They are associated with magic and oracles.

The cave dream in Jacobi's (1959) book is an excellent example of the power of this symbol of transformation. The dream ego goes into the cave to be shown by the unconscious that he is not the true healer but that "archetype of the spirit," the wise man in white robes, is his true inner healer. This healer shows the dreamer that the feminine, or feeling aspect of the dreamer, needs to be healed or transformed.

In myth the cave is often concealed by a labyrinth, an important symbol in itself. Traditionally a cave guarded by a monster, dragon, or supernatural being. Mysteries are contained in caves, along with possible riches and treasures. Caves are associated with pirates and hidden treasure. In fairy tales they are associated with dwarves, gnomes, and dragons.

Primitives use caves as totemic centers. Specifically, in Australia tchuringas are buried there. Tchuringas are "sacred" stones. See Burial, Rebirth and Tunnel.

CAVE MEN and WOMEN

Prehistoric figures are important as they represent man's capacity to survive under harsh circumstances. They might be seen to represent the primal world of feelings without the governor of the rational mind.

CHILD

The divine child is an archetype of the Self uncontaminated with personal problems and quirks. We have many images of children in our memories: the playful child, mischievous child, curious child, the happy, carefree child, innocent child, rebellious child, and the lonely child to name a few. Like the unconscious itself, the child is an embodiment of possibilities. A dark child may be a shadow figure representing the repressed portions of the personality. See Baby and Dark Man, Woman or Child.

CHURCH

Churches, temples, and religious figures are important in sandplay work. Children are often surprised and delighted to see churches and religious symbols available for play. Spiritual issues may involve the family's teachings, or the lack thereof, or be indicative of the child's yearnings and need for greater understanding, or for more loving parenting. See Religious Figures and Ladder.

CIRCLE

Circles are unique geometrical shapes. They are alike in all parts and are without points of division. Circles are associated with psychological wholeness. A circle symbolizes self-containment, unity, timelessness, completeness, infinity, perfection, and cyclic movement (this is especially true of spirals). The Celts and other ancient civilizations associated the circle with protection, and astronomical significance. Our word church is from the Celtic or Middle English word kirke, which means circle.

When a child uses a circle it may refer to the early experience of wholeness and containment. The circle that contains a cross represents a cosmic center; a union of masculine and feminine principles the life cycle; a paradisiacal state.

A circle enclosing a square represents heaven enclosing earth in both Eastern and Western traditions. The circle is associated with the sun, a masculine element, or with the womb, a feminine association. The uroboros, the snake with its tail in its mouth, forms a circle. Circling a sacred object (circumambulation) is common is many religious traditions. See Sphere, Spiral and Egg.

CLAM

"Happy as a clam" refers to the symbiotic containment in the maternal matrix experienced en utero or as an infant. The clam's association with birth is responsible for its use as a symbol of transformation. Botticelli's Venus is depicted as rising out of the sea on an open clam shell. This usage relates to fecundity, regeneration, and female sexuality. See Shells.

CLOWN

Silliness, playfulness, pranks or tricks, humor, and hiding one's true identity are suggested by the image of a clown. The exuberance of the playful clown can be indicative of sheer joy, or of a facade to hide one's fears, pain, and vulnerability. Tricks and games may thinly veil a child's anger, and feelings of inferiority, or may be indicative of a child's need for mastery or power.

The clown is associated with the fool and jester and the archetype of the trickster. . The trickster is a forerunner of the Hero. He is more closely identified with the unconscious than the Hero. He is a more instinctual figure, and tends to be chaotic and amoral. He shifts from consciousness to a falling backward into the unconscious because of his primitive lack of development. This archetype's weaknesses are more readily apparent than those of the Hero, and may be exaggerated and publicly displayed in order to obtain the laughter of one's companions.

The trickster, as a more primitive state of consciousness, represents the life of the body. Jung (1959) says that he often seems more stupid than the animals, and gets himself into a series of ridiculous difficulties because of sheer unconsciousness and lack of relatedness. Surprisingly, the resulting behaviors may prove to be beneficial, simply because he is not usually evil so much as an animalistic super being. He fails to carry the instinctive wisdom of the animal world in spite of his living closer to that realm. These defects are a result of the humanness of his nature. Jung further emphasizes an eagerness to learn inherent in this psychic condition that is indicative of a great capacity for psychological development.

Occasionally this image may be used as a contrast to the goodness of the true Hero. Because of their incomplete moral development many children play out archetypal trickster behaviors.

COLORS

Children will demonstrate preferences for colors in several ways. They may wear a color frequently, talk about their favorite color(s), or use certain colors in their artwork. It is important to be aware of some of the psychological and symbolic implications of color.

The rainbow colors: red, orange, yellow, green, blue, indigo, and violet result when light is divided into various wave lengths through a prism. Yogi and psychologist, Christopher Hills (Hills and Rozman, 1978) has experienced the colors of the rainbow associated with each of the seven psychic energy centers, or chakras, within the body.

The rainbow colors: red, orange, yellow, green, blue, indigo, violet, purple, the tints: pink and lavender and the neutral colors: white, gray, black and brown are discussed under the heading for each individual color. See individual colors.

CONTAINERS

Containers are symbols of the feminine principle. It is important to have a collection of small containers, such as: small flower pots, baskets, and cooking pots, ups and tea kettles. A miniature kettle is especially useful. Kettles and other cooking utensils symbolize nourishment and physical well being. The feminine principle in its positive aspects is receptive and nourishing. The kettle, cauldron, and crucible are potentially powerful symbols of transformation. They refer to the feminine power of transformation. The act of cooking transforms disparate elements into a new and nourishing form. As with many other symbols of transformation there is an association with renewal and rebirth.

The cup and the chalice share in some of these associations. These forms are open, receptive and form a container, thus are associated with the feminine principle. The simple cup may represent the humble aspects of the feminine, while the chalice represents an inexhaustible supply, therefore becomes symbolic of the spiritual transcendent principle, or God. The cornucopia, or horn of plenty, is also an ancient symbol of divine inexhaustible supply.

For children of alcoholic/addicts it is important to have small glasses and bottles that relate to drinking beverage alcohol, small medical syringes, and pill bottles as this may elicit strong memories. These containers must be emptied and refilled with colored water.

COTTAGE

Houses have generally been interpreted as symbolic of the self. The cottage stands in sharp contrast to the castle as a symbol of a quiet, simple life, or humble ego. The cottage is evocative of the hearth, long a symbol of the feminine principle. Cottages are close to the earth and gardens. Simple pleasant life is suggested, away from the bustle and striving of the cities, and the masculine realm of achievement.

Since it is symbolic of the ego or Self it is important to provide a wide variety of houses. See House and Castle.

COW

The cow is notable for its gentleness, its ability to be domesticated and its useful feminine gift of milk. The nourishing qualities of the mother archetype are suggested. In ancient times it was used as a symbol of the "Great

Mother," Mother Earth. Peace, tranquillity, and a life without conflict are evoked by this image. A female using this image may be working on accepting her sexuality in a psychological sense in the midst of a society that exalts masculine logic and demeans feminine Eros—feeling and instinct.

COYOTE

Native Americans consider the coyote the trickster of the animal kingdom. From him we learn about wildness, trickster energy, survival, humor, and creativity.

CRAB

The crab, like the octopus and the crocodile, appears frequently in the trays of disturbed children and psychotic adults. This primitive creature of the waters is associated with the devouring, destructive aspects of the "Great Mother." This image suggests the likelihood of a powerful mother-complex. The Terrible Mother is associated with what is now commonly referred to as the blind destructiveness of "mother" nature. See Crocodile, Octopus, Spider and Quicksand.

CROCODILE

Evocative of the R-complex, this beast is frequently used with the octopus, dragon, and crab. The crocodile is thought of as baring a similarity to the dragon and the serpent. This creature's instinctive nature evokes the image of devouring. Like the shark and the tyrannosaurus Rex, this beast is notable for its large mouth and multiplicity of teeth. The crocodile represents rage, viciousness, greed, and evil. For the ancients the crocodile was thought to represent the fertility and destructiveness of the watery world. Other associations to the crocodile are death, deceit and dishonesty. See Alligator, Crab, Octopus, Spider and Quicksand.

CROSS

The cross is now associated with Jesus' crucifixion, and as such represents salvation. It is an ancient symbol of cosmic energy, the Sun, divine energy, protection, and cosmic unity.

DARK MAN, WOMAN, OR CHILD

Does it refer to a person in the child's life? Is the use of a dark person symbolic? If the use is symbolic, as it often is, then the reference is likely to be repressed or unacceptable parts of the personality. Jung calls all that is repressed or rejected in the personality the shadow. A Native American guide is commonly used form of dark companion. In this case, primitive, earthy, wisdom may be embodied.

DEATH

Many children use imagery of characters or animals dying frequently only to resurrect these characters at will. What is especially notable is the permanent death of a character. Note which characters die, and how often these deaths occur. Is the death that of the protagonist in the play? Is it the death of an adversary? If the villain dies, does he die every session? In that case the child's rage has not yet been neutralized. Do some or all of the family members die? All these situations provide insights into the child's intrafamilial or intrapsychic dynamics, conflicts and fantasies.

A death figure may represent a vanquished foe, a fear of dying, a fear of loss, or a need for transformation. See Skull, Skeleton, Burial and Rebirth.

DEER

Female deer carry a particularly gentle aspect. These attractive animals are strictly vegetarian browsing on trees and plants. Quick and skittish, like most prey animals, they generally have a reticent nature. They are benevolent symbols. Deer are linked with supernatural powers, spirituality, purity, creativity, light, sensitivity, grace, alertness, and regeneration.

Bucks are associated with pride, strength, nobility and aggressiveness as much as the doe and fawn are associated with gentleness. The buck, or stag, is also associated with creativity. See Stag.

DEMONS

Demons are spirit beings. They are thought to be fallen angels who have given themselves over to the powers of darkness. Much like the Emperor, Darth Vader, and Darth Mael in the Star Wars series, these beings millennia ago abandoned the light and followed the being once called Lucifer (Light-bringer), in his fall (Isaiah 14:12) to the state of *ha satan* (the adversary in Hebrew).

With the tremendous popularity of Dungeons and Dragons, gargoyle cartoons, and Pokemon small plastic, or pewter, demonic figures have become more available to the child psychotherapist. It is important to find out if these fantasy games or gargoyle cartoons are a normal part of the child's play and fantasy life. If not typical, the use of these figures may gain additional import. The notion of shadow aspects of the personality are called up, along with that of the R-complex. Are family members or others are menacing the child? Family members are not always the culprits. Sometimes a child at school is victimizing the child.

Children who are extremely fascinated with or disturbed by these images may need to be assessed for exposure to Satanic or ritual abuse. See Angel.

DESERT

Unlike other forms of play therapy sandplay lends itself to the creation of snow storms, oceans, swamps, and deserts. Children have used desert scenes as places where treasures are sought; lives are lost; desolation prevails. Occasionally, a child will contrast a desert area with a fertile land within the same tray.

As the land of Biblical revelation, the desert is associated with pure spirituality. The desert opposes the lusty life of the body, and promotes concentration upon the one God who demands that He be worshipped in spirit and in truth. See Cirlot (1962) for an expansion of this theme. Does the child live in an emotional wasteland? Find out about the family situation. See Death.

DEVIL

See Demons.

DEVOUR

Years before the advent of the extremely graphic movie, Jurassic Park, I observed children using dinosaurs to devour humans, as well as other dinosaurs. Crocodiles and sharks are used to devour humans rather than preying upon fish or other animals. All of these beasts are evocative of the

R-complex, i.e. primitive oral, sadistic rage. Erik Erikson's (1950) concept of oral incorporation relates to these images of devouring.

The act of devouring, or the fear of being devoured, is associated with entanglement, sinking into a swamp, quicksand or mud. Jung (1956, CW 5) suggests that the fear of incest translates into a fear of being devoured by the mother.

This fear takes such forms as the witch in *Hansel and Gretel*, the wolf in Red Riding Hood, ogres, dragons, and so forth. Investigate the possibility of child molestation, inappropriate touching, lack of boundaries, etc. Be careful not to intrude upon the child's magical world of play. Of course, not all incest wounds are the result of overt behaviors, they can be covert. Intrusions into one's territory can bring an angry response from many individuals. See Dinosaurs, Crocodiles, Sharks and Quicksand.

DINOSAURS

The love of dinosaurs is typical of children who are not characterized by severe pathology. Katherine Bradway (1981, p.94) says, "Children use prehistoric animals more frequently than do adults, and their use seems to be more consistent with the chthonic (primitive, mysterious; also pertaining to the underworld) character of the vegetative stage than does the use of domesticated animals."

As the preeminent denizens of the primeval world dinosaurs have written an eloquent lesson for mankind in the sands of time. Older children usually make a clear distinction between flesh eating dinosaurs and placid plant eaters. Tyrannosaurus Rex appears as the unrivaled embodiment of primitive rage. Many children who need to deal with strong anger eagerly grasp this object, and act-out the devouring of their enemies. As Buhler (1941) points out, the devouring of humans is taken as a sign of greater pathology than is the devouring of animals. It is important to be in tune with the child's feeling tone during this enactment. The significance of this type of aggressive play may have to be gathered intuitively.

A tyrannosaurus rex that is made of soft rubber and that is hollow is a great delight to children to put objects—often symbolizing their perpetrator—into the mouth and body of this predator. The same is true for soft, hollow sharks. Jurassic Park toys, comics, videos, and other dinosaur related items are so prevalent and so graphic, one must be careful in interpreting children's play. Dinosaurs packaged with human figures with rip apart limbs encourage pathological play. See Dragon and Devour.

DOG

Dogs are pack animals and bond intensely to their group. Domesticated dogs are characterized by faithfulness to man, and are a symbol of loyalty. A good dog is seen as a faithful, long-suffering friend. Because of their subservience to man, dogs may be either greatly prized or despised. If dogs, or any animal, appear to be despised, humans may also be looked upon with contempt. The child's parent may be the source of this attitude, and may well hate any display of "weakness," i.e. sensitivity or compliance. The child may be the subject of ridicule. This is frequently true with children of alcoholic/addicts. Parents with low self-esteem project their self-hatred upon the child who in turn may feel like a whipped dog.

In ancient cultures the image of a dog or jackal stands at the entrance to the underworld (unconscious) in the myths of Cerberus (Greek), Anubis (Egyptian), and Xoltl (Aztec). Dogs are considered companion spirits for the dead.

DOLPHIN

Dolphin are much beloved for their playfulness, devotion to their offspring and intelligence. Native American say we can learn purity, lightness of being, communication, love , intelligence and spiritual attainments from the dolphin.

DONKEY

A donkey or burro is a beast of burden. For Christians the donkey is associated with humility, patience and poverty since Jesus chose it for his entry into Jerusalem.

Donkeys take on sinister, harmful roles in Egyptian, Greek, Roman and East Indian stories and myths. The donkey is associated with stubbornness and laziness. This image may represent the vulgarism for a stupid or foolish person, i.e. an "ass." Certain children love to demonstrate their knowledge of this usage. Ass can easily remind the child of the forbidden realm of adult sexuality and become an even funnier association for the child.

DOVE

These beautiful birds have a long association with peace. This is not the result of their nature as much as it is the result of their appearance. The white dove, is associated with the notions of purity, tranquillity, and peace. In Christianity the White Dove is associated with the Holy Spirit and chastity. Girls use these birds more frequently than males. Boys, who have created violent trays, have used the image of the dove as a note of resolution. See Spirituality and Deity.

DRAGON

Symbolically, dragons and serpents are interchangeable. They are associated with the life-giving element of water. These images are usually taken to represent unmanifest chaos; untamed nature; the undifferentiated. From Genesis to Revelation, the Bible uses serpent and dragon as symbolic of the fallen archangel, originally called, Lucifer.

Dragons may appear as a winged serpent. This image combines the concepts of matter and spirit. Depending upon the culture, he is thought of as an embodiment of evil or as the embodiment of wisdom. In the Orient the dragon is thought of as the embodiment of the highest spiritual power and supernatural wisdom. Native Americans saw the winged serpent as the thunder creature or rain-bearer. The Aztecs saw Quetzal, the plumed serpent, a combination of snake and bird, as the spirit of wind, rain, thunder and lightening; the spirit of ascension.

In mythology the dragon is a master of the ground and a protector of treasures. The Hero conquering the dragon is usually interpreted as: gaining the treasures of inner knowledge; subduing evil forces; overcoming one's nature and attaining self-mastery. Rescuing a maiden from the dragon is a releasing of pure forces after subduing evil powers.

Primitive rage and the R-complex are keys to understanding the negative symbol. See Serpent, Snake and Dinosaur.

DROWNING

Drowning is an important theme for many clients—a loss of ego consciousness in the ocean of non-differentiated unity. .Drowning may indicate submersion into the unconscious, possibly too close a relationship to the mother, enmeshment with an alcoholic, borderline or psychotic parent, or incipient psychosis. The theme of drowning may indicate an opportunity for the personality to reconstitute.

Drowning family members indicates unneutralized rage at the family. Family therapy and parenting classes should be helpful. If the child seems open, see if some of this rage might be vented in a more physical fashion, i.e. pounding clay, hitting with batakas, yelling in addition to sandplay. See Flood and Burial.

DWARVES

Little people appear in dreams, fairy tales and mythology. In mythology and folklore the dwarf was representative of mischievous forces. These images are masculine, phallic, and childish in character. Dwarves, elves, etc. are representative of forces that are outside the realm of the conscious mind. Jung (1953) regards this image as a guardian of the threshold of the unconscious.

The image of the dwarf can have an important role in psychological development. When Snow White was threatened by the witch mother, she was protected and nourished by seven dwarves, the contrasexual or animus portion of her personality. Inner archetypal figures will often come to the rescue of the abandoned child. See Little People, Elf, and the archetype of the trickster described under Clown.

EAGLE

The eagle is a masculine symbol that represents strength, pride, victory, the spiritual principle, royalty, authority, vision, clarity, inspiration, and ascension, Young boys are often keenly aware of the eagle's freedom, power, and ability to prey on other animals.

The eagle is a king of the heavens that holds a great fascination for many peoples, most notably certain tribes of Native Americans. For the

Native American the eagle represented the Great, or universal, Spirit, or a spiritual messenger. This creates a duality, the man of earth obsessed with the spirit of the air. An eagle vanquishing the serpent is symbolic of the higher instincts emerging victorious over the lower instincts.

EARTH

The earth may offer life and protection, or be representative of burial and dissolution. This parallels the dual concept of the protective Great Mother and the Terrible Mother. See Cave, Burial and Earth Mother.

EARTH MOTHER

Earth and the image of mother have been synonymous. Mother nourishes and shelters the infant as earth nourishes and shelters the human family. Conversely, a mother can destroy her offspring psychologically by tenaciously holding on to them. Anciently, pagans worshipped the Earth Mother as a goddess who provides fertility, and who must be propitiated by human sacrifice.

EATING

Eating can symbolize the child's need for emotional nourishment. Children have used toys to prepare a feast to feed the emotionally starved portion of the child's personality. Eating can represent oral incorporation, oral greed, or a mother-complex. Eating can also be a way of forcing down feelings. See Devour and Food.

EGGS

Like seeds, eggs carry the mystery of new life within them. They represent containment in the maternal matrix, the unconscious. Like the unconscious, eggs carry hidden potential. Eggs are often used to represent the concept of rebirth or renewal, and as such are symbolic of transformation. In archaic religions the cosmic egg was the life principle, the beginning of the universe, and the womb. The spherical egg suggests wholeness. The egg also suggests new beginnings. See Sphere and Rebirth.

EIGHT

Eight is a doubling of four and like four is static and stable. The octagon was thought to mediate between the square and the circle. It is associated with totality, stability, the four cardinal points and deity. Eight was associated with the Greek messenger god, Hermes. Personal associations to numbers should be investigated before assuming universal associations. See Four, Square and Circle.

ELEPHANT

An elephant has an overwhelming presence. Strength, patience, longevity, wisdom, and long memory are considered to be his attributes. He may be a willing servant of man, or a formidable adversary. A child who is feeling frail and weak may chose an elephant as a self-symbol to compensate her feelings of inferiority. The largest elephant in my collection, approximately 6" high, has been used by a large percentage of both my youthful and adult clients.

ELEVEN

Eleven is associated with being saved at the "eleventh hour," the last hour of the workday in Jesus' time. Personal associations to numbers should be investigated before assuming universal associations.

ELF

In most cultures elves are tiny, often mischievous spirits. Their character, which inclines toward mischief, gives them a resemblance to the archetype of the trickster. These figures are more Puer-like, youthful or Peter Pan-like, than are dwarves or gnomes. All these characters are associated with childishness. These fanciful creatures seem to be even more mercurial than are dwarves or gnomes. Elves are associated with the woods or forest. Forests are symbolic of the unknown, and of the unconscious. Elves, as other little people, are denizens of the unconscious. In sand trays, elves are typically used as helpful figures. See Little People and Dwarves. See Clown for a brief commentary on the archetype of the trickster.

ELK

Native Americans associate the elk with confidence, strength, joy, wisdom, and responsibility. See Deer and Stag.

ETHNIC FIGURES

Obtain as many different ethnic figures as possible. These figures may be used to represent an actual person of that ethnicity, a person who is revered, hated, or a shadow portion of the personality. Blacks in the dreams of Caucasians often seems to represent the untapped warmth of the feeling function. Katherine Bradway in *Sandplay Studies* (1981) says, Native American culture respects authority and instinct See Dark Man, Woman, and Child.

FAIRIES

Fairies are much like elves, but portrayed with a more feminine aspect. The quintessential fairy for most young children is Tinkerbell from Peter Pan. See Elf.

FAMILY FIGURES

See Mother, Father, Child, and Dark Man, Woman, Child.

FANTASY FIGURES

The meanings inherent in fantasy figures are as varied as the figures themselves. Here is a short list:

Aladdin: a poor boy with courage finds power and love that raises him to the nobility.

Alice in Wonderland: lost in a strange world, this heroine finds courage and learns to use her wits.

Batman: this hero appears like a dark figure, but serves the good.

Cat Woman: This image is power and cunning personified.

Cheshire Cat: this mocking and mischievous figure relates to the trickster. See Clown for a discussion of the archetypal trickster.

Cinderella: Cinderella is a psychological and emotional orphan in her own home. She finds help from magical, unconscious sources.

The Emperor, Darth Vader, and Darth Mael: These villains embody evil combined with mystical powers.

Dorothy and Toto: Dorothy from the Wizard of Oz is a great heroine figure for small children and others. She has warmth, honesty, compassion and loyalty.

ET: a Wise Old Man with mystical powers.

G.I. Joe: These once popular groups of super masculine combatants are hero figures. A few are still being made and similar figures are available.

Queen of Hearts: an archetypal authority figure that runs amuck. The Queen of Hearts is the embodiment of the narcissistic personality who does not care for those beneath her, and declares, "Off with their heads!"

Mermaid: the mermaid bridges between the realm of feelings (water) and the earth. The Disney figure, Ariel, from The Little Mermaid, represents a glamorous image to young girls.

Monsters: Monsters may scare off the child's symbolic enemies and may represent their primitive core.

Pokemon: This group of figures range from the cute to the grotesque. Humans and wild monsters with extraordinary traits populate this popular world. The object is for the humans (child) to capture and direct these monsters. One of the cuter monsters is Pikachu, a mouse with electrical bolt power.

Santa Claus: originally a saint, seems like a good grandfather figure, who in this materialistic age can be seen to encourage greed.

Snow White: the maiden is threatened by the Queen—negative mother—who transforms herself into a witch and plots to kill the maiden. This is a potent psychological tale.

Superman: archetypal early 20th Century American Hero figure who fights crime and stands for all that is good and noble. This type of Hero is definitely an alien by today's standards.

Scarecrow: The Scarecrow from the Wizard of Oz is a likeable character who is filled with self-doubt and insecurity.

Tin Man: This character from the Wizard of Oz is a wonderful symbol. Men cut off from their inner feminine tend to be like this Tin Man. Many fail to pursue having a heart as this character does.

Wizard of Oz: This character appears to be a failed Wise Old Man at first, but then is able to help the Tin Man, the Cowardly Lion and the Scarecrow. He just isn't quiet wise enough to help our heroine.

Yoda: a Wise Old Man with mystical powers.

FATHER

The use of a father figure may refer to the personal father and/or to the archetypal ideas associated with the image of father. The archetypal father is associated with structure, rules, laws, and governing principles of society, and with spiritual principles. This image relates to that of king, authority, and protector. A negative manifestation of this archetypal position is found in the tyrant. The Jungian view stresses that this paternal principle operates in a collective manner that acknowledges children as subjects rather than individuals. If a person has a positive relationship with his father, he or she will tend to have a positive relationship to the notion of a structured and ordered society. If the internal image of father is negative, or non-existent, this might indicate difficulties with the rules of society, or with spiritual principles. Enmeshment with mother may be a problem. The relation to the archetypal masculine may be formed from relationships to individuals other than the personal father. See Man, King, and King and Queen.

FEATHERS

Feathers represent ascension and prayer among Native American tribes. Eagle feathers were associated with the Great Spirit, God above all other gods. Shamans wearing feathers and bird masks were believed to fly to obtain higher knowledge. See Birds.

FENCES

Charlotte Buhler (1941) found that fenced worlds are usually created from age eight onwards. A less healthy response is the construction of fences without gates. Fences may be used to wall-off unacceptable portions of the personality, i.e. those parts that need to be integrated. This would indicate that the ego conscious is not yet strong enough to integrate this material. Fences may indicate the need for control or restriction. Fences are often associated with Kalff's third or community stage. Bowyer observes that fencing increases from 5 to 10 years. Ten years seems to be a peak in the use of fences for normal subjects.

Dundas (1978) found that girls often fenced in groups of animals that they particularly liked and identified with. My observations have confirmed this finding. From this type of play we see that girls seem to need to learn to relate to, and control, their instincts. This fencing off of animals could also indicate a feeling of being separated from their instinctual nature. When threatening monsters are fenced or walled-off, the threatening aspects of the unconscious cannot be faced or assimilated yet. It is important to respect this statement, and to comprehend its power upon the individual's psyche. See Walls.

FIRE

Fire may be warming and life giving or destructive. It is a potent symbol of transformation Fire makes a strong impression upon the unconscious. There is something numinous, i.e. that sets one in awe, about fire. Fire purifies and burns away the dross, and is indicative of spiritual purification. Fire is associated with sacrifice to the deity; with transformation as in alchemy.

Fire is associated with passion, strength, energy, creativity and the masculine principle. Hephaestus, the Greek god of fire and the forge, is associated with creativity and with passion. Aphrodite the goddess of love, chose creative, but crippled Hephaestus as a mate. Jung (1965) comments on fire as a libidinal symbol that can indicate passions, desire, and the emotional or affective side of the psyche. In its negative forms, fire is associated with destruction, immolation, and conflagration. Obsessive fire setting is associated with blocked sexuality.

A trial by fire (roasting) for some shamans results as their being reborn as men of power. Primitive people think of magico-religious power as burning. Heat, burn, and very hot are words they use to describe this power. The original meaning of the Sanskrit word *tapas* was extreme heat. Charismatic Christians speak of being touched by the fire of God.

As a transformative symbol fire represents a change of state, or a change of being and character.

Some children are particularly fascinated with fire, and seem both grateful and somewhat dumbfounded that candles are among the objects used in sandplay. The light of candles is thought to represent spiritual illumination; the power of fire; and the transitory nature of life. The qualities associated with fire and candles seem to invite ritualistic play. If a fireplace or small portable fire pit can be provided, intense play may be centered there for certain children.

FISH

The ocean is usually interpreted as being symbolic of the unconscious, and of feelings. Consequently, it is not surprising to find that peoples throughout the earth have used fish to symbolize the psychic structures within the unconscious. These include archetypes, parental introjects, and so forth. Since fish spring from the waters, they are associated with the abundance or fertility of the waters. As a Christian symbol fish stand for men that are redeemed. See Fishing, Whales and Sharks.

FISHING

The image of fishing relates to delving into the unconscious. When I first began to write down my dreams years ago one of the first images that appeared was that of learning to fish. Archetypes may be likened to fish. The figure of the Fisher King from the tale of the Quest for the Holy Grail, reflects this phenomenon of introspection.

One must also be aware of the individual's outer life. Children who are close to their father, who enjoys fishing, have created sand trays centered on this theme. In these cases both outer and inner meanings may be true. See Fish, Whales, and Shark.

FIVE

Five may represent the five senses; sensation. Jung associates five with man (CW, Vol. 9, Part I, p. 373). A man's head and outstretched limbs form a five-pointed star. Christians interpret five as the number of grace, and the number of Christ's wounds. Oriental cultures associate five with totality. Buddhists associate five with perfection. The Greeks and Romans associated five with Aphrodite/Venus, the goddess of love and beauty.

.Personal associations to numbers should be investigated before assuming universal associations.

FLAGS

Small paper flags that represent various countries and the Red Cross are available in party supply shops. Children delight in the color and variety of these flags. Often they are used as an image of celebration, or in conflicts between opposites or rivals. Sometimes the celebration seems to be of one's personal identity. Occasionally whole trays are filled with these identity symbols. Children ask for the flags of specific nations. "Do you have an English flag, a Jewish flag, a German?" While working in Texas I heard a boy call the American flag, "the Texas flag." Conflicts between "nations," i.e. army men, are marked with flags.

FLOOD

Like an avalanche, a flood may be an overwhelming of the established order— the ego by the unconscious. The child's rage may be experienced as a flood of emotion. Floods are associated with cyclic destruction and rebirth. Children who have a great deal of repressed rage have used images of flood and burial to symbolically destroy their enemies, often family members. Amatruda and Helm Simpson (1997) found a positive correlation between clients who flood the tray and with having been molested. Not all clients who do this have been molested, but those who have been abused feel a lack of control and a flooding of feelings. See Avalanche and Burial.

FLOWERS

Most flowers are characterized by openness, color, softness, vulnerability, receptivity, fragrance. Associations with the feminine principle are unmistakable. What is particularly to be noted is the use of flowers by young males. This may indicate a capacity for sensitivity, or when extreme, an over identification with the feminine, and possible sexual identity problems. See Garden.

FOOD

Plastic toys in the shape of various kinds of food and drink items are of great value. Many abused children will hoard food, even after being placed in foster homes where there is an abundance of food.

Preoccupation with food can represent the child's need to survive; a mother-complex; the loss of a mother figure; a feeling of emptiness; not having been adequately mirrored or accepted. See Devour.

FOREST

A single tree may represent the Self, while a forest represents the unknown or the unconscious. In fairy tales the forest is associated with the perilous aspects of the child's unconscious. Forests are mysterious, dark, and difficult to negotiate. Clear paths are not usually found through them. Being lost in a forest, like Alice in Wonderland, can symbolize inexperience, and the difficulties involved in the achievement of knowledge. New energy coming from the unconscious may be indicated by the image of a forest. Forests are filled with animals, representative of the instincts. The symbolism of the Great Mother, or feminine principle, is connected to the idea of the forest.

In the past, forests were thought to be the habitat of demons. The darkness of the forest is associated with a lack of spiritual awareness. A forest may represent a place of trial and testing in fairy tales. A confrontation with introjected negative parental images (such as a witch figure, or a wicked man), may be required before the child moves into another developmental phase. Entering a dark or enchanted forest may symbolize entering an altered state of consciousness. This represents a symbolic death. See Tree.

FORTIFICATIONS

There is a very different feeling when a child creates an open battle than when he creates battles that feature the use of fortifications. Fortifications might be indicative of the child's need for defenses. They might be compensatory to his feeling of weakness and vulnerability. See Fences, Castle, Tower.

FOUR

Four suggests psychological wholeness, and the unconscious Self. Four is symbolic of quaternary. It can represent the four functions that are inherent within the Self, i.e. the intuition, sensation, thinking and feeling functions. Four may also represent the four archaic elements: air, fire, earth, and water; the four seasons; the four cardinal points of the compass. Four denotes a solidity that gives the impression of firmness, intellect, comprehension, justice, organization, power, strength, and omnipotence. Four can be seen as foundational in the tetragrameton, YHVH, the four Hebrew letters in the sacred name of God. The four faces of the heavenly cherubim described in the Bible are another occurrence of this motif (Ezekiel 1:10) of quaternary. The four rivers that flowed out of Eden picture comprehensive spiritual nourishment. In the Cabbala the four worlds or cosmic cycles are Manifestation, Creation, Formation and Action. A different aspect of God is seen in each cycle. Personal associations to numbers should be investigated before assuming universal associations. See Square.

FOX

The fox is sleek, beautiful, and swift. Since it is a predator and will prey upon the animals man claims, the fox has a long association with cunning, craftiness, trickery, and deception. More recently, fox is associated with an attractive appearance.

FROG

Frogs are usually better received by humans than are reptiles and other amphibians. Clever frogs appear in many fairy tales. The frog and the toad have been used to represent sexuality in fairy tales. Bettelheim (1977) suggests that the child is not afraid of frogs, but may react with disgust. This is the same feeling of not being ready for sex that he or she may have before maturing enough to be aroused. Certain children seem delighted with miniature frogs that they carefully place in the sand tray.

Amphibians represent a transition between the waters and the land. This can be interpreted as the capacity to move from one state of consciousness to another. Like the beaver, or the seal, the frog can symbolize moving into the deeper areas of the psyche.

Since the frog's origin is in the waters it is associated with renewal of life. It has a strong traditional association with fertility, and with the feminine principle. The frog undergoes a transformation from tadpole to mature animal, and may represent the child's own capacity for development. Other associations are mystery, humor, and communication.

GATE

A gate, like a door, represents a point of entrance into another realm or state of consciousness. Any reference to a threshold is important. These images may relate to entrance into a new life task, or passage, or to a deeper state of consciousness.

GARDEN

Paradise is associated with a garden, as in the Garden of Eden. A garden is usually thought of as a small plot of land near a house in which vegetables, fruit, and flowers are raised. Plants are comforting symbols of divine benevolence. In the symbolic realm the mother archetype is associated with the garden, the ploughed field, and the feminine. Enclosed gardens are associated with virginity. Gardens are peaceful places, where one can work quietly, bask in the Sun, have her senses filled with continual beauty, or spend time in silent reflection. Associations with garden are a tamed and ordered nature, i.e. personality; the center of the psyche; an imago mundi, or world center, and harmony. An enclosed garden became the symbol of the Virgin Mary.

GREEN

The fourth color of the rainbow, green, is the color of the thymus and heart, chakra. It is associated with heart love that is expansive and generous. This center is indicative of our desires, which include our longing to belong to someone. In general it seems to represent attachment.

Green is further identified with security or insecurity, i.e. green with envy is a reflection of a feeling of insecurity. Possessiveness and the desire to acquire wealth are associated with green.

Vital force and healing are among the more positive associations for this color. The color of plant life, green is associated with fertility, renewal, youth, hope, and with change. As with other colors, the meaning of green changes greatly according to the particular hue. Bright, verdant green is positive, while pale green, especially a yellow-green or muted green, carries negative associations. Muddy green is associated with disease, death, and disintegration.

GOAT

Goats have a willful, independent quality. Unlike sheep, goats will not blindly, or trustfully, follow a leader. The goat is associated with the masculine principle; creative energy; sinfulness; lust; sacrifice. In the Bible a male goat was used as a sin offering. In the ancient Hebrew culture on Yom Kippur (Day of Atonement) a scapegoat symbolically discharged the sins of the people.

GOLD

Gold represents wealth since it is the color of one of the earth's most valuable, useful, and popular metals. The value placed upon gold is the highest of precious metals. Children use gold and wealth interchangeably. A treasure chest that contains a small piece of "gold" is greatly valued by children. Very elaborate stories have been created using these objects. Other associations are: glory, divinity, royalty, incorruptibility; wisdom; honor; the Sun; perfection; wholeness. Symbolically gold is similar to yellow and partakes of some of its characteristics. See Yellow.

GRADUATE

Small figures of a male and a female in cap and gown can be obtained in party shops and cake decorating supply stores.

GRAY

Gray is a quiet neutral that is associated with non-involvement. Dr. Max Lusher (1969) suggests that people who select gray want to wall everything off. Gray is associated with depression, blunted affect, and interestingly, with sophistication. Battleship gray helps to conceal a large object.

HEART

Children generally use this image to portray love, joy and sentiment. Many times children will use art materials to draw or make hearts, often for their mothers. To amplify we also understand the use of the heart to symbolize compassion, the emotional life, truth, positive feelings, joy, courage. The Bible uses heart in relation to an individual's deepest thoughts or inner life.

HEROES AND HEROINES

Heroes and heroines represent the powerful, outgoing aspect of the psyche. Heroic figures are a type of Savior or Messiah. As Adler pointed out, it is part of the human condition to experience oneself as weak and inferior, and to desire power. Heroic images are compensatory to these feelings. Heroes aid the child in the struggle toward separation and individuation from the all-powerful parents. The archetypal Hero is usually of royal or semi-divine birth, however he may not be aware of this. Sometimes he is of humble parentage. He must undergo various trials of his strength, and is sometimes accompanied by an animal or a weaker friend. For the hero truly to be an archetypal Hero he must intervene and rescue someone of importance, or save a group, a tribe or city. He must overcome evil and temptation in the process of this rescue. In ancient tales heroes often had to undergo great suffering and would sometimes die. Fictional American heroes such as Superman or Luke Skywalker may suffer loss and come close to death, but the themes of betrayal, sacrifice, and death are usually not so final and devastating.

During sandplay children may have their hero figures die repeatedly during cycles of battle. These cycles might indicate cyclical feelings of strength followed by feelings of weakness. A portion of the personality needs to be reintegrated on a higher level.

Notably, heroines such as Wonder Woman battle against evil, but the villains are imprisoned rather than executed, or killed in battle just like fictional American heroes Superman and Batman who typically have the

villains imprisoned. This may reflect a feminine influence upon the mid-20th Century American zeitgeist. See Death.
HORNS
Horns are representative of masculine power and strength. Horns used to adorn helmets were symbolic of royalty, power, and war. The phallic implications of the horn are readily apparent. The ancients used horns as symbols of fertility.
HORSE
Horses represent the faithful servant, free spirit, dynamic energy, the spiritual impulse, etc. As with other animals it is representative of the instincts. Further associations are: conquest and superiority, wisdom, intellect, swiftness of thought, wind, waves, running water, and the passage of life. In legends and fairy tales, the horse represents the psychic and intuitive aspect of the of protagonist. The horse may represent the darker or base side of the individual's instincts.

Ancients associated the horse with knowledge of the underworld. Later the horse was associated with the sky gods. The white horse is a particularly potent symbol. This is a masculine symbol associated with religion, the spiritual innocence, purity of thought, and light. Two white horses appear in the book of Revelation, one representing false religion, and the other carrying the Messiah. A white horse and black horse appearing together may represent life and death; a personal struggle of good against evil; the struggle of the carnal nature against the spiritual.

Jung (1965) comments on the horse as a libidinal symbol. See Unicorn.
HOUSE
The house is associated with the human body. Houses are usually interpreted as symbols of the Self; one's inner being. Dreams parallel this symbolism. The house represents the conscious and unconscious state of the subject. The type of house chosen is a reflection of the person's present state. The different floors of a house may represent different aspects or layers of mind. This was illustrated beautifully in the film *Being John Malkovich*.

A house may also represent the sheltering aspect of the archetypal mother, the family, and security. A clinician will extend the usefulness of the medium by purchasing a wide variety of houses: cottages; castles; Victorian; suburban; modern; medieval; Oriental; Native American teepees and hogans. See Cottage and Castle.

HUMMINGBIRD

Native Americans teach that we can learn energy, precision, lucidity, vibrancy, clarity, grace and healing from the hummingbird.

ICE

Ice is water that has altered form and has become rigid. It may represent a point of division between the conscious and unconscious, or between other states of consciousness. Children use sand to depict snow and ice. Coldness and freezing might refer to the emotional climate within the home, or to a certain quality of coldness that exists within a particular sphere of the child's experience. In the infant stage, the child may have been left in wet diapers too long and too frequently, and may unconsciously associate coldness, neglect, and mothering. Associations are rigid, brittle, and impermanent. See Snow.

INDIGO

Indigo, or midnight blue, is the sixth color of the rainbow. This is the color of the pituitary and medulla oblongata chakra, the intuitive center. Indigo is associated with psychic perception, the spiritual or third eye, future-orientation, and a tendency toward a lack of grounding in the here-and-now, i.e. spacey. This color represents the transpersonal dimension of consciousness. Certain personalities are so blocked by their emphasis on social, or intellectual, pursuits that this level is incomprehensible to them. Unfortunately, they tend to speak as if it cannot exist for anyone. Hills (1978) wisely states that being psychic is not identical with being a truly spiritual person.

INSECTS

A child's reaction to the creepy toys, such as insects, can give the therapist insight into whether there is denial of or acceptance of the dark side of life, as in a Histrionic Personality Disorder. See Spider.

JOURNEY

In psychological or spiritual growth a journey or pilgrimage is essential. Transformation does not occur without movement and the overcoming of obstacles.

KING AND QUEEN

The king and queen are often representative of the old ruling principle, generally the parents, parental introjects, or archaic superego. Cirlot (1962) believes that the king represents the royalty or grandeur in mankind. The image of the king often represents the Hero or Savior as well as the father. Since the idea of the king contains so many images that relate to archetypal maleness he may symbolize all of the potentialities inherent in the masculine realm. Just as the king may represent all of the archetypal potentialities inherent in the idea of maleness, the image of the queen may represent the full range of potentialities within the idea of woman or mother.

Together the king and queen may represent the royal union of masculine and feminine principles, the hieros gamos. The theme of the royal marriage will not have the same significance in a child's tray as it would in a mature adult's work. The uniting of opposites is a development in adult psychology. Ego formation, and the development of cognitive abilities, are the child's developmental tasks. Girls will often use a bride and groom to signify a marriage in the usual sense, rather than an inner union of opposite qualities. "Some day my prince will come...." See Castle.

LABYRINTH

The labyrinth is an archaic symbol that refers to the convoluted protective barriers surrounding the king's tomb and treasure. Labyrinths might be open or enclosed paths, buildings, designs, dances, games, or walls. Psychologically the labyrinth represents a return to the center. The difficulties involved with negotiating a complex labyrinth represent trial and testing; death and rebirth, initiation, and self-discovery. Most children love to solve the puzzle of a maze. It would be interesting to see what certain children would do with a small three-dimensional labyrinth that could be placed within a sand tray.

LADDER

A ladder traditionally represented the passage from one place or state of consciousness to another. It is a symbol of transcendence and ascension. Certain children use this symbol frequently. Ladder symbolism relates to the rainbow. See Stairs.

LAKE

Water is associated with feelings and emotions. They associated with the feminine principle, and often are the secret home of magical powers. Traditionally lakes are seen as two-way mirrors separating the natural and the supernatural realms. When children create a lake in the sand tray it often serves as a focal point around which the action of the figures takes place. See Water, Pond and Magic.

LAMB

A lamb has the compliant, obedient nature of its kind, and the innocent purity associated with the very young. The image of a lamb or a sheep is associated with that of an easy animal for the strong to prey upon. The lamb is considered a Christian symbol, but it should be referred to as a Judeo-Christian symbol. The Passover lamb was a sacrifice to provide protection for the Hebrew nation. Later, Messiah Yeshua (Jesus) was seen as a "our Passover who was sacrificed for us" (I Corinthians 5:7). See Sheep.

LAVENDER

Lavender is purple tinted with white. Like pink it's a favorite color of young girls and is associated with warmth, femininity, gentleness, and tender emotions. Lavender is closely related to the seventh color of the rainbow. Violet is the color of the pineal and brain chakra. This center is associated with imagination, fantasy, sense of eternity, spiritual yearnings, awareness of how we create our reality, and the magic or chaos that relates to the unconscious. See Purple, Violet and White.

LIGHT

Light is associated with consciousness and spirituality. See Candles.

LIGHTHOUSE

A lighthouse protects the traveler during dark or stormy situations by preventing a shipwreck. Light is associated with the spiritual. The ocean represents feelings; and the unconscious. A light in a dark and perilous place is a wondrous thing..

LION

Like other great cats, the lion is notable for strength and power exhibited during the kill. Like kings they were seen as great and terrible. Lions are associated with the power of the sun, and with royal ruling power. Richard the Lion-hearted, the royal crests of England and Scotland, and The Lion King film are examples of the long association between royalty and lion imagery.

The Buddha is depicted as sitting on a lion, and is considered a lion among men. Jesus is called the Lion of the House of Judah, and is expected to sit upon the throne of David ruling over Israel.

LITTLE PEOPLE

Little people, such as dwarves, elves, and the like appear regularly in dreams, mythology and fairy tales. The characters ET, Yoda, and the Ewoks from the Star Wars films are modern forms of this tendency to envision "little beings" that may be mischievous, have secret knowledge, may create difficulties, or prove to be helpful. In Star Wars, both Obi Wan Kenobi and Yoda were representative of the Wise Old Man, but the diminutive Yoda partook more of the magical, other-worldly quality that we find in dreams and the manifestations of the unconscious. See Elf, Dwarf and Magic.

LIQUOR BOTTLES

Small, individual serving size liquor bottles (cleaned out) need to be included in a sandplay collection. Some children will use these to deal with parental substance abuse, or their own substance abuse. Many children from substance abusing families are substance abusers from very early childhood. Bottles can symbolize poison.

MAGICAL FIGURES

Many children delight in magical figures, such as Mickey Mouse as the Sorcerer's Apprentice. A more traditional magician is also useful, especially for older children.

Gods and Goddesses: A shepherd holding a lamb represents the Christ; Buddha figures are thought to represent man's capacity to find god within.

Ghosts: The association of haunted castles is common. A ghost has often been placed on or near a castle tower. Ghost movies, or the idea of invisibility, is more than just curiosity. It may represent a longing for otherworldly power. There are times we would all like the power to walk through walls and spy upon people who are unaware of our presence.

Dark or satanic objects (coffins, blood, black, pentagrams or pentacles, etc.) are important for children who have been ritualistically abused or abused by satanic cults or have a fascination with the dark side of power. Children who are fascinated with or extremely disturbed by these images may need to be assessed for exposure to ritual abuse. Often children have been programmed to conceal this type of abuse from mental health professionals.

MANDALA

Mandala designs are carefully balanced and represent divine harmony. Mandalic forms symbolize cosmic order, the spiritual realm, sacred space, and progression toward a spiritual center.

Jung saw the mandala as a representation of psychic order, or the longing for psychic integration. The circle combined with a square is seen as a picture of the relationship between the psyche (circle) and the body (square), or material world.

First Nation peoples' Medicine Wheels are fascinating mandalic forms. There are hundreds, maybe thousands of different Medicine Wheels. The totemic animals may vary greatly from one tribe and region to another, but many elements remain similar. Amatruda and Helm Simpson (1997) see the process of sandplay in the journey through the Medicine Wheel from seeking a vision, returning to the inner child, moving into dark, introspective space, and emerging with increased wisdom and new light. See Circle and Square.

MAN

The common archetypal masculine images are those of the Hero, the Wise Old Man, the Father, and the Son. The Hero and king are often combined. The Hero figure represents dynamic, out-going masculine energy. The Hero archetype is characterized by the need to be assertive and courageous in the face of dangers, obstacles, and life-threatening situations. Goals and personal achievement are more important than relationships.

Heroes are expected to be loyal friends, but the principle of action always remains primary. This has been softened somewhat during the past thirty years, and the heroic spaceman more frequently wins the heroine than did the cowboys of the thirties, forties and fifties.

The Father is associated with the Sun and sky. The masculine principle is associated with law and order, reason and consciousness, and the spiritual. Many figures are available for sandplay that represent Hero principle. Superman, Batman and Robin, are frequently used hero figures. To cover other archetypes a wide variety of male figures, cowboys, road workers, firemen, spacemen, doctors, etc. need to be available for sandplay. Yoga and Obi Wan from Star Wars represent the Wise Old Man. A variety of figures can be used to represent the Son archetype. Robin, Batman's sidekick, is a heroic Son figure. See Father, Heroes and Heroines, King and Wise Old Man.

MONKEY

Quick, bright, alert, and mischievous are attributes associated with these primates. The idea of monkeyshines or pranks may be associated with the archetype of the trickster. Certain boys have been observed to associate sexuality and monkeys. These children have used these figures in "sex play," i.e. with a male mounting a female. See Clown for a brief explanation of the archetype of the trickster.

MOTHER

Jung repeatedly pointed out that he does not see the personal mother as being the sole cause of the origin of a disturbance. He believes that crediting the personal mother with the sole responsibility of a patient's etiology is due to a lack of breadth of understanding. The mother plays a part in the development of the mother-complex, but is not responsible for every psychological difficulty. Whenever the archetypal image of the mother, or simply the feminine principle, is activated it calls up the dark side of the archetype as well as the light. Negative characteristics may be projected upon and imputed to the personal mother that belong to the archetype, and not to the specific individual. This is much more common than many people realize.

The earth was considered the universal mother, and is linked with nature and goddess worship. Motherhood is associated with rebirth and renewal, protector, nourishing, warmth, sheltering, sustaining and destroying, and dissolution and devouring. It is interesting in regards devouring that some animals seem to re-absorb their fetuses.

Traditionally, motherhood was associated with weaving and spinning. This was by extension thought of as symbolizing the weaving of fate or the pattern of life, also ensnaring and binding. The images of spider, octopus, crab, quicksand, and crocodile relate to this ensnaring Terrible Mother image. The implication of dissolution into the unconscious makes the negative side of the Mother archetype particularly frightening. See Woman and Earth Mother.

MOTORCYCLE

All forms of transportation suggest energy. A motorcycle is an individual or personal conveyance. The motorcycle is seen as a masculine image. This toy suggests the concepts of mobility, speed, power, and immediacy.

The willingness to take physical risk is implied by the use of a motorcycle. As mentioned earlier, testosterone is associated a higher degree of aggression. Additionally, children from alcoholic/addict families may be high-risk takers. See the discussion of aircraft for a discussion of the Puer personality that appears to be positively correlated with dangerous, high-risk behaviors. See Aircraft.

MOUNTAIN

A mountain represents the meeting place of earth and heaven, and as such it represents transcendence. Other associations are spiritual ascent, the home of the immortals and prophets, firmness, constancy, stillness, and eternity. The cosmic mountain is an omphalos, a world center, or point of connection between ontological planes; a place where the spiritual realm can be sought or touched.

MOUSE

A mouse is a small, timid creature that seeks for food busily and stealthily. It is notable for its apparently incessant motion. The mouse, rabbit and owl have formed an interesting triad in many of the trays that my clients have created. This is fascinating, since this triad is formed of two prey animals and one predator. Owls prey on rabbits and mice, yet the trays I have observed have a peaceful aspect (see case stories).

Native Americans teach that we can learn introspection, innocence, trust, perception, resting and acceptance of others from this humble little brother.

Mickey and Minny Mouse are familiar friends to most children.

MYTHICAL CREATURES

Centaurs and satyrs combining the animal with male human carry a more bestial meaning than do the graceful mermaids and mermen. Centaurs and satyrs may represent poorly integrated instincts.

The centaur symbolizes man's dual nature. The centaur may have begun as a horse totem in prehistory. The earliest drawings of demon in human form show men wearing fetishes of hindquarters of horses joined at their waists. These fetishes were common in European fertility rituals. Of centaurs in myth and legend only Chiron was known for his wisdom and healing abilities. Hercules killed Nessus for trying to rape his wife. Other centaurs were known for their weakness for drink. Centaurs can also represent greater than human speed.

Satyrs are associated with Bacchus, wine, debauchery, lust and lechery. Mermen and mermaids combine human-like intelligence while the ability to move and live in the watery realms associated with feelings and emotions.

Amatruda and Helm Simpson (1997) state that two-headed monsters are associated with a substance abusing or inconsistent parent. See Pegasus and Unicorn.

NEST

These fragile structures are associated with protection and nurturance.

NINE

Since it is a triple triad nine is a powerful number in Celtic, Taoist, and Buddhist traditions. The Hebrews consider nine as a symbol of truth. Personal associations to numbers should be investigated before assuming universal associations.

NUMBERS

The numerical patterns that occur in a client's tray are likely to have personal significance. If it is possible see if a numerical pattern means something to the client first before going to archetypal or universal interpretation. See individual numbers.

OAK

"Mighty as an oak" is indicative of the strength associated with this great tree. Associations to the oak include the human body, nobility, durability, endurance, protection, courage, steadfastness, and fertility. Oaks were important natural temples in ancient Druidic nature worship. See Tree.

OCEAN

The ocean as a primordial symbol is truly beyond comprehension. The ocean represents the unconscious, and the emotions. Although these statements are true, these definitions seem too facile. An ocean generates a sense of awe, wonder, and fascination. It partakes of the numinous. Other associations include: formlessness, chaos, all potentialities, endless motion, the feminine principle, wisdom, the unfathomable and dissolution.

A whole ocean can be represented in a sand tray in the space of a few inches or feet. Often the sand in a dry tray will represent an ocean. It is invaluable to have three trays so that water may be added to two of the trays. One tray is used dry, one is used damp and the third is used very wet. I like to use quite a lot of sand as it facilitates burials, and provide as much water a child or adult wants to use. Some children have experimented with flooding the tray so that the sand representing land was minimal, while the waters were primary. Pushing the limits is both playful and psychologically powerful. This would type of play would be associated with Kalff's vegetative stage.

Objects associated with the sea, such as shells, fish, and ships, are valuable elements in a complete sandplay collection. See Lake, Pond, River and Water.

OCTOPUS

The most obvious feature of the octopus is its grasping nature. The power of an unconscious complex is experienced as grasping, as is any over powering of the ego by the forces within the unconscious. An octopus has appeared with great frequency in trays by children with an over-powering mother, and whose mother-complex activated the image of the Terrible Mother. Often the octopus, the crab, and the crocodile will be used together. All these images relate to the mother-complex. See Mother, Crab, Crocodile and Spider.

ONE

One is associated with beginning, the one God in monotheism, the self, and loneliness. Personal associations to numbers should be investigated before assuming universal associations.

ORANGE

Orange, the second color of the rainbow, is the color of the spleen and epigastrus chakra. Orange is associated with sociability and the herd instinct. People who love orange are considered to be dependent upon others politically and socially, yet are interested in advancing their social position. Orange is associated with food and with the appetite. Many restaurants are decorated with a red-orange color to stimulate the appetite.

OWL

Owls are associated with wisdom, yet how many people are aware of the owl's association with the Greek goddess Athena whose pet was a magical owl? Athena was born fully-grown from the head (intellect) of her father Zeus. The owl's round head and wide-eyed look suggests intelligence, as does the continual questioning, "who, who?"

Dundas (1978) writes, "As a creature of the night, his enormous eyes frighten the children. Nonetheless, they seem to know that owls offer a kind of protection and insight needed in life. They know that the frightening owl can also be an intelligent friend, a friend to light up the path for them at night." And further, "The fear of the owl is probably the fear of the night, and of all the unknown elements that are associated with darkness" (pp. 95-96).

One of my adult clients interpreted one of her sand trays which included two owls. She said these birds were "night watchers." While she slept one of the owls was always awake. This might be seen as analogous to the spirit in man that is our link to that vast spiritual realm termed the unconscious and superconscious minds.Native Americans teach that we can learn old wisdom, knowledge, vision, paradox, mystery, and femininity from the owl.

PEGASUS

Pegasus, the winged horse, carried the hero, Bellerophon, to victory over a lower animal hybrid, Chimera. This symbolizes victory of the spirit over matter.

PELICAN

A pelican is seen as a nourishing mother. Some associate its large pouch with greed, "its beak can hold more than its belly can."

PIG

The pig has a long association with the feminine principle, particularly with fertility, prosperity and happiness. Negative associations are gluttony, greed, selfishness, ignorance, uncontrolled passion, lust, obstinacy, and filth. People are described as "going hog wild."

PINE

Pine trees were selected as symbolic of the renewal or rebirth of the Sun in mid-winter because their evergreen color was associated with immortality, vitality, and fertility. Other associations are: straightness, uprightness, and strength of character, longevity, renewal, solitude, and masculinity.

PINK

Pink is a soft, warm, more delicate variant of red. Red is the color of the genital, chakra. It is associated with the gonads, and is considered to be sensual color. It is associated with the sensation function, i.e. the five senses. The addition of white to red softens it greatly.

The tint pink is usually selected by people who like to be pampered and sheltered from the world. Many women want this protection was suggested in the book *The Cinderella Complex*. This color is rightly associated with the more tender aspects of the feminine principle. Like lavender it is a favorite color of young girls and is associated with warmth, femininity, gentleness, positive emotions.

PLANES

See Aircraft.

POLICEMAN/WOMAN

This authority figure, like others, may symbolize the superego.

POND

A pond is a small body of water smaller than a lake. Ponds often appear as a focal point in a sand tray world. Idyllic pastoral scenes appear around a pond. Since water often appears in imagery as symbolic of the unconscious, of primal energy, i.e. libido, and of the emotions, its significance in the sand tray may lie in these areas. It is important to note whether it is placed in the center of the tray. This suggests an image of a center or of circumnambulation around an intrapsychic center point, an emotional core.

If it is placed on the left side of the tray, this suggests the unconscious portion of the psyche is particularly activated, while placement within the right portion of the tray suggests more ego consciousness. See Water and Lake.

PRINCE AND PRINCESS

A prince or princess may represent the desire of the child to assume the position of ruling authority that the parents (King and Queen) now hold. These images may be compensatory to feelings of rejection and inferiority, or may be indicative of inflation. Everyone wants to feel special. The child's history must always be considered. See King, Queen and Castle.

PURPLE

Purple is the color of royalty, power, authority, creativity, and the arts. Because of its associations with royalty, purple is also thought to be representative of pomp and pride. It is a blending of the colors red and blue, and partakes of their very different characteristics. See Violet, Red and Blue.

QUADRANTS

Theorists vary greatly in their interpretations of the portions of the sand tray. The four quadrants of the sand tray are associated with various parts of the Self. The left side of the paper or the tray often indicates the unconscious portion of the personality, and the right side of the paper or the tray is indicative of the conscious personality or ego.

In art therapy, Ogdon (1981) suggests that placement on the right side of a page indicates a degree of intellectualizing, control and the reality principle. Jolles (1971) suggests that this indicates the person is concerned with the future. Objects on the left are thought to indicate a person who is more impulsive or more focused on the past (Jolles, 1971; Ogdon, 1981).

Dora Kalff used a four quadrant system upper left=personal father, lower left=archetypal mother (unconscious), upper right=archetypal father (conscious), and lower right=personal mother. In later years she said that this model failed to take the three-dimensionality of sandplay into account.

Some theorists see the left side of the tray as associated with the feminine or the right brain, and the left side of the tray as masculine or associated with the left brain. Other theorists divide the tray into two portions horizontally. The upper portion is associated with consciousness and the lower section with unconsciousness.

QUEEN

The image of a queen suggests temporal power and strength. This has not always been the case. In medieval times even women of rank were totally dependent upon men. See King and Queen for additional commentary. See Mother and Woman.

QUICKSAND

Quicksand is evocative of the drawing downward into the depths of the unconscious that occurs with certain severe psychological wounds. It carries with it the notion of entrapment, and is associated with the mother-complex.

RABBIT

Rabbits have a charm and a beauty about them. They are quick, alert, skittish little creatures. They are associated with lunar symbolism, and the feminine principle. The rabbit has a long association with fertility and regeneration. The rabbit is of the flight mode, no fight here. Where is the anger in the personality?

Native Americans teach that we can learn lessons that pertain to growth, dealing with fear, innocence, productivity, creativity, and self-actualization from the rabbit.

RAT

Rats that are available for play are usually black, ugly creatures, rather than the cute pet rat type that a child may have at home. Pet rats may be gentle, but the first type of rat is not. These black rats are thought of as being among the most repulsive and least desirable of the small rodents. Rats are associated with the plague, death, decay, destructiveness, meanness, the Devil, and evil.

REBIRTH

Rebirth is an important archetypal notion. Rebirth and the transformation of intrapsychic processes may be considered to be synonymous. Jung (1959) says that although we cannot observe the notion of rebirth it is a reality of the psyche. He states that rebirth is among the "primordial affirmations of mankind" (1959, p.50). One can "see" the image of rebirth in the process of sandplay.

Children use the process of rebirth within some of their most destructive sand trays. This process of transformation usually refers to the reconstituting of the tray's protagonist, or possibly the anti-hero, but not to the villain. Villains may also be reborn, but the rationale is different. Sometimes the motivation seems to be sorrow at the destruction of the enemy, while other times the child's cycles of anger and mayhem cannot continue without the appropriate victim. When deep-seated rage is finally neutralized these children show us what the intrapsychic process of transformation and rebirth "looks like."

The notion of resurrection, which is somewhat different from that of rebirth, is one of the key concepts of the Judeo-Christian experience. This concept goes beyond that of psychic transformation, and speaks of a higher level change from flesh to spirit (I Corinthians 15:50-53). See Death.

RED

Red is the first color of the rainbow. Red is the color of the genital, chakra. It is associated with the gonads, and is considered a sensual color. It is associated with the sensation function, i.e. the five senses, with reactivity, physical activity, action orientation, anger, sexuality, and the instincts of self-preservation. Red is the favorite color of small children.

Traditionally it is thought of as a positive, masculine color. Other associations are: passion, love, joy, fire, war, blood, rage, fire, cruelty, health, aggression, strength, danger, and impulsivity.

RELIGIOUS FIGURES

Kalff (1980. p. 24) states that in about the third year of life the "Center of the Self is stabilized in the unconscious of the child and begins to manifest itself in symbols of wholeness." These images of wholeness may appear as squares, circles or religious figures.

BAR MITZVAH BOY: Jewish boy at his Bar Mitzvah: I have had a Jewish child exclaim with delight, "Oh, you have everything!" as she placed this figure in her tray.

BUDDHA: Buddha: These figures are thought to represent man's capacity to find god within. They are used as an image of serenity, and being focused inward.

CHRIST: Christ as the Good Shepherd carrying a lamb. The Judeo-Christian worldview is such that we cannot be our own savior and find our way back to God. We are inherently evil (self-centered and selfish), and need the redeemer God to pay the price for our sin. When we accept the forgiveness provided by God the Good Shepherd/redeemer tenderly cares for us.

CROSS: A small cross or crucifix represents Christianity, savior, and self-sacrifice.

MADONNA AND CHILD: This figure may speak to a person's spiritual beliefs, and/or his psychological needs

MENORAH: A small menorah represents the lamp of God in Heaven.

NATIVITY: Nativity sets represent Jesus' birth, the joy of Christmas, and the promise of peace on earth.

WIZARDS/WITCHES: Wizards and witches represent magical-spiritual powers.

See Church, Ladder, Circle and Square.

RIVER

Water is associated with the unconscious and the emotions. A river is associated with the passage of life; the creative source; change. A river flowing upstream is thought to represent a return to the paradisiacal state to find enlightenment. The mouth of a river is a threshold symbol, which represents a change of state. Crossing a river may also represent a change of state. It this way it becomes a threshold symbol

A river can be representative of spiritual power or nourishment. The "rivers of living water" (John 7:38) spoken of by the Messiah is clearly a symbol of spiritual power that emanates from God, and flows through certain individuals.

ROCK

See Stone.

SATAN

See Demons.

SEAHORSE

The seahorse may be used decoratively in a sand tray that depicts the ocean. Of course, it may picture a nurturing father, or the feminine principle in a boy.

SEAL

The seal functions well on land and in the water. In moving from one realm to another it symbolizes moving into the depths of the psyche. Many children associate the seal with the cute antics they have seen at Sea World shows.

SERPENT

Serpents or snakes represent the lower instincts. Serpents and dragons often appear to be used interchangeably. The serpent power of the kundalini represents the life force. Dragons or serpents are the guardians of the threshold, or entrance to other states of consciousness or esoteric knowledge that are symbolized by treasures, temples, or a "goddess." It may be seen as either a destructive or regenerative (shedding its skin) power; healing and poison; masculine or feminine; light and dark; good and evil. The serpent biting its tail, the uroboros, is symbolic of cyclic manifestation and re-absorption.

Two serpents entwined represent the uniting of opposites. Serpents entwined around a tree or staff represent the natural cycles and healing. Wound around each other the two serpents are thought of as time and fate. Other associations are: instinctual nature, guile, subtlety, cunning, power, knowledge, and evil.

The serpent as evil symbol occurs in the Biblical book Genesis. The fallen angel, originally called, Lucifer or light-bringer, is now called *ha satan*, or the adversary. He was described as a serpent in the first book of the Bible, and as a dragon in the last book, the book of Revelation. The serpent, or dragon, of the book of Genesis offered knowledge at the price of removal from the original closeness to the creator God that existed in Eden. The selfish, unfeeling, sociopathic traits that we associate with the R-complex have everything to do with this negative image.

Jung (1959) believes that when a snake dream occurs, this indicates that the conscious mind is moving away from the instinctual self. Later chapters include several images of psychic threat in which the serpent or snake represents the unconscious of the intruder. See Snake, Angels and Demons.

SEVEN

Seven is associated with completeness and perfection as seen in the seven days of the Biblical week of creation and the lunar calendar made-up of four seven day phases of the moon. Both Eastern and Western traditions associate this number with deity. Seven is used repeatedly in the Biblical Holy Days. The Mesopotamian's divided the heavens and earth into seven regions, and pictured the Tree of Life as having seven branches. In Hindu tradition the World Mountain has seven faces, and the sun has seven rays, the seventh being the center and power of God. Islamic adherents walk around the sacred Kaaba seven times. Personal associations to numbers should be investigated before assuming universal associations.

SHARK

The great white shark is among the most archaic and feared beasts upon the earth. Mankind has few living creatures that menace him so deeply as the man-eating shark. Sharks can be used as an embodiment of primitive rage. Like the tyrannosaurus rex, sharks introduce the image of devouring equated with the concept of oral, sadistic rage, as well as the swallowing up by unconscious forces. Movies like "Jaws" and "Jurassic Park" testify to the human fascination with this primitive, bestial process.

I have sharks that are made of soft rubber and that are hollow. It is a great delight to children to actually put objects (images of their perpetrator) into the mouth and body of this animal.

SHEEP

These gentle domesticated animals need care and protection. Sheep are useful to mankind for the wool and meat that they provide. They are trusting and obedient to the shepherd, and are associated with acceptance of fate, Christian nonviolence, innocence, and sacrifice, i.e. "going like sheep to the slaughter." Here they are associated with the idea of the innocent or weak victim and with the "Lamb of God." See von Franz's (1970) book on the archetype of the Puer for a further discussion of this image. See Lamb.

SHELLS

Children of both sexes love using shells in their sand tray worlds. Usually these items appear in appropriate sea scenes, but they may appear in trays that depict scenes that are set on the land. Shells used in a non-aquatic setting may be the most potent symbolically.

Shells have a long association with the feminine principle. Eliade (1961) says that shells partake of the "sacred powers" that are concentrated in the images of the moon, of women, and of the waters, i.e. the feminine principle. Shells and oysters were used to symbolize birth and rebirth. Certain Native American tribes used shells in the ritual enactment of death and rebirth. Shells were used in rituals in agricultural, nuptial or funerary ceremonies. Sexual imagery is suggested by the resemblance between the female genitalia and certain shells. This meaning was expanded to include the universal source of life.

The oyster, whose irritation by sand results in the formation of a pearl, is associated with transcendental reality, generative powers and embryological symbolism. See Clam.

SHELTER
Shelters are traditionally associated with the feminine principle. The house may symbolize either the Self or the Mother archetype. Houses, caves, villages, cities, walls, fences, and gates all serve to protect.

Although the home is usually associated with the female, the notion of shelter can also be indicative of the masculine desire to protect one's wife and children. Many women long for a male to shelter and protect them. See House, Nest, and Cave.

SHEPHERD
A shepherd is the protector of his flock. In this sense a shepherd would be a type of Messiah Yeshua (Jesus). This image can be used in a realistic pastoral scene, as a symbol of rescue, or as a religious symbol. The shepherd may be thought of as a spiritual hero, a savior figure who is filled with compassion and mercy for the lost sheep. The Messiah is the "Good Shepherd who gives his life for the sheep." John 10:11 See Hero, Lamb and Sheep.

SHIPS
The ocean represents the unconscious. Ships represent a way of being contained and protected in this unknown and potentially dangerous environment, or at least a means of venturing into this environment. It is helpful to obtain a variety of ships, these may be pirate ships, battleships, pleasure ships, lifeboats, etc. See Ocean and Transportation.

SILVER
Silver is associated with wealth and the quality of preciousness. Because of its reflective properties silver is thought to be representative of the moon and the feminine. In the Biblical economy, silver represents redemption.

SIX
Biblically, six is associated with man. Man was created on the sixth day and falls short of perfection. The antichrist is associated with 666, the number of the Beast. Other associations are equilibrium, stability, truth, and union.

The six-sided hexagram combining two triangles symbolizes the union of masculine and feminine principles. The triangle pointing up is associated with man and fire. The triangle pointing down is associated with female, water, and earth. This figure, called the Star of David is associated with the uniting of the tribes of Israel and Judah just before the Messiah returns. Because of Solomon's great wealth and wisdom other cultures have come to associate this figure with the occult. Personal associations to numbers should be investigated before assuming universal associations.

SKELETON

Adventurous children are delighted to find miniature skeletons among the sand tray materials. These objects give them an opportunity to deal with a facet of life that is shunned and neglected. Skeletons picture death, mortality, and time. Children most often use these objects in conjunction with the idea of a treasure hunt, shipwreck, and tropical island scenes. See Skull and Death.

SKULL

The skull represents man's mortality, death, danger, desolation, the transitory nature of life, the shades, the need to overcome fear, a wasteland or no-man's land, and time.

The skull and crossbones (the femur, or thighbone) were used to represent the vitality of the life force contained in the head and the loins. Skull and crossbones signifies pirates, poison, death and drugs. Children seem to react to these images as portraying power, and as issuing a warning to others to beware. See Skeleton and Death.

SNAKE

A snake or serpent may be either a positive or negative symbol. Jung (1959) believes that when a snake dream occurs, this is an indicator that the conscious mind is moving away from the instinctual self. The snake arouses fear and threatens to poison or kill, at the same time it is a "savior in animal form, representing the possibility of becoming conscious and whole" (von Franz, 1970, p. 78). The coiled snake represents latent power either for good or evil. It has also been thought of as representing cycles of manifestation.

Snakes may serve as representations of negative forces within the unconscious of the parent that are threatening to the child. The image of snake can represent the lower instincts of the parent or child.

In his preface to *Sandplay* (Kalff, 1980), Harold Stone states, "The snake expresses primitive emotion. It expresses sexuality. It expresses the whole realm of the imagination that became consigned to an increasingly inferior position as we moved more and more into our scientific age." Kalff (1980, p. 79) says that the snake shedding its skin represents a "renewal being prepared in the unconscious."

The eagle and the snake, or stag and snake, represent the struggle between higher and lower forms of the instinctual nature. The victory of the eagle or stag over the snake represents the victory of good over evil.

The snake is a symbol of libidinal energy in the widest sense. Kalff (1980, p. 75) says it often appears in puberty. Yogis speak of the force of the kundalini that flows through the seven chakras, or energy centers, from the base of the spine to the top of the head as being the serpent power. Is it possible this usage is related to the image of healing as two snakes flowing up the caduceus? Two snakes coiled around the caduceus represent the healing power of nature, also healing and poison, health and illness, much like the dual nature of the unconscious. See Serpent, Dragon and Uroborus.

SNOW

Certain children often use dry sand as snow, sprinkling it everywhere, especially on trees and rooftops. Some of these winter scenes are quite charming and attractive. Snow may be fun to play in, but is potentially very dangerous. Children with obvious pathology have used "snow" while talking about their sand tray figures freezing to death. See Ice.

SPACEMEN

As pioneers of the new frontier, spacemen have replaced cowboys s as folk heroes, pioneers, and adventurers. Planetary, earth and space images will mean a lot to some individuals. These images represent travel, adventure, curiosity or intellectual strivings. The use of spacemen may indicate a healthy desire for individuation, or as with aircraft, may indicate a desire to escape a overpowering mother, i.e. a Puer situation. See Aircraft, Heroes and Heroines.

SPHERE

The sphere symbolizes perfection, completeness, containment, eternity, unity, and the possibilities of other forms. Since it represents containment and possibilities, it is also seen as representing the abolition of time and space. The sphere is associated with the idea of the cosmic egg. The blue sphere is associated with the masculine spirit. (See Signell in *Sandplay Studies*, 1981, p. 106). See Egg.

SPIDER

Spiders have a traditional association with the archetype of the Terrible Mother. Historically, spiders were associated with the weaving of fate and time, and the entrapment of mankind. As with the octopus and the crab, a mother-complex may be indicated if the child frequently uses this image, or uses combinations of related images. See Octopus, Crab, Crocodile and Quicksand.

SPIRAL

The spiral appears as the typical form of a galaxy, certain types of shells, and other natural occurring forms. These naturally occurring spiral forms have intrapsychic counterparts. Spiral forms are a significant feature in sand tray work. Spirals are related to right-brain cyclical and holistic perception of time and conscious awareness. A spiral is a type of circumnambulation around a central point. These widening or decreasing patterns may be flat or three-dimensional. As a holistic perception of time, the spiral would have to be visualized as a three-dimensional form. The spiral was thought to represent both the masculine and feminine creative forces. It represents expansion or contraction, birth and death. It is associated with the serpent power of the coiled sleeping kundalini. The spiral shares the symbolism of the labyrinth. See Labyrinth.

SPORTS FIGURES

Figures playing soccer, tennis, basketball, football, skateboarding, doing gymnastics, etc. can be obtained from toy stores and cake decorating shops. These figures are extremely important for certain children.

SQUARE

The square is symbolic of quaternary. It can represent the four functions that are inherent within the Self, i.e. the intuition, sensation, thinking and feeling functions. It may also represent the four archaic elements: air, fire, earth, and water; the four seasons; the four cardinal points of the compass. It denotes a solidity that gives the impression of firmness, organization, and strength. The four faces of the heavenly cherubim described in the Bible are an occurrence of this motif (Ezekiel 1:10). The square suggests psychological wholeness, and the unconscious Self. See Four and Mandala.

STAFF

The staff is associated with masculine power or authority. Since a traveler uses a staff, it is associated with pilgrimages. The shepherd's staff is associated with "the good shepherd."

STAG

The buck or stag is associated with creation and The Tree of Life, the sun fertility and renewal. The stag trampling the serpent is seen as the victory of spirit over matter and good over evil. It is seen as the opposite of the chthonic serpent. The stag is associated with pride and nobility. In numerous religious systems, the stag is associated with deities and supernatural powers. See Deer.

STAIRS

The use of stairs is symbolic of ascension, transcendence, and change in the state of consciousness. See Ladder and Gate.

STAR

Stars are distant, heavenly bodies. They can be seen to represent the presence of divinity or the eternal; high attainment. In the Bible, stars are associated with angelic messengers. Messenger is the same word as angel in Hebrew.

The five-pointed star is seen by Jung to symbolize material, sensate man (CW, Vol. 9, Part I, p. 373). Pentagrams, the five-pointed star turned upside down, are associated with the occult, the demonic, or witchcraft.

The interlocking six pointed star, or Star of David or Seal of Solomon, is the symbol for the tribe of Judah. In the joining of the two triangles it is associated with creation; the joining of the masculine and feminine, and the reuniting of the tribes of Israel and Judah. Occult associations to the six-pointed star have been added by other cultures.

Biblical symbolism uses stars to represent angels.

STARFISH

The starfish combines the life of the ocean depths and an image that is associated with the heavenly realms. Ancient associations are with divine love, the Holy Spirit and Christianity.

STREAM

See River.

STREET SIGNS

The meanings may be self evident: stop, a blockage or barrier in energy; yield, give in to another with greater entitlement; an external danger; railroad crossing, one stream of energy crossing another, etc.

STONE

In the past a stone, tree, mountain, or grove were understood as symbolic of the cosmos. Pillars or tall stones were considered to represent an axis mundi, or point of entrance to different levels of consciousness. Stones are seen to be a symbolic of being and reconciliation with self. Common associations are strength, durability; permanence, imperishability; integrity, and immortality. The Rock of Gibraltar typifies this usage.

Standing stones are associated with the sacred, and the life force. Stones have a long history of usage in altars, the Hebrew Beith-el or bethels (God's house); the Irish Lia-Fail coronation stone. Omphalos or lingam stones are associated with human sacrifice. Notable uses of large stones are the Greek omphali, a rounded stone at the entrance to Apollo's temple at

Delphi that was considered the world's center; Stonehedge, the blarney Stone, and the black stone of Islam in Mecca.

Rounded stones may represent the moon, eggs, the feminine principle. Broken angular stones were associated with disintegration, dismemberment, weakness, annihilation and destruction. The ancient Hebrews used unhewn pillars as altars and as waymarks. A heavy stone can create an obstacle when it blocks the entrance to a cavern or well.

The alchemist's philosophers stone represents the joining of opposites or the fixing of volatile elements. Jung (1959) states that in alchemy the Philosopher's stone is a symbol of the Self.

The Sword in the Stone represents a messianic opportunity that was reserved for the Hero-King only.

The white stone of the book of Revelation represents being judged blameless, immortality that is a gift of God (Romans 6:23) and not inherent to physical life.

Cirlot (1962) associates stones "fallen from heaven" with the origin of life. "In volcanic eruptions, air turned to fire, fire became 'water' and 'water' changed to stone." Meteorites and other stones that contain black pigment were worshipped, for example, the black stone of Pessinus, and the Kaaba in Mecca. It is important to have rocks of various types, such as sedimentary, volcanic, metamorphic, small rounded river stones, geodes, and crystals. Cut and polished geodes have been used to represent a magical lake. See Rock.

SUN

Small images of the sun are important in a sandplay collection. These images are typically used by boys. The sun is symbolic of the masculine ego just as the moon is symbolic of the feminine ego. In addition, Neumann (1955 p. 57) states that the luminous bodies are symbolic of the spiritual side of the psyche. Jung (1953, p.84) sees the Sun as an image of God, of life and of wholeness. This association of the Sun and God is typical in numerous religious systems.

SWAN

Graceful and beautiful, regal and silent, swans are believed to represent solitude and retreat. The whiteness of the swan is associated with sincerity, purity, chastity, and love.

SWINE

See Pig.

TEN

Jewish sages associate ten with perfection since it is the number of the Ten Commandments. Ten is the number of digits on the human hand. The Greek mathematician, Pythagoras, associated ten with the whole of creation. As a combination of male and female numbers ten was considered a symbol of marriage. Personal associations to numbers should be investigated before assuming universal associations.

THREE

Three is a dynamic or uneven number. Three is associated with the unification of opposites; thesis, antithesis, synthesis. The union of opposites, masculine and feminine energy, is the goal of individuation. In Christianity three is important in the trinity, the triune God. Three might represent father, mother and child. In Hebrew many words are composed of three letters. The Celts taught in triads.

The third dimension is the dimension of depth. Jung states that the third dimension adds reality and solidity to what would be two-dimensional. The third eye represents psychic seeing.

Third class, poor. Third World stands for poor nations. .. Personal associations to numbers should be investigated before assuming universal associations. See Six, Nine, and Twelve.

THRONE

The throne is an image of authority. Signell (1981) states that a golden throne is an important image for men who use the sand tray. She states that the throne shows a man's position in relation to the archetype of the Father.

TIGER

In India and Asia tigers symbolize great and terrible power, much like the lion does in the West. These great cats are known for their power, quickness, quietness while stalking, and their ability to overpower their prey. Devouring is associated with the image of a tiger. There is a strong sense of body consciousness with the image of great cats. See Cat, Lion, and Devour.

TORTOISE

Tortoises are associated with the waters and the feminine principle. The tortoise is associated with slowness, ancient wisdom, longevity, patience, endurance, and self-protection, with its shell. The tortoise with its shell may be seen traveling within its home. Traditionally, the tortoise was believed to support the world. It was thought of as representing the four corners of the earth, and may picture the unconscious Self. See Turtle.

TOWER

Towers have a long association with the masculine principle. Erik Erikson (1950) found that boys were characterized by their tendency to create block towers. That towers have a phallic quality is readily apparent. Males create towers more frequently than do females and these towers tend to be more central and taller than girls' towers. They represent a striving, a strong desire to impact upon the world, an intense desire to be noticed, and to achieve in an outward sense. Towers are indicative of a desire to rise above the common level of society. The destruction of these creations may be just sheer exuberance, and typify the creator's power to destroy as well as to build. A negative meaning may be an emotional dropping off of energy/libido due to a sense of deficiency within the self, i.e. deep, narcissistic wounding. Like airplane crashes, the frequent fall of towers in a child older than preschool, may represent a sense of depression following inflation.

The tower can represent virginity, and the inaccessible aspects of the psyche. The tower itself has a phallic aspect, but its sheltering and containing aspects are associated with the feminine principle.

The Rapunzel tower is an interesting image. The tower is a shelter with a strongly masculine flavor in which an older woman holds a younger female captive. This image clearly speaks to the notion of the mother-complex. The witch-mother is ruled by a harsh negative animus, and therefore has a masculine quality, pictured by the phallic tower. The complex is experienced as an entrapment from which there is no escape, i.e. no stairs or ladder. The witch-mother and captive daughter "enjoy" an exclusive sadomasochistic relationship that is characterized by a love-hate ambivalence. Although the fairy tale ends on a positive note, a therapist working with either the child or parent caught within this archetypal situation will experience this relationship as sticky and problematic. Resistance to changing the relationship may come from either, or both, members of the couple. A child, of either gender caught in this type of relationship with either mother or father, needs to be helped and set free.

Plastic molds for creating castles and towers are important items in sandplay. Many children create these sandcastles and towers to achieve a sense of mastery. See Castle and Fortifications.

TRANSPORTATION

All modes of transportation relate to energy in motion. This can be understood as energy in the psyche that is in motion. Bicycles and motorcycles are personal conveyances. Cars may be personal conveyances, like sports cars, or relate to a small group, as does the family car. Buses may relate to energy in the collective. See Aircraft, Bus, Car, Ship, and Truck.

TREASURE

A treasure chest is an important item in the sandplay collection. Children have constructed marvelous and convoluted stories about the quest for hidden treasure. The search for treasure often includes delving within a cave for treasure that was secreted away. Material wealth is the most obvious and external form of wealth. The element of greed may be apparent. The deeper implications refer to self-knowledge, self-esteem, self-control and to spiritual treasure, such as the Biblical "pearl of great price" (Matthew 13:46). See Cave and Gold.

TREE

The sheer number of advertising logos that use an image of a single tree silently testifies to the power of this image. The single tree is representative of the psyche's power to connect the various elements or states of consciousness. The tree is rooted deep within the earth, in the darkness and unknown. It draws water and nutrients into itself from the earth, and it has its branches in the heavens. In this sense it symbolizes the joining of the worlds of the physical, emotional, and mental life, and connects the visible with the unseen. In ancient thought the tree connects the feminine, receptive earth with the masculine sun and air. In interpreting the projective test, House-Tree-Person, the clinician sees each of the images as representing the patient.

In addition to representing the Self, the tree may represent the Mother archetype (Jung, 1959). It serves to shelter, protect, and nourish, and in these ways is a symbol of the feminine principle. Its strength and uprightness appear to be masculine characteristics. In these ways, the tree can symbolize the androgynous qualities of the psyche.

The Biblical Tree of Life represents spiritual life and understanding as opposed to carnal, fleshly life without spiritual understanding. The Judaic understanding is that the Tree of Life represents the Torah. The Biblical Tree of the Knowledge of Good and Evil represents the necessity to make moral choices in life, yet apart from God we fail to obtain the results we desire.

A tree on an elevated place is often seen as announcing a "sacred place," or Biblical high place.

A barren tree may represent a time in which energy is at a low ebb; a time prior to renewal; a feeling of desolation. A flowering tree may represent a period of growth; a time of rebirth; a feeling of hope or joy. See Forest, Oak and Pine.

TRUCK

Trucks, like cars, are a means of getting around in the external world. In dreams they appear as images that refer to our motive power in either our inner or outer life. As masculine images, they also may imply a specific means of impacting upon the world.

Construction trucks and road building activity may indicate a positive change in the therapeutic process, a movement toward integration and constructive pursuits. See Car and Transportation.

TUNNEL

Going through a tunnel can be seen as a symbol of rebirth. See Burial and Cave.

TURTLE

The turtle is notable for its armored resistance to intrusions from the outside, its long life, and its vulnerability when flipped over. Among the world of the reptilian and amphibious forms, it carries a gentler aspect than do most other creatures. Common associations are slowness, stability, ancient wisdom, protection, and long-life. Aesop's fable the Tortoise and the Hare makes the point that, "slow and steady wins the race." See Tortoise.

TWELVE

Twelve months of the year, twelve inches in a foot, Twelve Apostles, twelve tribes of Israel, Western civilization has placed great importance of this multiple of three. Personal associations to numbers should be investigated before assuming universal associations.

TWO

Two is used to represent duality and opposing principles, synthesis and division, good and evil, a pair or couple such as Adam and Eve. It is linked to union, fertility, growth, love, and the feminine principle. The Gemini twins are an archetypal pattern. Personal associations to numbers should be investigated before assuming universal associations.

UNICORN

The unicorn was one of those mythological beasts that were largely forgotten until recently. Recently the unicorn seems to have become ubiquitous appearing as small statues, folder covers, and other uses. Traditional courtly meanings associated with this image are sublimated desire, chastity, virginity, virtue, incorruptibility, and strength of mind and body.

The unicorn is associated with the feminine principle. As a Christian symbol it is associated with the Incarnation.

The lion and the unicorn appear together as a pair of opposites representing the masculine and feminine principles. The most notable use of the lion and the unicorn is on the Seal of Great Britain. See Lion and Horse.

UROBORUS

The circular image of the snake devouring its tail is a symbol of undifferentiated wholeness, mother and child unity, or oceanic consciousness. See Snake.

VILLAINS

Well-known villains, such as the Joker, the Riddler, and Darth Vader, typically are guilty of great crimes. In a child's life these may be objectively existent crimes in which the child is involved, or they may be psychological or spiritual in nature. Child abuse comes in many forms.

Both in society, and in one's inner life, there is a need to struggle with good and evil, light and dark. Boys, more than girls, show an eagerness to alternately identify with, and to contend with, the dark side of life. Many girls, and adult women, compliantly identify with the stereotype of the "good little girl," and deny or avoid all objects that are indicative of conflict or evil. This tends to create an aura of unreality for this type of female, and definitely inhibits the process of individuation, and the development of creativity. See Demons

VIOLET

Violet, the seventh color of the rainbow, is the color of the pineal gland and brain chakra. This center is associated with imagination, fantasy, sense of eternity, spiritual yearnings, awareness of how we create our reality, and the magic or chaos that relates to the unconscious. Other associations are moderation, temperance, meekness, and virtue.

The unconscious may be conceived as being divided into the superconscious and subconscious realms. These realms would correspond to the ultra-violet and infrared portions of the spectrum, respectively. See Purple.

VOLCANO

Volcanoes present a fascinating phenomenon. These cone-shaped hills or mountains are the result of the movement of material from the depths of the earth to its surface. In this sense they can be seen as providing a connecting link between the transformative power of the unconscious and the conscious awareness of the ego. Anger and rage are associated with this image. The spewing forth of molten lava can be seen as similar to the bursting forth of primitive rage. Volcanoes may be used in the destruction of the old order in the process of reconstitution of the personality.

Von Franz (1970) states that an extinct volcano represents libido that is blocked and has returned to the unconscious. She has seen this image in post-psychotic individuals. During this stage in their life, the individual is functional, but the passion or fire has gone out of their lives. See Mountain and Fire.

VULTURE

Vultures are often associated with foreboding; a sense of immanent loss. Birds of prey remove the dead and purify the land. The vulture was seen as sacred to many of the pagan goddesses Isis, Hera, Nekhbet, Hathor, and Maat. The logical association with this is a "death mother," and the Terrible Mother.

WALL

Walls may appear as barriers and blockages. The child's fragile ego may be represented by a figure who hides behind the defense of walls, and is besieged by adversaries. If this imagery occurs, it is important to find out what is happening at home. If all negative images are totally walled off from other portions of the tray, the individual is not ready to consciously deal with the negative forces in his or her unconscious.

Walls are threshold symbols. The inner portion of walled cities was considered to be sacred. This sacred space may be thought of as representing the numinous feelings associated with the psyche. See Fences and Fortifications.

WAR

Warfare is a particularly masculine activity. This image may indicate the struggle to establish a masculine identity, a struggle against the maternal matrix, and is indicative of movement toward differentiation and individuation. Males exhibit a need to experience struggle and conflict. It is emasculating for therapists to deny this need. Not that war is a good thing. It is not. It is the necessity of a struggle or battle of some sort that seems essential to the development of masculine psychology, and to a lesser extent the establishment of feminine creativity and identity. In addition to the establishment of identity, war may symbolize intrapsychic conflict or interpersonal struggles. See Battle.

WATER

Water has a numinous quality to it. It is unique on the planet for its many different permutations and for its power to support life. Water may be found in liquid, gaseous and frozen states. When it is frozen it may take the form of snow, ice, icicles, sheets of ice, hail, or sleet. In addition to supporting life, water may be extremely destructive in floods, tidal waves, blizzards and storms. In sandplay dry sand frequently is used as torrents of water or snow in which people, or animals, are buried and entombed.

Water is representative of the potentialities of life. It is associated with the feminine principle, the Great Mother, the creativity of life, gestation, birth, and containment. Water can purify, wash way, and dissolve undesirable elements or experiences. Immersion in water can symbolize death and renewal. Baptism is symbolic of purification, and of death and spiritual rebirth. Water represents the unconscious with all it vastness and potentialities, or the emotions and their instability. Diving into water may represent searching the unconscious mind, or searching for the secrets of life and spiritual knowledge. Crossing water represents changing from one state of consciousness to another. Crossing water may also indicate separation, as in a death.

Watery, messy, flooded trays are associated with the vegetative stage. See Ocean, Pond, River, Flood, Waves, Bridge and Burial.

WAVES

Water in motion may be indicative of a stirring up of the unconscious or of feelings. Other meanings associated with waves are: change, agitation, futility, and instability. See Ocean.

WELL

A well is associated with the feminine principle and mother archetype. Most associations are positive. Wells may represent renewal, spiritual truth, and healing. Wells are associated with wish fulfillment. A feminine, sexual image may be meant.

WHALE

Whales are impressive because of their great size. Both the Jonah and the Pinocchio stories use the whale or great fish. The great white shark has also been suggested for the Jonah tale. Southeast Asia is the source of many spiritual myths where a great whale delivers the Hero. Being swallowed by the great fish is symbolic of a grave or a burial. Both the Jonah and Pinocchio tales end with the protagonist emerging from the grave.

Native Americans teach that we can learn knowledge based on experience, patience, strength, being in harmony with the environment, and the magnificence in all things from the whale. See Ark, Rebirth.

WHITE

White light results from the combination of all the prismatic colors. In Western tradition white is symbolic of spiritual purity, higher consciousness, illumination, holiness, chastity, and perfection.

WIND/WINDMILL

Wind is associated with the spirit or spiritual realm, the life-breath, and the notion of universal prana or life force. The Hebrew word, ruach, means both wind and spirit. Windmills are an important source of elemental power.

WISE OLD MAN

The Wise Old Man archetype is symbolic of inner wisdom, and suggestive of God. The Wise Old Man is characterized by his involvement with ideas, and the meanings associated with these ideas. He is the image of the capacity for reflection, for philosophical and spiritual understanding. A Wise Old Man may appear as a guide, a teacher, or a sage. Jung believes that as with other archetypes there will also be a dark side to the image of the wise man. A clever old man is not necessarily a good or moral man. See Man and Father.

WISE OLD WOMAN

Jung refers to the image of Sophia as associated with feminine wisdom, but his translated works have no indexed references to Wise Old Woman. Jung (1959) said that for the child the mother's attributes are often transferred to a person close to her, especially to the mother's mother. The grandmother frequently carries the projection of wisdom as well as that of a witch. Elevating an older woman to a more powerful status places her in a position of carrying the archetype of the "Great Mother." The light and dark duality contained within this basic archetype calls for a psychic splitting, i.e. fairy godmother and old witch or wicked fairy are typical Great Mother images. See Mother and Woman.

WITCH

The witch in fairy tales is a menacing negative mother that threatens the child's development. The beautiful, narcissistic Queen Mother in *Snow White* transforms herself into an old crone before seeking to kill the maiden.

Children are exposed to a wide variety of religious worldviews. The witch is a foremost image associated with the negative side of the maternal. In *Four Archetypes* (1959) Jung says, "The hunter or old magician and the witch correspond to the negative parental introjects in the magic world of the unconscious" (1959, p. 113). Jung formulated the ambivalence of the mother archetype in his book *Symbols of Transformation* (1956).

Practitioners of Wicca, see themselves involved in a search for power in harmony with the forces of nature and the feminine. In contrast, the Bible condemns witchcraft as working in collusion with the demonic realm, or the realm of fallen angels. See Mother and Woman.

WOLF

Historically, wolves were associated with evil, cruelty, greed, and craftiness. The wolf in the Bible, (i.e. wolves in sheep's clothing, Matthew 7:15) is a predator and a deceiver. In the Tale of Red Riding Hood he is thinly disguised as a helpful animal whose evil side becomes apparent. Bettelheim (1975) believes that the child has used the mechanism of splitting and that the grandmother and the wolf in "Little Red Riding Hood" are the loving and threatening aspects of the adult figure.

A more recent association of wolf is with sexual prowess, conquest, and Don Juanism. It is easy to see the wolf of Red Riding Hood as a dangerous predator as well as sexually threatening. Some fairy tales associate wolves with witches.

Jung (1959 Part I) interprets "The Princess in the Tree," a German fairy tale, in which a wolf truly does serve a helpful function to the hero. The conservation movement associates the wolf with the pristine wilderness.

Native Americans teach that we can learn lessons about healing relationships, love, fidelity, intimacy, forgiveness, community, generosity, and compatibility from the wolf.

WOMAN

Jungian psychologist Toni Wolff has described four general archetypal styles of womanhood. These types seem shallow and one-dimensional, but the closer one lives to an archetypal image, the more one-dimensional the person will be.

Jean Bolen in *Goddesses in Everywoman* gives a broader view of women. She sets forth seven archetypal patterns that may be lived singly or in various combinations. Bolen's archetypal figures seem closer to life. Since our topic is play therapy the four patterns are covered rather than the seven. I invite the reader to read Bolen's book.

The first of these archetypes is the mother who is impersonal in the sense that she is instinctual and conventional, serving the interests of her family in a very general way. This type of female is limited by her incapacity to perceive her husband and children as individuals. Simple mother figures created for doll housedoll play suit this type perfectly.

The second type is a polar opposite of the mother. The archetypal Hera is primarily concerned with getting and keeping a man. Her need is to relate to him in a very personal way. She shows little or no interest in creating a family and assuming the role of wife and mother. Miniature figures similar to Barbie dolls suit this type.

The tomboy may grow up to be the embodiment of the Amazon type, Artemisor Diana. There is nothing absolute about this tendency. The Amazon is the independent or self-sufficient type who places primary interest in her career or achievements. This tends to be very much a reaction against men, or identification with the father. See Bolen's 1984 book for a discussion of the archetypal Artemis. This type of woman will tend to behave as a friend or as a competitor with men, rather than a wife or a lover. If the archetype of the animus takes too strong hold of this type of female, she may become a tyrant whose primary interest is to control and organize others and bend them to her will.

The tomboy stage is not always negative, nor does it always result in such an extreme development. Experiencing this developmental course can permit a young woman to develop her creativity and interests in areas other than mothering, homemaking, or attracting a man. Bolen suggests that Artemis, Athena and Hestia type women have a capacity for independent thought not ruled by an unconscious and primitive animus which creates an inferior thinking function as Jung postulated. In this observation she has added an important shift in Jungian thought. Small figures of female athletes, women skin divers, and cowgirls are among the type of objects that appeal to a child who is following this developmental course.

The last type of woman is the medium. This intuitive woman or girl lives in close relationship to the collective unconscious. The sand tray work of this personality type will evidence an overlap of collective and personal symbols. I have not found a specific type of toy to portray this tendency, perhaps Native American storyteller figures come closest.

YELLOW

Yellow, the third color of the rainbow, is the color of the adrenal and solar plexus chakra. It is associated with linear, left brain processes, i.e. logical, sequential, analytic, reductive, and mechanical thinking. Other associations are cheeriness, lightness, sunny, and warm. Dark, muddy yellow carries such negative associations as: avarice, treachery, ambition, and betrayal. See Gold.

Appendix B

Guide to Resources

Childswork/Childsplay
135 Dupont Street
P.O. Box 760
Plainview, N.Y., 11803-0760
1-800-962-1141; e-mail: info@Childswork.com
This is an excellent source for therapeutic games, books for children with various problems, a few books for professionals. A free catalog is available.

Dover Publications, Inc.
31 E. 2nd Street
Mineola, N.Y., 11501
Dover has cardstock cut and assemble castles, villages, an ark, and a windmill. These are not rugged, but are relatively inexpensive and attractive.

Catherine Gould Ph.D., 16661 Ventura Bl., Encino, California, 91436, has developed a four page questionnaire to assess ritualistic abuse in children.

Lakeshore Learning Materials
2695 E. Dominguez Street
P.O. Box 6261
Carson, CA 90749
310-537-8600; 1-800-4215354; www.lakeshorelearning.com
Lakeshore manufactures and sells items for schools. This is an excellent source for child-sized furniture; shelves with cubbies for storage; activity

carpets for floor play; easels; play tables; rugged, wooden doll houses; flexible families (Asian, Hispanic, Black and White); animals; dolls with disabilities; hand puppets; puppet theater; dress-up clothes and more. Most of their items are built to last and are expensive. The Feelings and Faces Games listed in their catalog is perfect for therapists.

Lakeshore lists a Giant Sand and Water Table that is made of rugged plastic, supported on aluminum legs. It height is adjustable from 18" to 24". Older children or adults might have to sit on a chair to utilize this tray. It is less expensive than most sand trays made for play therapy, unfortunately it is red, not blue. They do offer a smaller sand tray that is blue that is 20" wide and 27 1/4" long, and is 18" to 21" high which is very adequate. If you are on a budget these are economical trays. A free catalog is available.

Lilly's Kids
1-800-545-5426; www.lillianvernon.com
This large mail-order house has produced a catalog filled with children's toys, furniture, puppet theater and more. Competitive pricing.

Oakhill Specialties
P.O. Box 152
Cloverdale, CA 95425
707-894-4856; www.sandtrays.com
Sand trays. portable stand, play center.

Playmobil, USA
11-E Nicholas Court
Dayton, N.J. 08810
908-274-0101; www.playmobil.com
Playmobil figures are stiff looking, but rugged. Playmobil produces outstanding accessories such as: pirate ship; circus; hospital operating room; hospital ward; surgery room; castles in several sizes; covered wagon,

jungle ruin, alligator swamp, Rockies landscape, rescue helicopter, ambulance, and more. Expensive.

Playrooms
P.O. Box 2660
Petaluma, CA 94953
707-763-2448; 800-667-2470; www.playrms.com
Rugged plastic sand trays. Their initial sandplay toy assortment appears to favor masculine items. Balance it out with small female figures, houses, miniature flowers, shells, and other feminine items and you would have a great start.

Sandplay Essentials
3544 Lincoln Avenue #64
Ogden, UT 84401
801-621-4105; www.sandplayessentials.com
This organization has a great name, and maybe someday will embody what the name suggests, however, right now their selection is small. They have very artistic creations by Gwen Pina—Native American figures, a unique Jewish male storyteller, wizards, and inexpensive and unusual skull hill. Expensive.

Sandplay Therapists of America
P.O. Box 4847
Walnut Creek, CA 94596
203-869-7307; www.sandplay.org
This organization offers training.

Sensational Beginnings
P.O. Box 2009
987 Steward Road
Monroe, MI, 48162

800-444-7147; www.sb-kids.com
Play stations, dollhouses, toys for younger children, and more. A free catalog is available.

The Family Clinic
www.familyclinic.simplenet.com
Wooden trays with removable lids.

Ther-a-Play Products
P.O. Box 761
Glen Ellen, CA 95442
707-938-3074
Wooden sand trays, projective storytelling cards, miniatures, books, puppets, anatomical dolls, videos and more.

University of North Texas
Center for Play Therapy
P.O. Box 311337

Denton, TX 76203-1337
Offers training, videos, Directory of graduate schools offering play therapy.

Uniquity
215 4th Street
P.O. Box 6
Galt, CA 95632
800-521-7771, 209-745-7771
Uniquity has one piece molded blue fiberglass sand trays that are wonderful for use with wet sand. Their prices are just right for those with tight budgets. The one-piece trays are leak proof and perfect for very wet sand. Fiberglass covers may be purchased separately, and inexpensive cloth

covers are available. In addition, they have sandplay videos, books, a sandplay cart, colored sands, plywood dollhouse, doll house furniture, family figures, communication games. Affordable. A free catalog is available.

SAND

Sandbox grade sand may be obtained at lumberyards or building supply yards. Do not buy the coarse sand used for making cement. If you get sand from the beach, rinse it many times, as the salt will corrode the paint on a painted sand tray. Lakeshore lists a plastic coated moldable sand. Uniquity lists sand in 23 colors.

Where to Shop

AIRCRAFT
Aircraft may be obtained in toyshops. Playmobil has a rescue copter.
ALLIGATOR
Alligators may be obtained in some toyshops. Playmobil has an alligator swamp
ANATOMICAL DOLLS
Ther-a-Play Products.
ANGEL
Angels might be obtained in hobby shops that have a cake-decorating department. Christmas shops, floral supply shops at Christmas, such as Michael's or Hobby Lobby.
ANIMALS
Animals may be obtained in toyshops, gift shops, Lakeshore, and hobby shops.
APE
Apes may be obtained in some toyshops, Ther-a-Play, and Lakeshore.
ARK

I obtained a Noah's Ark from a Christian mail order catalogue. Sensational Beginnings catalog has a rugged wooden ark. Dover Publications has a cut and assemble heavy paper ark.

BABY

African-American and Caucasian infants may be obtained from toy stores and from hobby shops that have cake-decorating supplies. Lakeshore Learning Materials has various ethnic figures family sets which includes infants.

BASKET

Small baskets may be obtained in some floral/hobby shops. Try Michael's or Hobby Lobby.

BEAR

Bears may be obtained in some toyshops and gift shops.

BEAVER

Beavers might be obtained in toy or gift shops in certain parts of the country. I haven't found a source for these interesting and unique animals.

BEE

Bees may be obtained in floral shops.

BELL

I obtained a small Liberty Bell in a floral and hobby store.

BIRD

Birds may be obtained in toy or floral shops.

BLACK PERSON

I obtained a Black skin driver in a toy shop, a Black spaceman in a toy store, a Black bride and groom in a hobby supply store that carries cake decorating items. I obtained Black infants from toy stores and from hobby shops that have cake-decorating supplies. Lakeshore has African-American family, Asian, and Hispanic family figures.

BLOOD

Vampire "blood" may be obtained in some toy or costume shops.

BRIDGE

Several wonderful Oriental bridges may be obtained in an aquarium shop. Train hobby shops may have bridges.
BULL
Bulls may be obtained in some toyshops.
BUS
Buses may be obtained in some toy or hobby shops. Playmobil have a school bus.
BUTTERFLY
Butterflies may be obtained in a floral supply shop.
CAR
Cars may be obtained in toyshops.
CASTLE
Castles may be obtained in toyshops, Dungeon and Dragons shops, i.e. shops that have role playing games and military games. Dover Publications has a beautiful cut and assemble heavy paper castle. Playmobil and Lakeshore have castles. Lincoln Logs have a castle building set.
CAT
Cats may be obtained in gift shops that carry small ceramic animals. Lions, tigers and panther may be obtained in some toy stores. Lakeshore has a wide variety of animal sets.
CAVE
A ceramic cave may be obtained in gift shops that carry small ceramic animals. Playmobil has a jungle cave.
CAVE MEN and WOMEN:
Prehistoric figures may be obtained in some toyshops.
CHILD
Infants and children may be obtained in toyshops and hobby shops that have cake-decorating supplies. Lakeshore has family sets that include children.
CHURCH
Churches may be obtained in hobby shops that carry train sets and in some gift shops.

CIRCUS

Playmobil has a beautiful circus tent with, a high wire act, grandstands and circus trailer. Toy stores or cake decorating shops may be a source for these items.

CLAM

Clamshells may be obtained in gift shops, especially in coastal towns. Shells may be found in some party decoration shops.

CLOWN

Clowns may be obtained in cake decorating shops.

CONTAINERS

Small containers may be found in gift shops or floral/craft shops.

COTTAGE

Cottages may be found in gift shops and discount stores.

COW

Cows may be obtained in toyshops along with farm sets.

CRAB

Small plastic crabs may be obtained in some toyshops or gift shops near the coast. Lilly's Kids catalogs list Sea Life sets that include crabs.

CROCODILE

Plastic crocodiles may be obtained in toyshops.

DEATH

A figure representing Death might be obtained in fantasy role playing shops.

DEER

Deer may be obtained in toyshops.

DEMONS

Plastic or pewter demons may be obtained in fantasy role playing shops or toyshops.

DEVIL

See Demons.

DINOSAURS

Dinosaurs may be obtained in toyshops or nature shops. Lakeshore has dinosaur sets.

DOG

Dogs may be obtained in toyshops or gift shops that have small ceramics figures.

DONKEY

Donkeys may be obtained from gift shops that have small ceramic figures.

DOVE

Doves may be obtained in cake decorating supply shops.

DRAGON

Dragons may be obtained in fantasy role playing shops, gift shops and China, Korea or Japan town shops.

DWARVES

Dwarves and elves may be obtained from cake decorating supply shops or some gift shops.

EAGLE

Eagles may be obtained in toyshops. Eagles fighting a serpent may be obtained from some toyshops.

EARTH

Nature shops may have small images of the earth and planets.

EGGS

Eggs may be obtained in floral supply shops, or may be packed amongst plastic foods for play in toyshops. Many toy stores have plastic play food sets. Lakeshore has the largest number of these sets that I have seen.

ELEPHANT

Elephants may be obtained in toyshops or gift shops. Lakeshore carries a jungle animal collection that includes and elephant.

ELF

Elves may be obtained in cake decorating supply shops.

ETHNIC FIGURES:

African-American, Asian and Hispanic family figures may be obtained from Lakeshore.

Native American figures may be obtained in toyshops, specialty mail houses for sandplay, cake decorating supply houses and in some gift shops. Native American women figures are difficult to obtain, but worth seeking out. Sandplay Essentials has some handcrafted Native American storyteller dolls.

FAIRIES

The quintessential fairy for most children is Tinkerbell from Peter Pan. This figure is available in The Disney Store. Other fairies may be obtained in cake decorating supply shops and some gift shops.

FAMILY FIGURES

Family figures may be obtained in toyshops, mail order catalogues for psychological games and supplies for play therapy, cake decorating supply shops. Lakeshore Learning Materials has flexible family figures, which include infants, and grandparent figures.

FANTASY FIGURES:

Sources are toyshops, thrift shops, antique shops, and gift shops:

Aladdin: The Disney Store, toyshops.

Alice in Wonderland: The Disney Stores.

Batman: Toy stores.

Cheshire Cat: The Disney Stores or antique shops.

Cinderella: Playrooms catalog.

Hansel and Gretel and Witch: Playrooms catalog used to carry this, but I am not certain where this could be obtained now. Check antique and collectible stores.

Pokemon: Many different figures of various types are available at toy stores in just the right size for sand trays.

Queen of Hearts: The Disney Stores, antique or thrift shops. I found one in an antique shop.

Mermaid: Ariel in toyshops, Disney Stores. Other mermaids may be found in gift shops.

Santa Claus: may be obtained from gift shops.

Snow White: The Disney Stores.

Superman: Toy shops.

FARM ANIMALS/BARN:

Toys stores, Playmobil and Lakeshore are likely to have these items.

FATHER

Lakeshore is a source of family figures. Many different masculine figures will serve to represent father depending on the individuals concerned.

FENCES

Various types of fences may be obtained in toyshops or hobby shops, usually as part of a set of small toys, such as a western set.

FISH

Plastic fish may be obtained in gift shops, especially near the coast. Some toy stores may carry plastic fish. Lakeshore carries a set of ocean animals.

FLAGS

Small paper flags may be obtained in party supply shops.

FLOWERS

Small flowers may be in floral supply and hobby shops.

FOOD:

Plastic food items may be obtained in toyshops or floral supply or hobby shops. Lakeshore has a nice collection of miniature groceries and a fruit and vegetable set.

FORTIFICATIONS

Toy stores, fantasy role playing shops or hobby shops may be good sources for these items. Playmobil has some beautiful items. Lincoln Logs have a fort building set.

FOX

Foxes might be obtained in toyshops or gift shops.

FROG

Frogs may be obtained in toyshops or gift shops. Certain children have been totally charmed by these items.

GATE

Gates of all sorts may be obtained in toyshops, hobby shops that carry train sets and related items.

GOAT
Goats may be obtained in toyshops.
GOLD
Real gold may be obtained in rock shops, however it is cheaper and safer to spray paint a few small stones with gold spray paint.
HEART:
Hearts may be obtained in gift shops.
HORSE
Horses may be obtained in toyshops.
HOUSE
Houses may be obtained in gift shops, hobby shops that carry train sets, toyshops. The Oriental house I have in my collection was purchased in an aquarium store.
ICE
Plastic ice cubes may be obtained from photo supply catalogues.
INSECTS
Plastic insects may be obtained in toyshops and nature shops.
KING AND QUEEN
King and Queen figures may be obtained in fantasy role playing shops and gift stores.
LADDER
Playmobil has excellent ladders in their firemen set.
LAMB
Lambs may be obtained in toyshops.
LIGHT, LIGHTHOUSE
Lamps of various types might be obtained in toyshops, but are not generally available. I have a plastic army lantern and a antique lantern, but cannot recall how I obtained these. An inexpensive lighthouse may be obtained in an aquarium supply shop.
LION
Lions may be obtained in toyshops.
LIQUOR BOTTLES

Small liquor bottles, the real thing, may be obtained at liquor stores or markets. The contents should be poured out and replaced with colored water.

MAGICAL FIGURES:

Magician: Mickey Mouse as the Sorcerer's Apprentice is available at The Disney Store, Disneyland or Disneyworld and some toy stores. A more traditional magician (wizard) maybe obtained in fantasy role playing shops or possibly some toy stores.

Gods and Goddesses: Sandplay specialty catalogues used to carry these, but currently do not.

Ghosts: Playmobil; gift shops before Halloween.

Satanic objects: Fantasy role playing shops that carry Dungeons and Dragons games may have some objects; some Heavy Metal music fans may have access to objects that fit this obsession.

Wizards are easily obtained from gift and toy stores.

MAN

Lakeshore, Ther-a-Play Products and toyshops are good sources for these items.

MEDICAL

Playmobil has a hospital operating room, hospital bed and ancillary equipment.

MONKEY

Monkeys may be obtained in toyshops, jungle animal sets.

MOTHER

I found a classic mother and child in a cake decorating shop in Los Angeles. Gift shops may be a good source for this item. Lakeshore has ethnic family figures.

MOTORCYCLE

Toy motorcycles may be obtained in toyshops.

MOUNTAIN

Foam or plastic mountains may be obtained in hobby shops where train sets are featured. Playmobil lists a Rockies landscape.

MOUSE
A mouse may be obtained in gift shops that have small ceramic animals.
OAK
The best source of small realistic trees is hobby shops that feature train sets.
OCTOPUS
Gift shops near the coast might have this item. Occasionally a set will include this very powerful item. The ones I have were part of a deep-sea diver set. Lakeshore's catalog lists a "Tub of Sea Creatures" that includes 144 creatures from 44 species.
OWL
Ceramic owls may be obtained in gift shops.
PELICAN
Pelicans might be obtained in toyshops or gift shops.
PIG
Pigs may be obtained in toyshop farm animal sets.
PINE
The best source of small realistic trees is hobby shops where train sets are featured.
PIRATES
Pirates may be obtained from cake decorating supply shops and Playmobil. Playmobil has a beautiful pirate's secret Treasure Island.
PLANES
Toy military and commercial planes may be obtained in toyshops.
POLICEMAN/WOMAN:
Policemen may be obtained in toyshops included in police vehicle sets.
POND
I found a beautiful little ceramic pond in one of the Oriental shops downtown Los Angeles.
PRINCE AND PRINCESS
These items might be obtained from fantasy role playing shops.
QUEEN

These items may be obtained at fantasy role playing shops.

RABBIT
Rabbits may be obtained in toyshops or gift shops

RAT
Rats may be obtained in toyshops.

RELIGIOUS FIGURES
Buddha: These images may be obtained in the Oriental shops in larger cities and some gift shops. Disneyland has a gift shop in Adventureland that carried this item.

The Good Shepherd carrying a lamb. I have a nice Good Shepherd figure, but cannot recall how I obtained this. Try cake-decorating shops.

Jewish boy at his Bar Mitzvah (obtainable at cake decorating stores).

Joseph, Mary and Jesus: Playrooms catalog; gift shops before Christmas.

ROCK
Rock and mineral shops for collectors, a gift shops, and, of course, rivers, mountains, deserts. Children love geodes that are sliced open to reveal the crystal interior.

SATAN
Demonic figures might be obtained from a Dungeons and Dragons shop (fantasy role-playing shop) and toy stores.

SCARECROW
Ther-a-Play and some toy shops.

SEAHORSES
Seahorses may be obtained in gift shops near the coast.

SEAL
Seals may be obtained in toyshops, Lakeshore, and gift shops.

SERPENT
Serpents (snakes) may be obtained from toyshops.

SHARK
Sharks may be obtained from toyshops, Lakeshore has a "Tub of Sea Creatures."

SHEEP

Sheep may be obtained from toyshops, and gift shops.

SHELLS

Shells may be obtained at gift shops and hobby shops that carry items for parties. Gift shops near the coast carry these. Party shops may carry a few shells.

SHEPHERD

Playrooms used to carry a shepherd holding a lamb. I do not know where this can currently be obtained. A cake decorating shop might have this, or a Christian catalog or gift shop.

SHIPS

Ships may be obtained from toyshops, Playmobil has several including a wonderful Pirate ship.

SILVER

Ordinary rocks can be painted silver. Iron pyrite, obtainable in rock shops, looks like it might be silver.

SKELETON

I have some miniature plastic skeletons but cannot remember where I found these. Check gift shops before Halloween, or cake decorating shops in early autumn.

SKULL

Aquarium shops and some gift shops may carry this item.

SNAKE

Small plastic snakes may be obtained from toyshops.

SPACEMEN

Spacemen may be obtained from toyshops. Playmobil has astronauts.

SPHERE

Polished spherical stones may be obtained from some rock shops.

SPIDER

Spiders can be obtained from party supply shops (party favors of little boys) and some toyshops.

STAG

Stags may be obtained from toyshops and gift stores.

STAIRS

May be obtained as part of a playhouse. Stairs that are suitable as an image of ascension might have to be made.

STAR

Stars can be made of stiff cardboard, painted silver and mounted on thin dowels inserted into small wooden base.

STARFISH

Miniature starfish replicas used to be available through Playrooms. I do not know where they obtained these. Lakeshore offers a "Tub of Sea Creatures" that includes 44 species. Hopefully, the starfish is among these.

STREET SIGNS:

Lakeshore has traffic signs, not as small as I'd like for the sand tray, but of excellent quality. Some small, plastic signs are available through toyshops, as part of a set.

STONE

Rock and mineral shops for collectors, gift shops, and, of course, rivers, mountains, deserts.

SUN

I have a beautiful sun magnet from a kitchen accessory shop. Playrooms used to list a sun on a plastic rod with a base. It would be easy to make one out of Sculpy, bake it in the oven and paint it with water-based paint mixed with glue.

SWAN

Swans may be obtained from cake decorating supply shops, and hobby shops, such as Michael's that carry items related to weddings.

THRONE

I do not have a throne and am not certain where one could be obtained. Since it was referred to in *Sandplay Studies*, I assume that one was found or made.

TIGER

Tigers may be obtained from toyshops and gift shops.

TORTOISE

See Turtle.
TOWER
Towers may be obtained from fantasy role playing shops that contained Dragons and Dungeons figures. Playmobil has medieval towers.
TREASURE CHEST
A treasure chest may be obtained from Playmobil along with other items for their pirate's secret island. Cake decorating shops may have this item.
TREE
Hobby shops that carry train sets often have a nice selection of trees.
TRUCK
Trucks may be obtained from toyshops.
TUNNEL
Tunnels may be obtained from hobby shops that carry train sets.
TURTLE
Turtles may be obtained from gift or toyshops.
UNICORN
May be obtained from gift shops, and fantasy role playing shops.
UROBORUS
A uroborus used to be available from Playrooms catalog, maybe they can help you locate a manufacturer.
VILLAINS
Villains can be obtained in toyshops.
VOLCANO
I made volcanoes and painted them so from one side red lava was seen and from the other it was not. I made mind out of clay and made a mold so I could make several copies in plaster. If you shape individual volcanoes out of Sculpy (make them hollow) they may be hardened by baking in an oven. Then they can be painted with water-based paint mixed with white glue.
VULTURE
Vultures are hard to obtain. One may be obtained from certain toy stores. Playrooms catalog used to carry one.
WALL

Walls may be obtained in hobby shops that carry train sets.

WELL

This hard to find item might be obtained in a gift store.

WHALE

Whales can be obtained from nature shops, some toyshops, and Lakeshore.

WISE OLD MAN

Gift shops might be the best place to find an attractive old man figure. If you can find a Yoda (from Star Wars) or an ET figure, they will serve as wise old men. The old couple that I have was found in a discount store.

WISE OLD WOMAN

Gift shops might be the best place to find an attractive old woman figure. Lakeshore has family figure sets that include grandparents.

WITCH

A witch may be obtained from gift or toyshops, or fantasy role playing shops.

WOLF

Wolves might be obtained from gift or toyshops.

WOMAN

Mother figures are easily obtainable. Ther-a-Play and Lakeshore have Caucasian, Oriental, Black and Hispanic family figures. They also have a farmer's wife. I obtained a classic mother and child from a cake decorating supply shop. Gift shops may also be the source of maternal looking figures.

Miniature versions of the Barbie type dolls may suit the Hera type.

Miniature women athletes may represent the tomboy or Amazon type figure, I obtained some of these from a cake decorating supply shop, Ther-a-Play lists a horsewoman and a pony girl.

And, of course—discount stores, garage and yard sales. Happy hunting.

Glossary

anima/animus: The anima is the unconscious feminine component within a male. The animus is the unconscious masculine component within a female.

archetype: An archetype is an original model after which other similar objects are patterned.

cathect (cathected): To concentrate psychic energy on (a person, thing, or idea).

collective unconscious: Jung's theory that a person inherits, in the unconscious mind, memories of certain ancestral experiences, which effect behavior in the present.

compensation: A mechanism by which an individual seeks to make up for a real or imagined psychological defect by developing or exaggerating a psychological strength.

complex: A complex is an integration of impulses, ideas and emotions related to a particular idea or activity, such as the person's mother or sense of self.

constellate: to unite in or as a constellation; cluster.

container: The therapeutic alliance and safe holding area are referred to as "a container" by Jungians.

cosmic egg: The life principle.

divine child: The divine child is usually seen as an archetype of the Self.

extroversion: An attitude characterized by an interest in people or things outside of oneself. Dr. Jung was the first to identify extroversion and introversion and these are basic to his typology. See typology.

feeling (function): In Jungian typology there are four functions: feeling which is the polar opposite of thinking, and sensation which is the polar opposite of intuition. See typology.

feminine principle: As the in the Oriental notion of yin and yang in all things, objects and styles of play, can often be seen to represent the feminine principle which is creative, nurturing, containing, soft, yielding, vulnerability. Other association to the feminine principle are dark, mysterious, the unknown. The negative feminine is harsh, aggressive, cold, unyielding. Gardens, flowers, and containers are images associated with the feminine principle.

functions: In Jungian typology there are four functions: feeling which is the polar opposite of thinking, and sensation which is the polar opposite of intuition. See typology.

identification: Identification is a mainly unconscious process by which a person formulates a mental image of another person and then thinks, feels or acts in a way which resembles this image.

imago: In psychoanalysis this word refers to image, for example, a parental imago may be idealized.

imago mundi: An imago mundi is a world image.

individuation: In the process of individuation a person differentiates himself from others.

inflation: A person whose self-image is inflated thinks he can accomplish more or is entitled to more than his innate abilities, training or character would support.

introversion: A basic personality style in which one directs one's own interests to one's own experiences and feelings rather than to external objects, events or persons; a subjective personality style.

intuition (function): In Jungian typology there are four functions: feeling which is the polar opposite of thinking, and sensation which is the polar opposite of intuition. A person whose strength is in the intuition function often knows something without being able to tell another how he came to that conclusion. The sixth sense is a popular way of describing this function. See typology.

libido: In analysis this term refers to psychic energy, which comprises the loving, positive and creative energies; sexual energy.

mandala; A circular design containing concentric geometric forms and may contain images of deities. A mandala symbolizes the universe, totality or wholeness in Buddhism and Hinduism. In nature one can see spiral forms which may seem mandala-like.

masculine principle: As the in the Oriental notion of yin and yang in all things, objects and styles of play, can be seen to represent the masculine principle which is dominant, strong, assertive, given to leadership.

neurosis: Any of various mental dysfunctions characterized by guilt, anxiety, compulsions, phobias, depression, conversion reactions, etc.

numinous: Having a supernatural, , divine, mystical or spiritual effect.

objective psyche: During the process of Jung's exploration of consciousness and of the unconscioushe employed the term, the "objective psyche" to make clear his conviction that the inner world of the psyche is just as much a valid object of study as the outer world of material objects.

object relations: Object relations refer to an individual's responses to parental introjects.

omphalos: A navel or centerpoint that permits entrance into this deeper world, such as the Temple of Delphi in ancient Greece.

persona: The outer personality or facade presented to others.

projection: The unconscious process of attributing to other's one's own ideas, impulses, or emotions, especially when they are considered undesirable and provoke anxiety.

psychic image: An image that arises spontaneously from the unconscious.

Puer: Eternal youth. A man who has a Puer complex may be described as a Peter Pan type.

R-complex: The reptilian complex is the knot at the top of the brain stem. It governs primitive behaviors such as, territorial displays, rage, and sexuality. See Triune brain.

separation: In the process of separation and individuation a child must separate from his parents, especially from his mother.
Self: The Self consists of the conscious and unconscious minds. The ego complex is specific and unique to that individual, while the Self carries a full range of human potentialities.
Senex: The Senex is the archetype of the Old Man and contrasts with the Puer.
sensation (function): In Jungian typology there are four functions: feeling which is the polar opposite of thinking, and sensation which is the polar opposite of intuition. A person whose strength is in the sensation function depends heavily on the five senses. See typology.
shadow: The shadow consists of all the repressed, split-off and rejected parts of the personality. Not all shadow material is negative. Some individuals may repress or reject their good qualities.
superego: The part of the psyche which carries and enforces moral judgments; at an unconscious level it may block unacceptable impulses. This portion of the psyche may be filled with critical parental introjects.
symbol: An act or object that represents and unconscious desire.
symbols of transformation: With symbols of transformation there is an association with renewal and rebirth, for example, butterflies, cooking pots, a chalice.

transcendent principle: God, or the spiritual realm.
Terrible Mother: The dark side of the Great Mother archetype is destructive, rather than creative.

thinking (function): In Jungian typology there are four functions: feeling which is the polar opposite of thinking, and sensation which is the polar opposite of intuition. A person whose strength is in the thinking function depends heavily on his logical, rational ability as opposed to feeling. See typology.

threshold symbol: A door, bridge, gates, or other images that are a passage or link from one realm to another may be a threshold symbol.

trickster: The trickster is a more instinctual figure than the Hero archetype, and tends to be chaotic and amoral. He shifts from consciousness to a falling backward into the unconscious because of his primitive lack of development. This archetype's weaknesses are more readily apparent than those of the Hero, and may be exaggerated and publicly displayed in order to obtain the laughter of one's companions. The trickster, as a more primitive state of consciousness, represents the life of the body. He is associated with the fool and jester. Dr. Jung (1959) says that he often seems stupider than the animals, and gets himself into a series of ridiculous difficulties because of sheer unconsciousness and lack of relatedness. Surprisingly, the resulting behaviors may prove to be beneficial, simply because he is not usually evil so much as an animalistic super being. He fails to carry the instinctive wisdom of the animalworld in spite of his living closer to that realm. These defects are a result of the humanness of his nature. Dr. Jungfurther emphasizes an eagerness to learn about this psychic condition that is indicative of a great capacity for psychological development. When we work with delinquents we may run into behaviors that relate to this archetype.

triune brain: The reptilian complex is the knot at the top of the brain stem. It governs primitive behaviors such as, territorial displays, rage, and sexuality. This is the part of the brain we have in common with reptiles. The second part of the human brain is the affective brain, or the limbic system. We have this part in common with mammals. This portion of the brain is involved with feelings of nurturance, warmth and affection, and is involved in dreaming. The affective, or feeling brain is also called the mammalian brain. The newest portion of the brain is the neo-cortex. This portion is the part that governs our moral abilities and these need to be developed in early childhood, and strengthen during the latency and adolescent years. When there are liaisons to the forebrain (part of the neo-cortex) conscience that has been developed can be damaged and lost.

typology: Generally this means the study of types or symbols. In Jungian analytic psychology it means the construct of personality which uses the styles of extroversion and introversion as combined with the four functions: sensation, intuition, feeling and thinking from which individuals learn and make their choices about life.

unconscious (personal and collective): The personal unconscious is the sum of all the thoughts, memories, impulses, desires, feelings, etc. of which the individual is not conscious, but which influence the emotions and behavior. The collective unconscious is the Jungian theory that a person inherits, in the unconscious mind, memories of certain ancestral experiences, which effect behavior in the present.

union of opposites: The union of opposites, masculine and feminine energy, is the goal of individuation.

uroborus: The image of snake with its tail in its mouth is symbolic of cyclic manifestation and re-absorption.

Bibliography

Amatruda, Kate and Phoenix Helm Simpson, *Sandplay the sacred healing.* Novato: Trance*Sand*Dance*Press: 1997.

Axline, V.M., *Play therapy.* Boston: Houghton Mifflin, 1947.

_____, *Dibs: In search of self.* Boston: Houghton Mifflin, 1964.

Bachelard, G., *The psychoanalysis of fire.* Boston: Beacon Press, 1968

Baruch, D., *One little boy.* New York: Dell, 1952.

Bettelheim, B., *The uses of enchantment: The meaning and importance of fairy tales.* New York: Random House, 1975.

Bolen, J.S., *Goddesses in everywoman: A new psychology of women.* San Francisco: Harper and Row, 1984.

Bowyer, L.R., *The Lowenfeld World Technique.* Oxford: Pergamon Press, 1970.

Bradway, K., In *Sandplay studies.* San Francisco: C.G. Jung Institute, 1981.

Buhler, C. and G. Kelley, *The world test: A measurement of emotional disturbance.* New York: Psychological Corp., 1941.

Campbell, J., *The hero with a thousand faces.* Princeton: Princeton University Press, 1949.

Chappel, G.E., and Johnson, G.A. (1976) *Evaluation of cognitive behavior in the young nonverbal child.* Language speech and hearing services in the schools, 7, 17-27.

Cirlot, J.E., *A dictionary of symbols*, translated by Jack Sage. London: Routledge and Kegan Paul Ltd., 1962.

Cooper, J.C., *An illustrated encyclopaedia of traditional symbols.* London: Thames and Hudson, 1978.

Dement, W.and N. Kleitman, "Cyclic variations in EEG during sleep and their relation to eye movements, body mobility and dreaming," *Electroencephalography and Clinical neurophysiology*, 9:673-90: 1957.

Dundas, E., *Symbols come alive in the sand.* 552 Bean Creek Rd., #93, Scotts Valley, CA: Privately printed by the author, 1978.

Freud, A(1927), *The psychoanalytical treatment of children.* New York: International Universities Press, 1946.

_____, "An introduction to the techniques of child analysis," Nervous and mental disease monographs, No. 48,1928.

_____, *The ego and the mechanisms of defense.* London: Hogarth, 1937.

Gardner, R., *Handbook of play therapy.* Schaefer, C.E. and K.J. O'Connor, Eds. New York: John Wiley and Sons, 1983.

Gil, Eliana, *The healing power of play: Working with abused children.* New York: Guilford Press, 1991.

Ginott, H., *Group psychotherapy with children.* New York: Mc Graw-Hill, 1961.

Hammond, Mary, L., *Children of alcoholics in play therapy.* Pompano Beach: Health Communications, Inc., 1985.

Hillman, J., What does the psyche want?. Lecture given for the C.G. Jung Institute, Los Angeles, 1979.

Hills, C. and D. Rozman, *Exploring inner space.* Boulder Creek: University of the Trees Press, 1978.

Irvin, E., in *Handbook of play therapy.* Schaefer, C.E. and K.J. O'Connor, Eds.. New York: John Wiley and Sons, 1983.

Jernberg, A., *Theraplay.* San Francisco: Jossey-Bass, 1979.

Jolles, I., *The catalogue for the qualitative interpretation of the House-Tree-Person.* Los Angeles: Western Psychological Services, 1971.

Jourard, Sidney M., *The transparent self: self-disclosure and well-being.* Princeton: Van Nostrand, 1964.

Jung, C.G., In *The collected works of C.G. Jung.* Read, Forham, Adler, and McGuire, Eds.; Hull, trans. Princeton: Princeton University Press, Vol. 8, *On the nature of the psyche,* 1947/ 1954.

_____, *Memories, dreams, reflections.* New York: Pantheon Books, 1961. Also New York: Vintage Books, 1965.

_____, "On the psychology of the unconscious." In *collected works,* Vol. 7, R.F.C. Hull, translator: Princeton University Press, 1953.

_____, *The archetypes and the collective unconscious.* Vol. 9, part 1 *Collected works.* Princeton: Princeton University Press, 1959; 2nd ed., 1968.

_____, *Four archetypes*, R.F.C. Hull, trans.. Princeton: Princeton University Press, 1959.

_____, *Symbols of transformation.* R.F.C. Hull, trans.. Princeton: Princeton University Press, 1956.

Kalff, D.M. , "Symbolism and child analysis." A seminar given at the Footlighter's Child Guidance Clinic of the Hollywood Presbyterian Hospital, 1966a. Paper in the library of the C.G. Jung Institute Library, 10349 W. Pico Bl., L.A., CA.

_____, *The archetype as a healing factor.* Psycholgia, 1966b, 9, 177-184.

Kalverboer, A.F. Measurement of play: Clinical applications. In *Biology of play*, B. Tizard and D. Harvey, Eds., London: Heineman, 1979.

Kirsh, H., Ed., *The well-tended tree.* New York: G.P. Putnam's Sons, 1971.

Klein, M., Infant analysis, in *Contributions to psychoanalysis.* London: Hogarth Press, 1948.

Kramer, E., *Art as therapy with children.* New York: Schocken, 1971.

Largo, R.H., and Howard, J.A. (1979) "Developmental progression in play behavior of children between nine and thirty months: I: Spontaneous play and imitation. Developmental and medical child neurology, 21, 299-310.

Lewis, E., In T*he Lowenfeld world technique*. L.R. Bowyer, Ed.. Oxford: Pergamon Press, 1970.

Lowe, M. and Costello, A. J. *The symbolic play test*. National Foundation for Educational Research, 1976.

Lowenfeld, M., *The world technique*. London: George Allen and Unwin, 1979.

Luscher, M., *The Luscher color test*, trans. and ed. by Ian Scott. New York: Random House, 1969.

Machover, K. *Personality projection in the drawing of the human figure: A method of personality investigation*. Springfield: Thomas, pub., 1965.

MacLean, Paul D., *A triune concept of the brain and behavior*. Toronto: University of Toronto Press, 1973.

Magid, Ken and Carole A. McKelvey, *High risk: Children without a conscience*. New York: Bantam pub., 1988. Originally published in 1987 by M and M.

Mussen, P., *Child development and personality*. New York: Harper and Row, 1979.

Oaklander, V., *Windows to our children*. Moab: Real People Press, 1978.

Ogdon, D.P., *Psychodiagnostics and personality assessment: A handbook*. Los Angeles Psychological Services, 1981.

Ornstein, Robert E., *The psychology of consciousness*. New York: Harcourt, Brace Jovanovich, 1977.

Perry, J.W., *The far side of madness*. Englewood Cliffs: Prentice-Hall, 1974.

Rosenblatt, D. Developmental trends in infant play. In *Biology of play*. B. Tizard and D. Harvey, Eds.. London: Heineman, 1977.

Samples, Bob, *The metaphoric mind: a celebration of creative consciousness*. Reading: Addison-Wesley Publishing, 1976.

Sanford, J., *Dreams and healing*. New York: Paulist Press, 1978.

Schaefer, C.E. and K.J. O'Connor, Eds., *Handbook of play therapy*. New York: John Wiley and Sons, 1983.

Schwartz-Salant, N., *Narcissism and character transformation*. Toronto: Inner City Books, 1982

Signell, K., In *Sandplay studies*. San Francisco: C.G. Jung Institute, 1981.

Smith, Ed M., *Beyond tolerable recovery*. Campbellsville, KY: Alathia Inc., 1999. www.theophostic.com

Stein, M., Editor, *Jungian Analysis*. LaSalle and London: Open Court, 1982.

Charles Stewart, published in *Sandplay studies: Origins, theory and practice*. Bradway, et. al.. San Francisco: C.G. Jung Institute of San Francisco pub. 1981)

Sullwold, E., in *Jungian analysis*, M. Stein, Ed. London: Open Court, 1982.

_____, Eagle eye. In *Jungian analysis*, M. Stein, Ed. LaSalle and London: Open Court, 1982.

Terr, L.C., (1981) *Forbidden games: Post-traumatic child's play.* J. Amer. Acad. Ch. Psychiat., 20, 741-760.

Tresidder, Jack, *Symbols and their meanings.* London: Duncan Baird Pub., 2000.

von Franz, *Puer aeternus.* Santa Monica: Sigo Press, 1970.

Whitmont, E., *The symbolic quest: Basic concepts of archetypal psychology.* New York: Harper, 1969.

Wickes, F., (1927, D. Appleton and Co.) *The inner world of childhood.* New York: Appleton Century Croft, 1955.

Winnicott, D.W., (1941) The observation of infants in a set situation, in *Collected papers.* London: Tavistock, 1958.

_____, (1948) Paediatrics and psychiatry, in *Collected papers.* London: Tavistock, 1958.

Index

abandon, 12, 73
  -ed, 21, 23, 40, 226-228,
  reality, 12-13, 20, 47, 111, 160, 170-171, 176, 184, 189
abuse, 13, 23, 117, 127, 139, 161-162, 189, 197
  child, 6, 8-15, 17-22, 24-35, 37-43, 45, 48-49, 52-54, 57-63, 66, 69, 71, 73-75, 77-78, 84-86, 88, 93-94, 99, 103-105, 110-111, 114-117, 119-120, 122-124, 127, 130-131, 133-134, 137-141, 143-147, 151-154, 156, 158-159, 162, 169-173, 178, 180, 184-186, 188-190, 192-193, 195, 203, 209, 215, 217, 220, 224, 226-227, 229
  ritual, 21, 46, 127, 139, 162, 176
accept, 2, 20, 53, 60, 69, 71, 173
accident, 100, 102, 111
  prone, 93, 100, 102, 111
Adler, 156, 225
adolescent, 75, 124, 222
adopted, 32, 40, 69
aggression, 48-49, 83, 102, 121, 164, 172
  neutralizing, 102,
aggressive, 51-52, 62, 70, 90, 92-93, 101, 106, 114, 128, 131-132, 140, 218,
air, 41, 43, 120, 128, 130-131, 143-144, 153, 180, 183, 186,
  -craft, 204
  -plane, 55,
  spirit of the ___, 143-144,
Aladdin, 94, 146, 206,
alcoholic, 74, 99, 105, 136, 141, 143, 164,
Alice in Wonderland, 146, 152, 206
alien, 64, 66, 147

alligator, 91, 121, 137, 199, 201,
altered state, 11, 126, 152,
amazon, 194, 215,
amphibians, 121, 153,
angel, 121, 139, 174, 181, 201,
anger, 19, 54, 71, 91, 100, 102, 106, 110-111, 124, 134, 140, 171-172, 189
animal, 25, 41, 109, 122-123, 125, 135, 137, 141, 154, 156, 160, 165, 168, 175, 178, 193, 203, 205, 209-210,
  helpful, 5, 24-25, 28, 32, 89, 121-122, 126, 143, 145, 161, 177, 193
  pack, 141,
  predator, 122, 140, 153, 165, 193
  prehistoric, 133, 140, 203,
  prey, 90, 121-122, 126, 138, 143, 153, 160, 165, 184, 190,
  totemic, 122, 133, 162,
animus, 36, 84, 89, 99, 105, 108, 110, 143, 185, 194-195, 217,
Anubis, 141,
anxiety, 52, 59, 62, 73, 96, 219,
archetypal, 9, 14-16, 18-19, 22, 44, 48, 62, 66, 80-81, 88, 108, 112, 115-116, 122, 124, 135, 143, 146-148, 156-157, 159, 162-163, 166, 170-171, 185, 188, 194, 229,
  connection to joy, 62,
  maleness, 159,
  patterns, 8, 41, 60, 70, 166, 180, 194,
  styles of womanhood, 194,
archetype, 14-20, 40, 60, 75, 84, 108, 115, 120, 124, 127, 132-134, 136, 143, 145, 154, 163-164, 176, 180, 184, 187, 191-194, 217, 220-221, 226
  as dark and light, 15, 239
  of the Self, 16-18, 20, 22, 39-41, 60, 82, 89, 108-109, 115, 121, 124, 133, 136, 157, 170, 172, 182, 217
ark, 73, 123, 192, 197, 201-202

art, 6, 9, 12, 14, 19, 21, 25-26, 29, 35, 39, 82-83, 117, 119, 123, 155, 170, 226
  therapy, 6, 8-11, 13, 18-21, 25, 28-29, 33-34, 38-39, 41-42, 44, 46, 53-54, 57, 59, 65, 68-69, 72, 90, 102, 109, 111, 113, 117, 119, 139, 143, 170, 194, 198, 200, 206, 223-226, 228
Artemis, 194-195
ascension, 84, 142-143, 148, 159, 181, 213
asthma, 35-36
attachment, 68, 85, 154
attack, 49, 57, 59, 61, 64, 102, 114
authority, 128, 130-131, 143, 146-148, 169-170, 181, 184
avalanche, 123, 151
avoid, 4, 54, 189
Axline, 3, 12, 20, 114, 223
baby, 22, 25, 52, 61, 84, 86, 95, 124, 133, 202
Bachelard, 63, 223
basket, 26, 124, 202
Batman, 75, 146, 156, 163, 206
battle, 16, 66, 71-73, 99, 124, 152, 156, 190
beach, 33, 52-53, 86, 106, 124, 201, 225
bear, 84, 86, 89, 95, 122-123, 125, 202
  mother and baby, 86, 95
beaver, 125, 153, 202
bee, 125, 202
bell, 126, 202
Bettelheim, 12-13, 22, 104, 114-115, 153, 193, 223
bird, 58, 126, 142, 148, 202
birth, 14-15, 17, 134, 156, 173, 176, 180, 191
black, 59-60, 126-127, 131, 135, 157, 162, 171, 182-183, 198, 202, 215
block, 9, 70, 73, 106, 120, 185, 220,
blood, 38, 53, 127, 162, 172, 202,

blue, 10, 127-128, 135, 158, 170, 180, 198, 200
body, 46, 88, 120, 129, 135, 139-140, 157, 162, 166, 169, 175, 184, 188, 221, 224
Bolen, 194-195, 223
borderline, 43, 48, 143
bossy, 52, 99
bottles, 3, 25, 136, 161, 208-209
nursing, 3, 121
boundary, 58, 71, 74
  lack of, 1, 13, 39-40, 58-59, 134-135, 140, 151-152, 158, 163, 221
  setting, 54, 99, 149, 176
  violation, 58, 74
Bowyer, 6-7, 79, 88, 129, 148, 223, 227
boy, 21-22, 32, 42, 50-51, 55, 57-58, 64, 68, 74, 81, 84, 92-94, 114, 146, 151, 172, 174, 211, 223
Bradway, 7, 140, 146, 223, 228
brain, 1, 6, 46-47, 75, 82, 121, 128, 160, 170, 189, 195, 220-221, 227
  affective, 47, 82, 121, 149, 221
    left, 1, 22, 44, 48, 59, 68, 71-72, 80-83, 90-92, 95, 106, 108, 115, 128, 158, 169-170, 195
    R-complex, 46-47, 49, 82, 121, 137, 139, 142, 175, 220, , 237, 247
    right, 1, 6, 15, 20, 37, 44-47, 64, 67, 71-72, 76, 80-83, 86, 90, 92, 94-95, 97, 108, 110, 114, 116, 128, 169-170, 199-200, 206
  triune, 47, 121, 184, 220-221, 227
bride and groom, 82-83, 89, 159, 202
bridge, 4, 24, 74, 94-95, 102, 106-108, 111, 119, 128, 191, 202, 221
brown, 129, 135
Buddha, 161, 173, 211
Buhler, 33, 41, 49, 70-71, 129, 140, 148, 223
bull, 129, 203
bullying, 100, 102, 130

burial, 48, 53, 75, 86-88, 106, 108-109, 111, 124, 129-130, 133, 138, 143-144, 151, 187, 191-192
  as acceptance into the unconscious,
  pathological, 48, 79, 88, 141
  ritualistic, 23, 47, 63, 79, 86, 127, 150, 197
  bus, 130, 186, 203
butterfly, 130, 203
Campbell, 78, 111, 223
candles, 10, 63-64, 130, 150, 160
cannibal, 55, 107
captive, 97, 99, 101, 108, 111, 185
car, 75-76, 130, 186-187, 203
castle, 26, 94, 96-98, 106, 130-131, 136, 152, 157, 159, 162, 170, 186, 203
  mold, 106, 214,
cat, 47, 75, 122-123, 131, 146, 184, 203, 206
cathected, 41, 217
cauldron, 136
cave, 25, 33, 41, 82-84, 86, 107-109, 132-133, 144, 176, 186-187, 203
center, 32, 37, 40-41, 43-44, 48, 59, 61, 67, 70-71, 79, 82, 86-87, 90-91, 108, 116, 128, 132, 134, 154, 158-160, 162, 164, 169, 172, 175, 182, 189, 198, 200
  right of, 86, 95
chakra, 67, 127, 154, 158, 160, 167, 169, 172, 189, 195
chalice, 136, 220
change of state, 84, 107-108, 132, 149, 173
characterlogical, 107
Cheshire Cat, 146, 206
child, 6, 8-15, 17-22, 24-35, 37-43, 45, 48-49, 52-54, 57-63, 66, 69, 71, 73-75, 77-78, 84-86, 88, 93-94, 99, 103-105, 110-111, 114-117, 119-120, 122-124, 127, 130-131, 133-134, 137-141,

143-147, 151-154, 156, 158-159, 162, 169-173, 178, 180, 184-186, 188-190, 192-193, 195, 203, 209, 215, 217, 220, 224, 226-227, 229
-hood, 140, 193
abandoned, 13, 43, 85, 96, 122, 138, 143
competitive, 5, 53, 81, 99, 106, 198
dark, 13, 15-16, 19, 47, 60-62, 69, 75, 84-85, 88, 93, 108-109, 111, 124, 126-127, 133, 137-138, 146, 152, 158, 160, 162, 164, 174, 189, 192, 195, 218, 220
difficult, 17, 21, 31, 39-40, 52-53, 71, 74, 91, 94, 103, 113, 131, 152, 206
disturbed, 2, 21, 53, 75, 92, 127, 137, 139, 162
divine, 61-62, 116, 124, 127, 132-133, 136-137, 154, 162, 182, 217, 219
inner, 5, 12-15, 18, 36, 44-45, 61-62, 67, 73-74, 80, 84, 89-90, 93, 96, 99, 108-109, 111, 114-116, 124, 131-132, 142-143, 147, 150, 156-157, 159, 162, 187, 189-190, 192, 219, 225, 228-229
male, 10, 35, 68, 70, 75, 80-81, 84, 89-90, 102-105, 108, 111, 115, 124, 155, 163, 165, 176, 199, 217,
masochistic, 61-62, 130
neglected, 8, 13, 53, 99, 116, 178
non-verbal communication of, 1
poorly socialized, 51
repressed, 5, 13, 61, 93, 133, 138, 151, 220
resistant, 5
wounded, 43, 76, 88, 116
Children's Apperception Test, 32
Christ, 150, 161, 173
church, 133-134, 173, 203
Cinderella, 122, 146, 169, 206
Cinderella Complex, 169

circle, 36, 44, 86-87, 133-134, 144-145, 162, 173
  squared, 15
circumnambulation, 39, 169, 180
Cirlot, 139, 159, 183, 224
clam, 44, 111, 134, 176, 204
clay, 3, 19, 25, 27, 116, 143, 214
climb, 98
clown, 92, 134, 143, 145-146, 163, 204
color, 25, 53, 61, 67-68, 108, 127-129, 135, 151, 154-155, 158, 160, 167-170, 172, 189, 195, 227
combat, 71, 120, 123, 127
community, 29, 74, 110, 117, 126, 148, 194
  stage, 29, 42, 64, 74-76, 86, 110, 114, 132, 140, 148, 158, 167, 189, 191, 195
compensation, 130, 217
complex, 12, 14-15, 17-18, 31, 59, 62-63, 82, 88, 90, 99, 103-104, 114, 121, 159, 167, 169, 185, 217, 220-221
compliant, 61, 92, 160
compulsive, 3, 74
conflict, 2, 29, 31, 42, 83, 102, 124, 130, 137, 189-190
conjoint, 6, 32, 38, 44, 53, 64, 71
conscious, 6, 8, 12, 14, 18-19, 21-22, 43, 59, 72, 83, 85, 88, 93, 115, 128, 132, 143, 148, 157-158, 170, 175, 178, 180, 189, 220, 222, 227
consciousness, 8, 11, 14-16, 43, 80-81, 84, 100, 119-120, 122-123, 126, 128, 134-135, 152-154, 158-160, 163, 169-170, 174, 181-182, 184, 186, 188, 191-192, 219, 221, 227-228
  altered state of, 11, 126, 152
container, 9-10, 68, 74, 102, 116, 124, 136, 217
containment, 9, 132, 134, 144, 179, 191
contrasexual, 143

cooking utensils, 136
cosmic, 108, 122, 132, 134, 137, 144, 153, 162, 164, 180, 217
center, 32, 37, 40-41, 43-44, 48, 59, 61, 67, 70-71, 79, 82, 86-87, 90-91, 108, 116, 128, 132, 134, 154, 158-160, 162, 164, 169, 172, 175, 182, 189, 198, 200
cottage, 97, 136, 157, 204
courage, 146, 156, 166
cow, 136, 204
cowboys, 10, 26, 73, 92, 94, 163, 179
cowgirls, 195
crab, 121, 137, 164, 167, 180, 204
crafts, 3, 25
crash, 111, 120
creativity, 13, 40, 65, 81, 85, 89, 93, 103-104, 115, 120, 137-138, 149, 170-171, 189-191, 195
crocodile, 121, 137, 164, 167, 180, 204
crone, 193
cross, 134, 137, 151, 173
cross-gender identified, 32, 52
crucible, 136
cup, 136
danger, 74, 91, 172, 178, 182
dark, 13, 15-16, 19, 47, 60-62, 69, 75, 84-85, 88, 93, 108-109, 111, 124, 126-127, 133, 137-138, 146, 152, 158, 160, 162, 164, 174, 189, 192, 195, 218, 220
death, 15, 36, 38, 73, 87, 102, 111, 126-128, 130-132, 137-139, 152, 155-157, 159, 171-172, 176, 178-180, 190-191, 204
 and rebirth, 108-109, 111, 130, 132, 136, 138, 144, 151, 159, 172, 176, 220
deer, 33, 138, 145, 181, 204
defense, 11, 31, 126, 190, 224
 mechanisms, 11, 224

rigid, 11, 19, 70, 72, 96, 158
Dement and Kleitman, 16
demon, 121, 165
dependency, 103, 105, 117
depression, 11, 26, 54, 120, 126, 155, 185, 219
desert, 38, 76, 139
desolation, 139, 178, 187
destruction, 47, 54, 74, 111, 126, 149, 151, 172, 182, 185, 189, , 249
destructive, 20, 48-49, 51, 53, 58, 65, 70, 107, 109, 111, 114, 120, 126, 137, 149, 172, 174, 191, 220
developmentally disabled, 26
devil, 125, 139, 171, 204
devour, 71, 121, 139, 141, 144, 152, 184
diagnosis, 2, 32, 35
dinosaur, 140, 142, 205
disease, 88, 129, 155, 224
dishes, 3
disintegration, 155, 182
disorganized, 40-41, 94
diver, 107-108, 210
divine, 61-62, 116, 124, 127, 132-133, 136-137, 154, 162, 182, 217, 219
divorce, 36, 79, 82, 89
dog, 82, 87, 89, 92, 123, 141, 205
doll, 3, 25, 81, 88-89, 194, 198, 201
  broken, 34, 129, 182
  house, 3, 22, 25, 28, 48-51, 55, 81, 83-84, 94-95, 97, 114, 131, 136, 154, 157, 161, 176, 182, 198, 201, 208, 223, 227
donkey, 141, 205
dove, 107, 126, 142, 205
dragon, 82-83, 91, 99, 106-109, 121, 133, 137, 141-142, 174, 179, 205

dreams, 2, 6, 16, 18, 20-21, 43, 46, 57, 84, 111, 121, 143, 146, 150, 157, 161, 187, 225, 228
  and healing, 19, 65, 68, 125, 154, 158, 165, 174, 191, 228
drown, 100
drugs, 12, 178
Dundas, 29, 115, 125, 149, 168, 224
dungeon, 203
dwarves, 36, 82-84, 133, 143, 145, 161, 205
eagle, 123, 126, 143-144, 148, 179, 205, 228
earth, 15, 68, 120, 125, 127-129, 132, 134, 136-137, 143-144, 147, 150, 153, 155, 164, 173, 175, 177, 179-180, 185-186, 189, 205
  down to, 68
earthquake, 52-53
eat, 107-108
egg, 132, 134, 144, 180, 217
  cosmic, 108, 122, 132, 134, 137, 144, 153, 162, 164, 180, 217, 235,
ego, 3, 8, 11-13, 16-18, 20, 22, 25, 29, 31, 33, 39, 42-43, 49, 54, 57, 62, 75, 80, 82, 99, 105, 107-109, 115, 119, 123-124, 130, 132, 136, 142, 148, 151, 159, 167, 169-170, 183, 189-190, 220, 224
  -mind, 2, 9, 11, 14, 16, 19, 21, 41, 43, 47, 59, 82, 93, 113, 133, 143, 157, 175, 178, 188, 191, 214, 217, 222, 228
  building, 3, 95-96, 187, 201, 203, 207
  complex, 12, 14-15, 17-18, 31, 59, 62-63, 82, 88, 90, 99, 103-104, 114, 121, 159, 167, 169, 185, 217, 220-221
  development, 2, 6, 8, 11, 14, 16-18, 22-23, 39, 42, 85, 88, 90, 93, 99, 115, 124, 132, 134-135, 143, 154, 159, 163, 189-190, 193, 195, 221, 227
  formation, 31, 39, 119, 153, 159, 176
  loss of, 44, 88, 109, 120, 142, 152
  masculine, 13, 19, 33, 41-42, 58-59, 65, 75, 81-82, 85, 89, 92, 99, 105, 120, 125, 129-130, 134, 136-137, 143, 146, 148-

149, 155-157, 159, 162-164, 170, 172, 174, 176-177, 180-181, 183-188, 190, 199, 207, 217, 219, 222
  nascent, 12, 43
  overwhelmed, 27, 40, 42, 49, 54, 59, 75, 123
  rigid, 11, 19, 70, 72, 96, 158
  weak, 6, 119, 130, 145, 156, 176
elephant, 82, 89, 129, 145, 205
elf, 92, 143, 145-146, 161, 205
Eliade, 176
emotions, 10, 15, 37-38, 47, 93, 126-127, 160, 165-166, 169, 173, 191, 217, 219, 222
  and R-complex, 6, 7, 57, 8, 89
  associated with water, 123
  conflicting, 37-38
  associated with black, 126-127
  associated with blue, 10, 127, 128, 135, 158, 170, 180, 198
  associated with gray, 135, 155
  associated with green, 68, 154
  associated with ocean, 91, 109, 111, 161, 166, 207
  associated with pink, 102, 106, 108, 111, 135, 160
  associated with violet or lavender, 135, 160, 170, 189
  associated with yellow, 128
  primitive, 39, 46-47, 53-54, 65, 70, 72, 106-108, 111, 125, 127, 130, 134-135, 137-140, 142, 147, 149, 175, 178, 189, 195, 220-221
  violent, 69, 71-72, 142
energy, 5, 9, 14-16, 19, 39, 49, 59, 62, 65-66, 81, 83, 106, 108, 115, 127-130, 135, 137, 149, 152, 155, 157-158, 163-164, 169, 179, 182, 184-187, 217, 219, 222
  blocked, 5, 19, 34-35, 105, 108, 123, 128, 149, 158, 189, , 247, 249
  psychic, 13, 15-16, 19, 39, 43, 57, 59, 61, 79, 84, 102, 106, 123, 130, 135, 150, 157-158, 162, 172, 175, 184, 217, 219, 221

enmeshment, 106, 143, 148
entanglement, 140
entrapment, 106, 171, 180, 185
envy, 68, 154
Erikson, 7-8, 139, 185
eternal youth, 18, 120, 220
ethnic figures, 145, 202, 205
evil, 13, 16, 19, 76, 85, 90, 109, 121, 124-126, 135, 137, 142, 146,
    156-157, 171, 173-174, 178-179, 181, 187-189, 193, 221
externalize, 12, 114
extroversion, 17, 217, 222
failure, 5, 7, 11, 13
fear of, 5, 36, 53-54, 102-103, 124, 138, 140, 168
fairy, 12, 26, 97, 99, 101, 104, 126, 133, 143, 146, 152-153, 157,
    161, 185, 193, 206, 223
  godmother, 193
  tale, 11-12, 26, 97, 99, 101, 104, 111-112, 119, 147, 150, 185,
    191, 193
family, 3, 22, 26, 28, 32, 34-35, 37-39, 44-45, 52-54, 57, 59, 74, 76,
    79-80, 86, 95, 97, 99-100, 103, 115, 117, 123-124, 129, 133,
    138-139, 143-144, 146, 151, 157, 186, 194, 200-203, 205-
    207, 209, 215
  figures, 10, 26, 32, 34, 36, 40-41, 44, 52, 54, 59, 74-76, 78-80, 84,
    86, 89-90, 93, 96, 103, 108, 115, 133, 139, 141, 143, 145-
    147, 155-156, 160-161, 163, 172-173, 179-180, 194-195,
    198-199, 201-203, 205-209, 211, 214-215
  pathology, 7, 32, 48-49, 52-53, 59, 62, 70, 74, 110, 129, 140, 179
fantasy, 6, 9-13, 20, 31, 35, 41, 54, 102, 111, 139, 146, 160, 189,
    204-211, 214-215
  figures, 10, 26, 32, 34, 36, 40-41, 44, 52, 54, 59, 74-76, 78-80, 84, 86,
    89-90, 93, 96, 103, 108, 115, 133, 139, 141, 143, 145-147,

155-156, 160-161, 163, 172-173, 179-180, 194-195, 198-199, 201-203, 205-209, 211, 214-215
play, 6, 8-13, 18-21, 24, 26, 29, 31-33, 39-43, 45, 47, 50, 52, 54, 57, 63-64, 67, 69-72, 74-76, 86, 90, 92-94, 102, 106, 113-114, 116, 119-120, 122, 132-133, 135, 138-141, 149-150, 163, 167, 171, 179, 194, 198, 200, 205-206, 218-219, 223-229,
father, 16, 34-36, 38, 58, 64, 69-71, 76, 79, 84, 88-89, 91-93, 95, 99-101, 103, 106, 108, 110-111, 146, 148, 150, 159, 162-163, 167-168, 170, 174, 184, 186, 192, 194, 207,
   -complex, 12, 14-15, 17-18, 31, 59, 62-63, 82, 88, 90, 99, 103-104, 114, 121, 159, 167, 169, 185, 217, 220-221
   adoptive, 40, 42, 69-70,
   archetype, 14-20, 40, 60, 75, 84, 108, 115, 120, 124, 127, 132-134, 136, 143, 145, 154, 163-164, 176, 180, 184, 187, 191-194, 217, 220-221, 226
   loss of, 44, 88, 109, 120, 142, 152
   separating from,
feeling, 3, 5, 21, 43, 53, 56, 68, 95, 100, 103, 130, 132, 137, 140, 145-146, 149, 152-154, 180, 187, 218, 220-222
   function, 18, 33, 146, 169, 172, 193, 195, 218-221
   lack of __, 1, 13, 39-40, 58-59, 134-135, 140, 151-152, 158, 163, 221
   of insecurity, 68, 154
   unacceptable, 12, 114-115, 138, 148, 220
feminine, 13, 19, 33, 37, 44, 68, 70, 74, 81-83, 89, 93, 103, 105, 108-110, 122, 124, 132, 134-137, 146-147, 151-154, 156, 159-160, 164, 166, 168-171, 174, 176-177, 180-188, 190-193, 199, 217-218, 222
   creativity and struggle, 16, 29, 42, 64, 67, 68, 86, 103, 109, 110, 124, 156, 157, 179, 189

principle, 37, 65, 83, 103, 108, 122, 124, 132, 135-136, 143-144, 148-149, 151-152, 154-155, 159-160, 163-164, 166, 168-171, 174, 176, 182, 184-185, 187-188, 191, 217-220
  principle as dark and light,
  wisdom, 84, 115, 122, 125-126, 128-129, 135, 138, 142, 145, 155, 157, 162, 165-168, 177, 184, 188, 192, 221
fence, 10, 33, 70, 71, 73, 148, 149, 152, 177, 190, 207
  without gates, 70-71, 148
fertility, 14, 121, 131, 137, 144, 150, 153-154, 157, 165-166, 168-169, 171, 181, 188
fight or flight, 122
fighting, 29, 64, 68, 71, 75-76, 82, 93, 114, 205
phase, 8, 29, 68, 104, 152
figures, 10, 26, 32, 34, 36, 40-41, 44, 52, 54, 59, 74-76, 78-80, 84, 86, 89-90, 93, 96, 103, 108, 115, 133, 139, 141, 143, 145-147, 155-156, 160-161, 163, 172-173, 179-180, 194-195, 198-199, 201-203, 205-209, 211, 214-215
  religious, 13, 18, 40, 64, 73, 114, 119, 123, 132-134, 172, 177, 181, 183, 193, 211
fire, 25, 33, 63, 65, 68, 130, 149-150, 153, 172, 177, 180, 183, 189-190, 223
  and God, 183,
  setting, 54, 99, 149, 176
  trial by, 65, 149
fish, 26, 33, 85, 123, 139, 150, 167, 191-192, 207
flags, 86, 151, 207
flood, 6, 43, 103, 123-124, 143, 151, 191
flower, 135
food, 81-82, 104, 144, 151-152, 165, 167, 205, 207
  and neglect of child,
forest, 94-95, 97-99, 103-104, 115, 145, 152, 187
  as a place of trial,

enchanted, 97-98, 152
fortifications, 152, 186, 190, 207
four, 7, 10, 16, 21-22, 31-32, 34, 42-43, 45, 59, 99, 116, 124, 129, 144-145, 152-153, 170, 175, 180-181, 184-185, 193-194, 197, 218, 220-222, 226
symbolism associated with, 2, 88, 152, 157, 171, 176, 182, 226
fox, 153, 207
Freud, 2, 11, 16, 20, 22, 46, 82, 114, 224
  Anna, 2, 11, 20, 114
frog, 123, 125, 153-154, 207
and sexuality, 129, 220-221
G.I. Joe, 146
games, 2-8, 11, 24, 26, 29, 51, 90, 99, 114, 116, 134, 139, 159, 197-198, 201, 203, 206, 209, 229
  therapeutic, 3-6, 9, 12, 17, 20-21, 25, 29, 50, 53, 62, 70, 93, 112, 119, 187, 197, 217
garden, 37, 151, 154
Gardner, 5, 224
gate, 154, 181, 207
ghost, 162
gifted, 104
gifts, 78, 85, 90
Gil, 3, 25, 69, 74, 224
Ginott, 6, 225
girl, 32, 37, 44-45, 52, 59, 79, 81-84, 87-89, 93, 100-101, 103-104, 108-109, 111, 115-116, 120, 189, 195, 215
goat, 155, 208
God, 15-16, 23, 61, 121, 128, 136, 139, 144, 148-149, 153, 161, 167, 173-176, 182-184, 187, 192, 220
  and three, 69, 117
goddess, 127, 144, 149-150, 164, 167, 174
Goddesses in Everywoman, 194, 223

gold, 98, 155, 186, 195, 208
Gould, 127, 197
grandmother, 54-55, 94, 192-193
gray, 135, 155
greed, 105, 121, 125, 137, 144, 147, 168, 186, 193
  and desire, 90
grotto, 43-44
guilt, 11, 53, 89, 219
Hampden-Turner, 47
Hansel and Gretel, 104, 140, 206
healthy, 3, 90, 106, 115, 148, 179
heart, 9, 12, 22, 36, 67-68, 119, 147, 154-156, 208
Henry, 48
hero, 12, 15, 87, 109, 111-112, 126, 128, 131, 134-135, 142, 146-147, 156, 159, 162-163, 168, 177, 191, 193, 221, 223,
  -king, 36, 129, 131, 143, 148, 150, 159, 161-163, 169-171, 208
  myth, 31, 78, 96, 108-109, 123, 133, 165
Hero with a Thousand Faces, The, 112, 223
heroic, 13-14, 34, 87, 156, 163
heroine, 44, 89, 99, 111, 146-147, 163
hieros gamos, 159
Hillman, 15, 225
Hills, 128, 132, 135, 158, 189, 225
Histrionic Personality, 158
honor, 44, 155
horse, 38, 84-85, 111, 157, 165, 168, 188, 208
  as libidinal symbol
  representing the base instincts,
  representing the spiritual,
  white, 25, 37, 50, 59-61, 84-85, 87, 111, 132, 135, 142-143, 147, 157, 160, 169, 175, 183, 191-193, 198, 206, 214
  white and black,

house, 3, 22, 25, 28, 48-51, 55, 81, 83-84, 94-95, 97, 114, 131, 136, 154, 157, 161, 176, 182, 198, 201, 208, 223, 227
  doll, 3, 25, 81, 88-89, 194, 198, 201
  symbolizing the body,
House-Tree-Person, 28, 186, 225
Human Figure Drawing, 33, 39, 42, 69, 90
ice, 158, 179, 191, 208
identity, 29, 36, 41-42, 58, 60, 103, 106, 134, 151, 190, 241, 243, 249
  loss of, 44, 88, 109, 120, 142, 152
illumination, 132, 150, 192
imago mundi, 154, 218
impulsive, 170
incest, 140
incorruptibility, 155, 188
Indian, 141
indigo, 135, 158
individuation, 9, 15, 19, 39, 58, 84, 131, 156, 179, 184, 189-190, 218, 220, 222
inexhaustible supply, 136
infant, 17, 32, 40, 42, 52, 59-60, 90, 92, 124, 134, 144, 158, 226, 228
  neglected, 8, 13, 53, 99, 116, 178
infantile, 104
inferior, 156, 178, 195
  -ity, 169
infinity, 128, 133
inflation, 120, 170, 185, 218
initiation, 108, 130, 132, 159
insects, 158, 208
insecurity, 68, 147, 154
instinct, 137, 146, 167
  herd, 167
  mastery over, 115

intelligence, 32-33, 40-41, 52, 64, 70, 76, 126, 141, 165, 168
  low, 38, 52, 99, 141, 187
interpersonal, 19, 22, 32, 190
  struggles, 16, 42, 190
interpret, 2, 12, 22, 59, 74, 100, 105, 115, 150
intimacy, 5, 194
  fear of, 5, 36, 53-54, 102-103, 124, 138, 140, 168
intrapsychic, 11, 13, 19, 32, 90, 110-111, 130, 138, 169, 171-172, 180, 190
introject, 108, 122, 131, 150, 152, 159, 193
introversion, 17, 128, 217-218
intuition, 41, 43, 153, 180, 218, 220-222
invader, 64, 131
Irvin, 6, 225
island, 90, 97-98, 104, 178, 210, 214
Jacobi, 132
Jewish, 151, 172, 183, 199, 211
Jolles, 170, 225
journey, 87, 111-112, 158, 162
joy, 19, 62, 66, 95, 126, 130, 134, 145, 155-156, 172-173, 187
Jung, 13-18, 21, 31, 39, 43, 47, 59, 80, 84, 88, 96, 99, 111, 119, 121, 135, 138, 140, 143, 149-150, 157, 162-163, 171, 175, 178, 181-184, 187, 192-193, 195, 217, 219, 221, 223, 225-226, 228
Kalff, 7, 9-10, 17-18, 22, 28-29, 40-41, 74, 110, 115, 148, 167, 170, 172, 178-179, 226
kettle, 44, 136
kinesthetic, 9
Kinetic Family Drawing, 28
king, 36, 129, 131, 143, 148, 150, 159, 161-163, 169-171, 208
  and queen, 131, 148, 159, 169, 171, 208
Fisher, 150
Klein, 11, 20, 226

Kramer, 4, 226
kundalini, 174, 179-180
labyrinth, 133, 159, 180
ladder, 84, 98, 133, 159-160, 173, 181, 185, 208
lake, 160, 167, 169, 183
lamb, 160-161, 173, 176-177, 208, 211-212
latency, 21, 222
left, 1, 22, 44, 48, 59, 68, 71-72, 80-83, 90-92, 95, 106, 108, 115, 128, 158, 169-170, 195
  side, 15, 22, 25, 44, 55, 59, 62, 64, 71-72, 75, 81-82, 85, 88, 90, 92-93, 95, 108, 110, 127-128, 149, 157-158, 162, 164, 169-170, 183, 189, 192-193, 214, 220, 228
  side and the past,
Lewis, 7, 79, 88, 129, 227
libidinal, 19, 58-59, 84, 89, 123, 149, 157, 179
libido, 169, 185, 189, 219
life and death, 157
light, 15-16, 60-61, 64, 84, 93, 113, 126, 135, 138, 150, 157, 160, 162, 164, 168, 174, 189, 192, 208
  associated with the spiritual, 120, 160
lighthouse, 160, 208
limbic system, 47, 221,
lion, 123, 132, 147, 161, 184, 188, 208
Lowenfeld, 6, 223, 227
luminous bodies, 183
Lusher, 127, 129, 155
Machover, 90, 227
MacLean, 46-47, 227
magic, 87, 89, 97, 131-132, 160-161, 189, 193
  helper, 87, 89, 121
magician, 161, 193, 209
maiden, 97, 109-110, 122, 142, 147, 193

male-female relationship, 103, 106
mammals, 5, 121-122, 125, 221
mandala, 39, 162, 181, 219
masculine, 13, 19, 33, 41-42, 58-59, 65, 75, 81-82, 85, 89, 92, 99, 105, 120, 125, 129-130, 134, 136-137, 143, 146, 148-149, 155-157, 159, 162-164, 170, 172, 174, 176-177, 180-181, 183-188, 190, 199, 207, 217, 219, 222
  identity, 29, 36, 41-42, 58, 60, 103, 106, 134, 151, 190
  principle, 37, 65, 83, 103, 108, 122, 124, 132, 135-136, 143-144, 148-149, 151-152, 154-155, 159-160, 163-164, 166, 168-171, 174, 176, 182, 184-185, 187-188, 191, 217-220
  symbol, 14, 18, 22, 31, 41, 44, 65, 67, 82, 84-85, 103, 107, 109, 119, 123-125, 128, 130-134, 136-137, 141-143, 147, 149-150, 154, 157, 159-160, 166, 173-174, 177-179, 181-182, 184, 187-188, 220-221
masochistic, 61-62, 130
mastery, 9, 12, 25, 31, 109, 114-115, 134, 186
maternal, 8, 41, 58-59, 62, 75, 84, 124, 127, 134, 144, 190, 193, 215
matrix, 8, 41, 43, 58, 124, 134, 144, 190
maturation, 21, 32
meat cleaver, 52
menstrual cycle, 103
mermaid, 147, 206
mirror, 61,
moat, 106, 111, 131
monkey, 47, 123, 163, 209
monster, 71, 75, 108, 111, 133
moon, 129, 175-177, 182-183
moral, 16, 124, 135, 187, 192, 220, 222
  development, 2, 6, 8, 11, 14, 16-18, 22-23, 39, 42, 85, 88, 90, 93, 99, 115, 124, 132, 134-135, 143, 154, 159, 163, 189-190, 193, 195, 221, 227

mother, 7, 14-15, 31, 34-36, 38, 42-45, 49-50, 53-55, 58-59, 61, 68-71, 75-76, 78, 84-86, 88-89, 91, 94-96, 99, 101-104, 106, 108, 111, 116, 120, 125, 127, 132, 136-137, 140, 143-144, 146-148, 152, 154, 157, 159, 163-164, 167-168, 170-171, 176, 179-180, 184, 186-188, 190-194, 209, 215, 217, 220
  -complex, 12, 14-15, 17-18, 31, 59, 62-63, 82, 88, 90, 99, 103-104, 114, 121, 159, 167, 169, 185, 217, 220-221, 235
  -complex and eating disorders,
  -hood, 140, 193,
  and child unity, 111, 188
  archetype, 14-20, 40, 60, 75, 84, 108, 115, 120, 124, 127, 132-134, 136, 143, 145, 154, 163-164, 176, 180, 184, 187, 191-194, 217, 220-221, 226
  death __, 15, 36, 38, 73, 87, 102, 111, 126-128, 130-132, 137-139, 152, 155-157, 159, 171-172, 176, 178-180, 190-191, 204
  devouring, 70, 106, 137, 139-140, 164, 175, 184, 188
  earth, 15, 68, 120, 125, 127-129, 132, 134, 136-137, 143-144, 147, 150, 153, 155, 164, 173, 175, 177, 179-180, 185-186, 189, 205
  great, 14, 22-23, 39, 42, 54, 74, 76, 81, 84-85, 105, 108, 122, 127, 135-137, 140, 143-144, 146, 148, 151-152, 156, 161, 166-167, 175, 177, 184, 186, 188, 191-193, 199, 220-221
  negative, 15, 57, 65, 70, 84, 88-89, 99-100, 108, 123, 130-131, 142, 147-149, 152, 155, 164, 168, 175, 178, 185, 190, 193, 195, 218, 220
  over-protective, 58
  separating from,
  single parent, 78
  Terrible, 75, 108, 127, 137, 144, 161, 164, 167, 180, 184, 190, 220,
  witch __, 15, 97, 140, 143, 147, 152, 192-193, 206, 215
motorcycle, 25, 41-42, 130, 164, 209
mountain, 25, 97-98, 164, 175, 182, 190, 209

mouse, 44, 86, 147, 161, 165, 209-210
Multiple Personality Disorder, 21
music, 3, 24, 128, 209
Mussen, 17, 227
myth, 31, 78, 96, 108-109, 123, 133, 165
personal, 11, 15-16, 19, 22, 31, 88, 99, 112, 123, 130, 133, 144-145, 148, 151, 153, 157, 163-164, 166-167, 170, 175, 177, 184, 186, 188, 194-195, 222
Narcissism and Character Transformation, 60, 228
narcissistic, 5, 59-61, 88, 105, 120, 124, 147, 185, 193
  character disorder, 60
Native American, 94, 111, 125, 138, 141, 143, 146, 148, 157, 176, 195, 199, 206
Neumann, 7, 183
nourishment, 126, 136, 144, 153, 173
numinous, 18, 149, 166, 190, 219
nurturance, 25, 45, 61, 90, 166, 221
  need for, 3, 12-13, 25, 29, 31, 34, 59, 86, 90, 133-134, 138, 144, 148, 152
oak, 166, 187, 210
Oaklander, 3, 6, 227
object, 7-8, 13, 15, 24, 28, 41, 52, 75-76, 88, 94, 103, 119, 129, 134, 140, 147, 155, 219-220
  constancy, 52, 76, 164
  relations, 8, 13, 219
  objects, 2-3, 5-7, 10, 12-15, 19, 21, 24-27, 33, 41, 43-44, 52, 54, 61-62, 70, 75-76, 81, 96, 114, 122, 129, 140, 150, 155, 162, 167, 170, 175, 178, 189, 195, 209, 217-219
  for sandplay, 52, 163, 206
obsessive, 26, 47, 52, 71-72, 114, 149
ocean, 91, 101, 109, 111, 150, 160, 166, 174, 177, 182, 191, 207
  -ic consciousness,

and unconscious, 43, 157-158, 220
octopus, 84, 89, 91, 101-102, 106, 108, 121, 137, 164, 167, 180, 210
Oedipal, 11, 62
Ogdon, 170, 227
omphalos, 132, 164, 182, 219
opposites, 18, 64, 128, 151, 159, 174, 182, 184, 188, 222
oral, 55, 104-105, 107, 121, 139, 144, 175, 245
  greed, 105, 121, 125, 137, 144, 147, 168, 186, 193
  incorporation, 139, 144
orange, 135, 167
  associated with appetite,
owl, 44, 125-126, 165, 167-168, 210
paradise, 63, 126, 154
paradisiacal state, 122, 134, 173
parent, 12, 34-36, 38, 43, 57, 60, 62, 78, 82, 89, 114, 131, 141, 143, 165, 178, 185, -246, 248
  inner, 5, 12-15, 18, 36, 44-45, 61-62, 67, 73-74, 80, 84, 89-90, 93, 96, 99, 108-109, 111, 114-116, 124, 131-132, 142-143, 147, 150, 156-157, 159, 162, 187, 189-190, 192, 219, 225, 228-229
  narcissistic, 5, 59-61, 88, 105, 120, 124, 147, 185, 193
  rejecting, 8, 108
  single, 9, 26, 32, 43, 55, 78, 106, 152, 186
passion, 65, 108, 149, 168, 172, 189-190
passive-aggressive, 92
paternal, 148
  principle, 37, 65, 83, 103, 108, 122, 124, 132, 135-136, 143-144, 148-149, 151-152, 154-155, 159-160, 163-164, 166, 168-171, 174, 176, 182, 184-185, 187-188, 191, 217-220
pathology, 7, 32, 48-49, 52-53, 59, 62, 70, 74, 110, 129, 140, 179
peace, 114, 128, 137, 142, 173
peers, 70, 94

lack of acceptance by,
pelican, 168, 210
perpetrator, 70, 131, 140, 175
Perry, 20, 75, 228
personality, 3-4, 12, 16-18, 20-21, 43-44, 48, 58, 61, 75, 80, 84-85, 89, 93, 96, 103, 108, 114-115, 120, 124, 128, 130-133, 138-139, 143-145, 147-148, 154, 156, 158, 164, 170-171, 189, 195, 218-220, 222, 227
   type, 9, 14-15, 17, 25, 43, 53, 57, 71, 76, 92, 101-102, 120, 124, 130-131, 140, 147, 149, 156-157, 162, 167, 171, 177, 180, 186, 189, 194-195, 215, 220
phallic, 48, 55, 143, 156, 185
pig, 14, 168, 183, 210
pilgrimage, 158
pilot, 55
pink, 102, 105-108, 110-111, 135, 160, 169
planet, 64, 90, 190
play, 6, 8-13, 18-21, 24, 26, 29, 31-33, 39-43, 45, 47, 50, 52, 54, 57, 63-64, 67, 69-72, 74-76, 86, 90, 92-94, 102, 106, 113-114, 116, 119-120, 122, 132-133, 135, 138-141, 149-150, 163, 167, 171, 179, 194, 198, 200, 205-206, 218-219, 223-229
   compulsive, 3, 74
   fantasy, 6, 9-13, 20, 31, 35, 41, 54, 102, 111, 139, 146, 160, 189, 204-211, 214-215
   floor, 24, 26, 198
   need for privacy during, 86
   of boys, 74, 124
   poorly organized, 50, 94
   posttraumatic, 3, 69, 74, 229
   ritualistic, 23, 47, 63, 79, 86, 127, 150, 197
   sex, 28, 153, 163

therapeutic, 3-6, 9, 12, 17, 20-21, 25, 29, 50, 53, 62, 70, 93, 112, 119, 187, 197, 217
unproductive, 106
poison, 20, 57, 161, 174, 178-179
pond, 82, 84-85, 97-98, 160, 167, 169, 191, 210
Post Traumatic Stress Disorder, 21
power, 4, 9, 11-12, 20-21, 46-47, 54, 60, 64-65, 68, 70, 82-83, 86, 92, 99, 119-120, 127, 130-132, 134, 136, 142-143, 146-147, 149-150, 153, 156, 161-162, 164, 167, 170-171, 173-175, 178-181, 184-187, 189-190, 192-193
predator, 122, 140, 153, 165, 193
pretend, 8, 11
primary process, 16, 20
primitive, 39, 46-47, 53-54, 65, 70, 72, 106-108, 111, 125, 127, 130, 134-135, 137-140, 142, 147, 149, 175, 178, 189, 195, 220-221
  brain, 1, 6, 46-47, 75, 82, 121, 128, 160, 170, 189, 195, 220-221, 227
  drawing, 3, 9, 11, 28, 33, 39, 42, 52, 55, 69, 90, 99-100, 115-116, 171, 227
prince, 97-98, 127, 159, 169, 210
princess, 97-98, 169, 193, 210
prison, 131
projection, 9, 60, 192, 219, 227
protagonist, 66, 138, 157, 172, 192
psyche, 3, 6, 9, 11, 13-15, 17-18, 20-21, 41-43, 53, 57, 74, 78-79, 87-88, 93, 99, 103, 111, 115, 121, 124-125, 128, 149, 153-154, 156, 162, 169, 171, 174, 183, 185-187, 190, 219-220, 225, 246, 252
  and healing, 19, 65, 68, 125, 154, 158, 165, 174, 191, 228
  inaccessible aspects of, 185
  language of, 2, 9, 14

movement of, 5, 16, 189
parent's, 34, 36, 43, 57, 62, 82, 89, 114
rejected parts of, 13, 220
psychic, 13, 15-16, 19, 39, 43, 57, 59, 61, 79, 84, 102, 106, 123, 130, 135, 150, 157-158, 162, 172, 175, 184, 217, 219, 221
  attack, 49, 57, 59, 61, 64, 102, 114
  burden, 13, 42, 45, 82, 115, 141
  energy, 5, 9, 14-16, 19, 39, 49, 59, 62, 65-66, 81, 83, 106, 108, 115, 127-130, 135, 137, 149, 152, 155, 157-158, 163-164, 169, 179, 182, 184-187, 217, 219, 222
psychotic, 48, 74, 76, 137, 143
puberty, 103, 179
puer, 18, 120, 164, 176, 179, 220, 229
purple, 135, 160, 170, 189
quadrants, 22, 170
quaternary, 152-153, 180
queen, 131, 147-148, 159, 169-171, 193, 206, 208, 210,
Queen of Hearts, 147, 206
quicksand, 106, 137, 140, 164, 171, 180, 247
R-complex, 46-47, 49, 82, 121, 137, 139, 142, 175, 220
rabbit, 44, 92, 165, 171, 211
rage, 10, 19, 34-35, 48-49, 51, 53-56, 65, 70, 75, 93, 102, 106-108, 111, 114, 121, 130, 137-140, 142-143, 151, 172, 175, 189, 220-221
  blocked, 5, 19, 34-35, 105, 108, 123, 128, 149, 158, 189
  oral sadistic, 55, 107, 139, 175
  primitive, 39, 46-47, 53-54, 65, 70, 72, 106-108, 111, 125, 127, 130, 134-135, 137-140, 142, 147, 149, 175, 178, 189, 195, 220-221
repressed, 5, 13, 61, 93, 133, 138, 151, 220
Rapunzel, 99-101, 109, 111, 131, 185
rat, 171, 211

rebirth, 15, 58, 82, 108-109, 111, 123, 125, 130, 132-133, 136, 138, 144, 151, 159, 164, 168, 171-172, 176, 187, 191-192, 220
red, 5, 108, 135, 140, 151, 169-170, 172, 193, 198, 214
regeneration, 123, 126, 129, 134, 138, 171
regressive, 47, 76, 85, 103, 109, 111
rejection, 56, 170
  of child, 2, 11, 13, 140, 224
relationship, 3, 5, 8, 11, 18, 28, 44, 59, 76, 84, 86, 88, 103, 106, 122, 143, 148, 162, 185-186, 195
  building, 3, 95-96, 187, 201, 203, 207
religious, 13, 18, 40, 64, 73, 114, 119, 123, 132-134, 172, 177, 181, 183, 193, 211
renewal, 41, 58, 68, 84, 89, 130, 136, 144, 153-154, 164, 168-169, 179, 181, 187, 191, 220
repetition, 3, 15, 20-21, 74
  compulsion, 3, 20-21, 70, 74
repress, 220
  -ed, 21, 23, 40, 226-228
reproachmont, 86
reptiles, 16, 121, 153, 221
resistance, 2, 51, 53-54, 73, 105, 185, 187
resolution, 55, 66, 74, 76, 110, 114, 142
resurrection, 125, 130, 172
right, 1, 6, 15, 20, 37, 44-47, 64, 67, 71-72, 76, 80-83, 86, 90, 92, 94-95, 97, 108, 110, 114, 116, 128, 169-170, 199-200, 206
  brain, 1, 6, 46-47, 75, 82, 121, 128, 160, 170, 189, 195, 220-221, 227
  side, 15, 22, 25, 44, 55, 59, 62, 64, 71-72, 75, 81-82, 85, 88, 90, 92-93, 95, 108, 110, 127-128, 149, 157-158, 162, 164, 169-170, 183, 189, 192-193, 214, 220, 228
rigid, 11, 19, 70, 72, 96, 158,
  defenses, 13, 19, 52, 70, 123, 131, 152

ritual, 21, 46, 127, 139, 162, 176
ritualistic, 23, 47, 63, 79, 86, 127, 150, 197
  play, 6, 8-13, 18-21, 24, 26, 29, 31-33, 39-43, 45, 47, 50, 52, 54, 57, 63-64, 67, 69-72, 74-76, 86, 90, 92-94, 102, 106, 113-114, 116, 119-120, 122, 132-133, 135, 138-141, 149-150, 163, 167, 171, 179, 194, 198, 200, 205-206, 218-219, 223-229
river, 82, 94, 106-107, 167, 173, 182-183, 191
rock, 10, 43, 173, 182-183, 208, 211-213
Rorschach, 32
rulership, 130-131
  sacred, 8, 80, 133-134, 153, 162, 175-176, 182, 187, 190, 223, 248
  powers, 49, 97, 109, 121, 126, 129-130, 138, 142, 146-147, 160, 173, 176, 181
space, 7-10, 19, 24, 26, 71, 81, 90, 94, 162, 166, 179-180, 190, 225
sadistic, 55, 61-62, 72, 107, 139, 175
sadomasochistic, 102, 185
sand, 4, 6-8, 10-12, 21-22, 24-26, 28, 30, 32-33, 35, 38-39, 41-43, 45-46, 48, 52-55, 57-59, 61, 63-64, 66-67, 70, 72, 74-76, 80, 83-84, 87, 89-90, 93-94, 99-103, 106, 119-121, 123-124, 127, 145, 150, 153, 158-160, 166-170, 172, 174, 176, 178-180, 184, 191, 195, 198-201, 206, 213, 223-224
  advantage of, 9-10
  damp, 24, 26, 166
  regressive use of, 48-49, 52-53, 75-76, 100-101, 106
  shaping, 33, 41, 52, 64
  tray of adult, 6, 94, 170
  used to hide objects, 52, 75-76
  wet, 8, 24, 26, 53, 106, 158, 166, 200
sand tray, 1, 3-4, 6, 10-12, 21-22, 24, 28, 30, 32, 38-39, 41-43, 45, 48, 52-55, 57-59, 61, 63, 66, 70, 72, 74, 76, 80, 83, 89, 93, 100-102, 106, 119, 127, 153, 159-160, 166, 169-170, 174, 176, 178-180, 184, 195, 198, 201, 213

sandplay, 2-10, 12-14, 16-22, 24, 26-34, 36, 38, 40, 42, 44, 46, 48, 50-52, 54, 56, 58-60, 62, 64, 66, 68-70, 72, 74-76, 78, 80, 82, 84, 86, 88, 90, 92, 94, 96, 98, 100, 102, 104, 106, 108, 110, 112, 114-120, 122, 124, 126-128, 130, 132-134, 136, 138-140, 142-144, 146, 148, 150, 152, 154, 156, 158, 160-164, 166-168, 170-172, 174, 176, 178, 180, 182-184, 186, 188, 190-192, 194, 196, 198-202, 204, 206, 208-210, 212-214, 216, 218, 220, 222-224, 226, 228, 230
  advantage of, 9-10
  collection, 4, 21, 95, 135, 145, 161, 167, 183, 186, 205, 207-208
  inwardly focused, 4
Sanford, 1, 19-20, 228
Santa Claus, 147, 206
satan, 127, 138, 174, 211
scapegoat, 54, 100, 155
Schaefer and O'Connor, 6
Schwartz-Salant, 60-62, 228
sea, 26, 41, 97, 134, 167, 174, 176, 204, 210-211, 213
seahorse, 174
security, 8, 18, 68, 79, 84, 125, 129, 154, 157
self, 8, 13, 15-20, 22, 39-42, 44-45, 59-61, 67, 82, 88-89, 93, 108-109, 115-116, 121, 124, 130, 132-133, 136, 152-153, 157, 167, 170, 172, 175-176, 178, 180-182, 185, 187, 217, 220, 223, 225
  -concept, 44, 58, 82, 107, 139, 144, 172, 175, 227, 249
  -destruction, 47, 54, 74, 111, 126, 149, 151, 172, 182, 185, 189
  -mastery, 9, 12, 25, 31, 109, 114-115, 134, 186
senex, 18, 220
sensation, 43, 92, 150, 153, 169, 172, 180, 218, 220-222
separation, 39, 41, 58, 82, 86, 128, 131, 156, 191, 220
  -individuation, 9, 15, 19, 39, 58, 84, 131, 156, 179, 184, 189-190, 218, 220, 222

lack of, 1, 13, 39-40, 58-59, 134-135, 140, 151-152, 158, 163, 221
serpent, 58, 121, 126, 137, 142-144, 174-175, 178-181, 205, 211
sexual, 7, 108, 130, 151, 176, 191, 193, 219
  -ity, 169
  identity, 29, 36, 41-42, 58, 60, 103, 106, 134, 151, 190
shadow, 16, 61, 93, 133, 138-139, 145, 220
shame, 8-9, 126
shark, 91, 121, 137, 150, 175, 191, 211
sheep, 155, 160, 175-177, 193, 211-212
shell, 44, 103, 134, 184
shelter, 176, 185, 187
  -ed, 21, 23, 40, 226-228
shepherd, 161, 173, 175, 177, 181, 211-212
ship, 91, 94, 186, 198, 212
sibling rivalry, 82
Signell, 180, 184, 228
silver, 177, 212-213
skeleton, 36, 90, 138, 178, 212
skull, 94, 138, 178, 199, 212
snake, 57-59, 91-92, 123, 126, 134, 142, 175, 178-179, 188, 212, 222
  as libidinal energy, 19, 59, 179
  dream, 1, 14, 16, 19, 59, 61, 78, 93, 113, 132, 175, 178
  symbolic of renewal, 174, 178-179
snow, 139, 143, 147, 158, 179, 191, 193, 206
Snow White, 143, 147, 193, 206
socialized, 51
  poorly, 50-51, 94, 121, 165
sociopathic, 175
son, 52, 58-59, 69, 162-163
Sorcerer's Apprentice, 86, 161, 209
space, 7-10, 19, 24, 26, 71, 81, 90, 94, 162, 166, 179-180, 190, 225

-men, 50, 64-65, 72, 75, 82, 120, 131, 133, 147, 149-151, 161, 165, 171, 184, 194, 203, 215
-ship, 91, 94, 186, 198, 212
child's, 1, 4-5, 8-9, 11-13, 19-21, 30-32, 34-35, 38-39, 42-43, 49, 57, 59-61, 66, 71, 75, 84, 86, 93, 99, 104, 110, 120, 123, 133-134, 137-141, 144, 147, 151-152, 154, 158-159, 170, 172, 188, 190, 193, 229
dominated by, 108
men, 50, 64-65, 72, 75, 82, 120, 131, 133, 147, 149-151, 161, 165, 171, 184, 194, 203, 215
sacred, 8, 80, 133-134, 153, 162, 175-176, 182, 187, 190, 223
storage, 26, 197
sphere, 120, 134, 144, 158, 179-180, 212
spider, 137, 158, 164, 167, 180, 212
spiral, 42-43, 86, 134, 180, 219
spirit, 108, 121, 130, 132, 138-139, 142-144, 148, 157, 168, 172, 180-182, 192
and wind, 128
beings, 61, 121, 132, 138, 161
spiritual, 18-19, 65, 67-68, 74, 84-85, 114, 120, 123, 126, 128, 130-131, 133, 136, 141-143, 148-150, 152-153, 157-158, 160, 162-165, 168, 173, 177, 183, 186-187, 189, 191-192, 219-220
-ity, 169
and horse, 188
conflict, 2, 29, 31, 42, 83, 102, 124, 130, 137, 189-190
lack of __ awareness, 1
purification, 65, 68, 123, 149, 191
purity, 126, 138, 141-142, 157, 160, 183, 192
struggle of carnal nature against, 64-65, 144

transformation, 4, 31, 41, 58, 60, 65, 107, 111, 124, 130-132, 134, 136, 138, 144, 149, 154, 158, 171-172, 193, 220, 226, 228
understanding, 1-2, 9, 12, 14, 18, 20-22, 28, 113, 122, 133, 142, 163, 187, 192
values, 63, 74, 127
splitting, 61, 193
square, 134, 144-145, 153, 162, 173, 180-181
staff, 174, 181
stag, 138, 145, 179, 181, 212
stairs, 84, 160, 181, 185, 213
stone, 66-67, 80, 115, 173, 178, 182-183, 213
  black, 59-60, 126-127, 131, 135, 157, 162, 171, 182-183, 198, 202, 215
  green, 66-68, 135, 154-155
sacred, 8, 80, 133-134, 153, 162, 175-176, 182, 187, 190, 223, 248
substance abuse, 161
suicidal, 54, 56, 100
Sullwold, 21, 40, 228
Sun, 134, 137, 154-155, 161, 163, 168, 175, 181, 183, 186, 213
super, 135, 146, 221
  -conscious, 6, 8, 12, 14, 18-19, 21-22, 43, 59, 72, 83, 85, 88, 93, 115, 128, 132, 143, 148, 157-158, 170, 175, 178, 180, 189, 220, 222, 227
  -ego, 3, 8, 11-13, 16-18, 20, 22, 25, 29, 31, 33, 39, 42-43, 49, 54, 57, 62, 75, 80, 82, 99, 105, 107-109, 115, 119, 123-124, 130, 132, 136, 142, 148, 151, 159, 167, 169-170, 183, 189-190, 220, 224
  -natural, 4-5, 15, 17, 19, 32, 42, 69-70, 160, 166, 174, 180
Superman, 53, 147, 156, 163, 207
swamp, 140, 199, 201
swan, 97-99, 183, 213

symbiotic, 111, 132, 134
symbol, 14, 18, 22, 31, 41, 44, 65, 67, 82, 84-85, 103, 107, 109, 119, 123-125, 128, 130-134, 136-137, 141-143, 147, 149-150, 154, 157, 159-160, 166, 173-174, 177-179, 181-182, 184, 187-188, 220-221
   amplification, 119
   of ascension, 84, 142, 181, 213
   of transformation, 58, 65, 107, 124, 130, 132, 134, 136, 144, 149, 172, 193, 220, 226
   universal, 7, 13, 76, 143, 145, 151, 153, 164, 166-167, 175-177, 184, 188, 192
symptom, 13
tchuringas, 133
temenos, 132
temple, 182, 219
Terr, 70, 74, 229
testing, 47, 131, 152, 159
   spiritual, 18-19, 65, 67-68, 74, 84-85, 114, 120, 123, 126, 128, 130-131, 133, 136, 141-143, 148-150, 152-153, 157-158, 160, 162-165, 168, 173, 177, 183, 186-187, 189, 191-192, 219-220
therapeutic alliance, 4, 9, 12, 50, 119, 217
therapist, 2-5, 10, 12-13, 19-21, 25-27, 29, 34, 38, 45, 50, 59, 61, 71, 88, 106, 114, 119, 132, 158, 185, 246
   intervention, 76
thinking, 1, 16, 20, 42-43, 113, 153, 180, 195, 218, 220-222
threshold, 84, 128, 143, 154, 173-174, 190, 221
   symbol, 14, 18, 22, 31, 41, 44, 65, 67, 82, 84-85, 103, 107, 109, 119, 123-125, 128, 130-134, 136-137, 141-143, 147, 149-150, 154, 157, 159-160, 166, 173-174, 177-179, 181-182, 184, 187-188, 220-221
throne, 161, 184, 213

tiger, 132, 184, 213
timelessness, 133
tomboy, 194-195, 215
tortoise, 184, 188, 213
totem, 41, 165
  -ic, 245, 248
tower, 97-101, 106, 111, 130-131, 152, 162, 185, 214
  Rapunzel, 99-101, 109, 111, 131, 185
transcendence, 159, 164, 181
transference, 50, 68, 106
transformation, 4, 31, 41, 58, 60, 65, 107, 111, 124, 130-132, 134, 136, 138, 144, 149, 154, 158, 171-172, 193, 220, 226, 228
  -al, 7, 17, 228
transition, 153
  -al, 7, 17, 228
transpersonal, 12, 22, 119, 158
  bond, 20, 119, 141
transportation, 120, 130, 164, 177, 186-187
treasure, 26, 43-45, 98, 116, 131, 133, 155, 159, 178, 186, 210, 214
  chest, 24, 26, 155, 186, 214
tree, 28, 82, 89, 94-95, 110, 152, 166, 174-175, 181-182, 186-187, 193, 214, 226
  of life, 40, 85, 103, 107, 120, 127, 129, 150, 153, 157-158, 164, 172-173, 175-176, 178, 181, 183, 187, 189, 191
trial, 65, 123, 149, 152, 159
trickster, 15, 134-135, 137, 143, 145-146, 163, 221
truck, 79, 130, 186-187, 214
trust, 11, 13, 99, 165
tunnel, 133, 187, 214
turtle, 185, 187, 214
typology, 17, 43, 88, 217-222

tyrannosaurus rex, 71, 93-94, 121, 137, 140, 175
unconscious, 1, 6-7, 12-16, 19-22, 28, 31, 38-41, 43, 48-49, 57, 62, 65, 68, 72, 78-79, 82-83, 86, 88-90, 92-93, 105-108, 111, 114-115, 123-126, 128-130, 132-134, 141, 143-146, 149-152, 157-158, 160-161, 164, 166-173, 175, 177-179, 181, 185, 189-191, 193, 195, 217-222, 225-226
  and fire, 177, 190
  and parental introjects, 122
  and transformation, 41, 132
  as helpful, 89, 145
  collective, 13-16, 19, 29, 48, 125, 130, 148, 186, 195, 217, 222, 226
  complex, 12, 14-15, 17-18, 31, 59, 62-63, 82, 88, 90, 99, 103-104, 114, 121, 159, 167, 169, 185, 217, 220-221
  dangerous, 85, 164, 177, 179, 193
  dual nature of, 20, 179
  healing tendency of
  language of, 2, 9, 14, 246
  overwhelming, 13, 22, 54, 115, 123-124, 130, 145, 151, 253
  parental, 13, 44, 103, 108, 122, 131, 150, 152, 159, 161, 193, 218-220
  personal, 11, 15-16, 19, 22, 31, 88, 99, 112, 123, 130, 133, 144-145, 148, 151, 153, 157, 163-164, 166-167, 170, 175, 177, 184, 186, 188, 194-195, 222
  pressures, 12
  threatening, 5, 19, 33, 36, 89, 92, 149, 178, 193
ungrounded, 120
unicorn, 36, 97, 99, 157, 165, 188, 214
uroboros, 134, 174
vegetative, 29, 42, 75, 110, 140, 167, 191
  stage, 29, 42, 64, 74-76, 86, 110, 114, 132, 140, 148, 158, 167, 189, 191, 195
victim, 51, 70, 92, 102, 108, 114, 122, 172, 176

villain, 138, 172
violence, 46, 69-73
  domestic, 47, 69
violet, 3, 6, 135, 160, 170, 189
virginity, 126, 154, 185, 188
visual, 9, 16, 34, 59
volcano, 84-85, 87, 94, 189, 214
  extinct, 189
von Franz, 120, 176, 178, 189, 229
wall, 155, 190, 214
war, 79, 115, 124, 128-129, 156, 172, 190
water, 3, 10, 22, 24-26, 29, 38, 91, 94, 106-107, 123-125, 136, 142, 147, 153, 157-158, 160, 166-167, 169, 173-174, 177, 180, 183, 186, 190-191, 198, 209
  crossing, 173, 182, 191
  supply for projects,
waves, 157, 191
Weinrib, 20, 24
well, 1, 10, 12, 19, 27, 30, 32, 42, 52, 59, 76, 116-117, 125, 131, 136, 139, 141, 159, 164, 174-175, 182, 185, 191-193, 215
whale, 123, 191-192, 215
white, 25, 37, 50, 59-61, 84-85, 87, 111, 132, 135, 142-143, 147, 157, 160, 169, 175, 183, 191-193, 198, 206, 214
  horse, 38, 84-85, 111, 157, 165, 168, 188, 208
  stone, 66-67, 80, 115, 173, 178, 182-183, 213
wholeness, 18-20, 39-40, 60, 88, 133-134, 144, 152, 155, 172, 181, 183, 188, 219
wicked, 64, 114, 131, 152, 193
Wickes, 13, 57, 229
wind, 128, 142, 157, 192
Winnicott, 11, 24, 229
WISC, 90

wisdom, 84, 115, 122, 125-126, 128-129, 135, 138, 142, 145, 155, 157, 162, 165-168, 177, 184, 188, 192, 221
  instinctual, 29, 37, 44, 46, 59, 79, 82, 84, 87, 99, 103, 115, 121-123, 125, 134, 149, 174-175, 178-179, 194, 221
Wise Old Man, 15, 44, 80, 89, 146-147, 161-163, 192, 215
Wise Old Woman, 89, 192, 215
wish, 98, 191
witch, 15, 97, 140, 143, 147, 152, 192-193, 206, 215
withdrawn, 51
wolf, 140, 193-194, 215
world center, 132, 154, 164
wound, 14, 36, 43, 61, 102, 174
  psychological __, 11, 13-14, 20, 26, 41, 43, 48, 54, 61, 63, 83, 88-89, 99, 101, 133, 135, 137, 143, 146-147, 152, 158, 163, 171, 173, 181, 189, 206, 217, 221, 223, 225, 227
WPPSI, 32
yellow, 127-128, 135, 155, 195
zoo, 33

Made in the USA
Lexington, KY
05 September 2012